Real-Resumes For Jobs in Nonprofit Organizations

...including real resumes used to change careers
and gain federal employment

Anne McKinney, Editor

PREP PUBLISHING

FAYETTEVILLE, NC

PREP Publishing

1110 ½ Hay Street
Fayetteville, NC 28305
(910) 483-6611

Library of Congress Cataloging-in-Publication Data

Real-resumes for jobs in nonprofit organizations--including real resumes used to change careers and gain federal employment / Anne McKinney, editor.
      p. cm. -- (Real-resumes series)
  ISBN 1-885288-40-9 (alk. paper)
  1. Resumes (Employment)--United States. 2. Nonprofit organizations--United States--Employees. 3. Career changes--United States. 4. Civil service positions--United States. I. McKinney, Anne, 1948- II. Series.

  HF5383.R395864 2004
  650.14'2--dc22   2004041419

PREP Publishing

Business and Career Series:

RESUMES AND COVER LETTERS THAT HAVE WORKED, Revised Edition

RESUMES AND COVER LETTERS THAT HAVE WORKED FOR MILITARY PROFESSIONALS

GOVERNMENT JOB APPLICATIONS AND FEDERAL RESUMES

COVER LETTERS THAT BLOW DOORS OPEN

LETTERS FOR SPECIAL SITUATIONS

RESUMES AND COVER LETTERS FOR MANAGERS

REAL-RESUMES FOR COMPUTER JOBS

REAL-RESUMES FOR MEDICAL JOBS

REAL-RESUMES FOR FINANCIAL JOBS

REAL-RESUMES FOR TEACHERS

REAL-RESUMES FOR STUDENTS

REAL-RESUMES FOR CAREER CHANGERS

REAL-RESUMES FOR SALES

REAL ESSAYS FOR COLLEGE & GRADUATE SCHOOL

REAL-RESUMES FOR AVIATION & TRAVEL JOBS

REAL-RESUMES FOR POLICE, LAW ENFORCEMENT & SECURITY JOBS

REAL-RESUMES FOR SOCIAL WORK & COUNSELING JOBS

REAL-RESUMES FOR CONSTRUCTION JOBS

REAL-RESUMES FOR MANUFACTURING JOBS

REAL-RESUMES FOR RESTAURANT, FOOD SERVICE & HOTEL JOBS

REAL-RESUMES FOR MEDIA, NEWSPAPER, BROADCASTING & PUBLIC AFFAIRS JOBS

REAL-RESUMES FOR RETAILING, MODELING, FASHION & BEAUTY JOBS

REAL-RESUMES FOR HUMAN RESOURCES & PERSONNEL JOBS

REAL-RESUMES FOR NURSING JOBS

REAL-RESUMES FOR AUTO INDUSTRY JOBS

REAL RESUMIX & OTHER RESUMES FOR FEDERAL GOVERNMENT JOBS

REAL KSAS--KNOWLEDGE, SKILLS & ABILITIES--FOR GOVERNMENT JOBS

REAL BUSINESS PLANS & MARKETING TOOLS

REAL-RESUMES FOR ADMINISTRATIVE SUPPORT, OFFICE & SECRETARIAL JOBS

REAL-RESUMES FOR FIREFIGHTING JOBS

REAL-RESUMES FOR JOBS IN NONPROFIT ORGANIZATIONS

REAL-RESUMES FOR SPORTS INDUSTRY JOBS

REAL-RESUMES FOR LEGAL & PARALEGAL JOBS

Judeo-Christian Ethics Series:

SECOND TIME AROUND

BACK IN TIME

WHAT THE BIBLE SAYS ABOUT...Words that can lead to success and happiness

A GENTLE BREEZE FROM GOSSAMER WINGS

BIBLE STORIES FROM THE OLD TESTAMENT

Contents

Real-Resumes For Jobs in Nonprofit Organizations

Anne McKinney, Editor

A WORD FROM THE EDITOR:
ABOUT THE REAL-RESUMES SERIES

Welcome to the Real-Resumes Series. The Real-Resumes Series is a series of books which have been developed based on the experiences of real job hunters and which target specialized fields or types of resumes. As the editor of the series, I have carefully selected resumes and cover letters (with names and other key data disguised, of course) which have been used successfully in real job hunts. That's what we mean by "Real-Resumes." What you see in this book are *real* resumes and cover letters which helped real people get ahead in their careers.

The Real-Resumes Series is based on the work of the country's oldest resume-preparation company known as PREP Resumes. If you would like a free information packet describing the company's resume preparation services, call 910-483-6611 or write to PREP at 1110½ Hay Street, Fayetteville, NC 28305. If you have a job hunting experience you would like to share with our staff at the Real-Resumes Series, please contact us at preppub@aol.com or visit our website at http://www.prep-pub.com.

The resumes and cover letters in this book are designed to be of most value to people already in a job hunt or contemplating a career change. If we could give you one word of advice about your career, here's what we would say: Manage your career and don't stumble from job to job in an incoherent pattern. Try to find work that interests you, and then identify prosperous industries which need work performed of the type you want to do. Learn early in your working life that a great resume and cover letter can blow doors open for you and help you maximize your salary.

We hope the superior samples will help you manage your current job campaign and your career so that you will find work aligned to your career interests.

As the editor of this book, I would like to give you some tips on how to make the best use of the information you will find here. Because you are considering a career change, you already understand the concept of managing your career for maximum enjoyment and self-fulfillment. The purpose of this book is to provide expert tools and advice so that you *can* manage your career. Inside these pages you will find resumes and cover letters that will help you find not just a job but the type of work you want to do.

Overview of the Book

Every resume and cover letter in this book actually worked. And most of the resumes and cover letters have common features: most are one-page, most are in the chronological format, and most resumes are accompanied by a companion cover letter. In this section you will find helpful advice about job hunting. Step One begins with a discussion of why employers prefer the one-page, chronological resume. In Step Two you are introduced to the direct approach and to the proper format for a cover letter. In Step Three you learn the 14 main reasons why job hunters are not offered the jobs they want, and you learn the six key areas employers focus on when they interview you. Step Four gives nuts-and-bolts advice on how to handle the interview, send a follow-up letter after an interview, and negotiate your salary.

The cover letter plays such a critical role in a career change. You will learn from the experts how to format your cover letters and you will see suggested language to use in particular career-change situations. It has been said that "A picture is worth a thousand words" and, for that reason, you will see numerous examples of effective cover letters used by real individuals to change fields, functions, and industries.

The most important part of the book is the Real-Resumes section. Some of the individuals whose resumes and cover letters you see spent a lengthy career in an industry they loved. Then there are resumes and cover letters of people who wanted a change but who probably wanted to remain in their industry. Many of you will be especially interested by the resumes and cover letters of individuals who knew they definitely wanted a career change but had no idea what they wanted to do next. Other resumes and cover letters show individuals who knew they wanted to change fields and had a pretty good idea of what they wanted to do next.

Whatever your field, and whatever your circumstances, you'll find resumes and cover letters that will "show you the ropes" in terms of successfully changing jobs and switching careers.

Before you proceed further, think about why you picked up this book.
- Are you dissatisfied with the type of work you are now doing?
- Would you like to change careers, change companies, or change industries?
- Are you satisfied with your industry but not with your niche or function within it?
- Do you want to transfer your skills to a new product or service?
- Even if you have excelled in your field, have you "had enough"? Would you like the stimulation of a new challenge?
- Are you aware of the importance of a great cover letter but unsure of how to write one?
- Are you preparing to launch a second career after retirement?
- Have you been downsized, or do you anticipate becoming a victim of downsizing?
- Do you need expert advice on how to plan and implement a job campaign that will open the maximum number of doors?
- Do you want to make sure you handle an interview to your maximum advantage?

- Would you like to master the techniques of negotiating salary and benefits?
- Do you want to learn the secrets and shortcuts of professional resume writers?

Using the Direct Approach

As you consider the possibility of a job hunt or career change, you need to be aware that most people end up having at least three distinctly different careers in their working lifetimes, and often those careers are different from each other. Yet people usually stumble through each job campaign, unsure of what they should be doing. Whether you find yourself voluntarily or unexpectedly in a job hunt, the direct approach is the job hunting strategy most likely to yield a full-time permanent job. The direct approach is an active, take-the-initiative style of job hunting in which you choose your next employer rather than relying on responding to ads, using employment agencies, or depending on other methods of finding jobs. You will learn how to use the direct approach in this book, and you will see that an effective cover letter is a critical ingredient in using the direct approach.

The "direct approach" is the style of job hunting most likely to yield the maximum number of job interviews.

Lack of Industry Experience Not a Major Barrier to Entering New Field

"Lack of experience" is often the last reason people are not offered jobs, according to the companies who do the hiring. If you are changing careers, you will be glad to learn that experienced professionals often are selling "potential" rather than experience in a job hunt. Companies look for personal qualities that they know tend to be present in their most effective professionals, such as communication skills, initiative, persistence, organizational and time management skills, and creativity. Frequently companies are trying to discover "personality type," "talent," "ability," "aptitude," and "potential" rather than seeking actual hands-on experience, so your resume should be designed to aggressively present your accomplishments. Attitude, enthusiasm, personality, and a track record of achievements in any type of work are the primary "indicators of success" which employers are seeking, and you will see numerous examples in this book of resumes written in an all-purpose fashion so that the professional can approach various industries and companies.

Using references in a skillful fashion in your job hunt will inspire confidence in prospective employers and help you "close the sale" after interviews.

The Art of Using References in a Job Hunt

You probably already know that you need to provide references during a job hunt, but you may not be sure of how and when to use references for maximum advantage. You can use references very creatively during a job hunt to call attention to your strengths and make yourself "stand out." Your references will rarely get you a job, no matter how impressive the names, but the way you use references can boost the employer's confidence in you and lead to a job offer in the least time.

You should ask from three to five people, including people who have supervised you, if you can use them as a reference during your job hunt. You may not be able to ask your current boss since your job hunt is probably confidential.

A common question in resume preparation is: "Do I need to put my references on my resume?" No, you don't. Even if you create a references page at the same time you prepare your resume, you don't need to mail, e-mail, or fax your references page with the resume and cover letter. Usually the potential employer is not interested in references until he meets you, so the earliest you need to have references ready is at the first interview. Obviously there are exceptions to this standard rule of thumb; sometimes an ad will ask you to send references with your first response. Wait until the employer requests references before providing them.

An excellent attention-getting technique is to take to the first interview not just a page of references (giving names, addresses, and telephone numbers) but an actual letter of reference written by someone who knows you well and who preferably has supervised or employed you. A professional way to close the first interview is to thank the interviewer, shake his or her hand, and then say you'd like to give him or her a copy of a letter of reference from a previous employer. Hopefully you already made a good impression during the interview, but you'll "close the sale" in a dynamic fashion if you leave a letter praising you and your accomplishments. For that reason, it's a good idea to ask supervisors during your final weeks in a job if they will provide you with a written letter of recommendation which you can use in future job hunts. Most employers will oblige, and you will have a letter that has a useful "shelf life" of many years. Such a letter often gives the prospective employer enough confidence in his opinion of you that he may forego checking out other references and decide to offer you the job on the spot or in the next few days.

With regard to references, it's best to provide the names and addresses of people who have supervised you or observed you in a work situation.

Whom should you ask to serve as references? References should be people who have known or supervised you in a professional, academic, or work situation. References with big titles, like school superintendent or congressman, are fine, but remind busy people when you get to the interview stage that they may be contacted soon. Make sure the busy official recognizes your name and has instant positive recall of you! If you're asked to provide references on a formal company application, you can simply transcribe names from your references list. In summary, follow this rule in using references: If you've got them, flaunt them! If you've obtained well-written letters of reference, make sure you find a polite way to push those references under the nose of the interviewer so he or she can hear someone other than you describing your strengths. Your references probably won't ever get you a job, but glowing letters of reference can give you credibility and visibility that can make you stand out among candidates with similar credentials and potential!

The approach taken by this book is to (1) help you master the proven best techniques of conducting a job hunt and (2) show you how to stand out in a job hunt through your resume, cover letter, interviewing skills, as well as the way in which you present your references and follow up on interviews. Now, the best way to "get in the mood" for writing your own resume and cover letter is to select samples from the Table of Contents that interest you and then read them. A great resume is a "photograph," usually on one page, of an individual. If you wish to seek professional advice in preparing your resume, you may contact one of the professional writers at Professional Resume & Employment Publishing (PREP) for a brief free consultation by calling 1-910-483-6611.

Part One: Some Advice About Your Job Hunt

What if you don't know what you want to do?

Your job hunt will be more comfortable if you can figure out what type of work you want to do. But you are not alone if you have no idea what you want to do next! You may have knowledge and skills in certain areas but want to get into another type of work. What *The Wall Street Journal* has discovered in its research on careers is that most of us end up having at least three distinctly different careers in our working lives; it seems that, even if we really like a particular kind of activity, twenty years of doing it is enough for most of us and we want to move on to something else!

Figure out what interests you and you will hold the key to a successful job hunt and working career. (And be prepared for your interests to change over time!)

That's why we strongly believe that you need to spend some time figuring out *what interests you* rather than taking an inventory of the skills you have. You may have skills that you simply don't want to use, but if you can build your career on the things that interest you, you will be more likely to be happy and satisfied in your job. Realize, too, that interests can change over time; the activities that interest you now may not be the ones that interested you years ago. For example, some professionals may decide that they've had enough of retail sales and want a job selling another product or service, even though they have earned a reputation for being an excellent retail manager. We strongly believe that interests rather than skills should be the determining factor in deciding what types of jobs you want to apply for and what directions you explore in your job hunt. Obviously one cannot be a lawyer without a law degree or a secretary without secretarial skills; but a professional can embark on a next career as a financial consultant, property manager, plant manager, production supervisor, retail manager, or other occupation if he/she has a strong interest in that type of work and can provide a resume that clearly demonstrates past excellent performance in *any* field and *potential* to excel in another field. As you will see later in this book, "lack of exact experience" is the last reason why people are turned down for the jobs they apply for.

How can you have a resume prepared if you don't know what you want to do?

"Lack of exact experience" is the last reason people are turned down for the jobs for which they apply.

You may be wondering how you can have a resume prepared if you don't know what you want to do next. The approach to resume writing which PREP, the country's oldest resume-preparation company, has used successfully for many years is to develop an "all-purpose" resume that translates your skills, experience, and accomplishments into language employers can understand. What most people need in a job hunt is a versatile resume that will allow them to apply for numerous types of jobs. For example, you may want to apply for a job in pharmaceutical sales but you may also want to have a resume that will be versatile enough for you to apply for jobs in the construction, financial services, or automotive industries.

Based on more than 20 years of serving job hunters, we at PREP have found that your best approach to job hunting is **an all-purpose resume** and **specific cover letters tailored to specific fields** rather than using the approach of trying to create different resumes for every job. If you are remaining in your field, you may not even need more than one "all-purpose" cover letter, although the cover letter rather than the resume is the place to communicate your interest in a narrow or specific field. An all-purpose resume and cover letter that translate your experience and accomplishments into plain English are the tools that will maximize the number of doors which open for you while permitting you to "fish" in the widest range of job areas.

Your resume will provide the script for your job interview.

When you get down to it, your resume has a simple job to do: Its purpose is to blow as many doors open as possible and to make as many people as possible want to meet you. So a well-written resume that really "sells" you is a key that will create opportunities for you in a job hunt.

This statistic explains why: The typical newspaper advertisement for a job opening receives more than 245 replies. And normally only 10 or 12 will be invited to an interview.

But here's another purpose of the resume: it provides the "script" the employer uses when he interviews you. If your resume has been written in such a way that your strengths and achievements are revealed, that's what you'll end up talking about at the job interview. Since the resume will govern what you get asked about at your interviews, you can't overestimate the importance of making sure your resume makes you look and sound as good as you are.

Your resume is the "script" for your job interviews. Make sure you put on your resume what you want to talk about or be asked about at the job interview.

So what is a "good" resume?

Very literally, your resume should motivate the person reading it to dial the phone number or e-mail the screen name you have put on the resume. When you are relocating, you should put a local phone number on your resume if your physical address is several states away; employers are more likely to dial a local telephone number than a long-distance number when they're looking for potential employees.

If you have a resume already, look at it objectively. Is it a limp, colorless "laundry list" of your job titles and duties? Or does it "paint a picture" of your skills, abilities, and accomplishments in a way that would make someone want to meet you? Can people understand what you're saying? If you are attempting to change fields or industries, can potential employers see that your skills and knowledge are transferable to other environments? For example, have you described accomplishments which reveal your problem-solving abilities or communication skills?

The one-page resume in chronological format is the format preferred by most employers.

How long should your resume be?

One page, maybe two. Usually only people in the academic community have a resume (which they usually call a *curriculum vitae*) longer than one or two pages. Remember that your resume is almost always accompanied by a cover letter, and a potential employer does not want to read more than two or three pages about a total stranger in order to decide if he wants to meet that person! Besides, don't forget that the more you tell someone about yourself, the more opportunity you are providing for the employer to screen you out at the "first-cut" stage. A resume should be concise and exciting and designed to make the reader want to meet you in person!

Should resumes be functional or chronological?

Employers almost always prefer a chronological resume; in other words, an employer will find a resume easier to read if it is immediately apparent what your current or most recent job is, what you did before that, and so forth, in reverse chronological order. A resume that goes back in detail for the last ten years of employment will generally satisfy the employer's curiosity about your background. Employment more than ten years old can be shown even more briefly in an "Other Experience" section at the end of your "Experience" section. Remember that your intention is not to tell everything you've done but to "hit the high points" and especially impress the employer with what you learned, contributed, or accomplished in each job you describe.

Once you get your resume, what do you do with it?

You will be using your resume to answer ads, as a tool to use in talking with friends and relatives about your job search, and, most importantly, in using the "direct approach" described in this book.

When you mail your resume, always send a "cover letter."

A "cover letter," sometimes called a "resume letter" or "letter of interest," is a letter that accompanies and introduces your resume. Your cover letter is a way of personalizing the resume by sending it to the specific person you think you might want to work for at each company. Your cover letter should contain a few highlights from your resume—just enough to make someone want to meet you. Cover letters should always be typed or word processed on a computer—never handwritten.

Never mail or fax your resume without a cover letter.

1. Learn the art of answering ads.

There is an "art," part of which can be learned, in using your "bestselling" resume to reply to advertisements.

Sometimes an exciting job lurks behind a boring ad that someone dictated in a hurry, so reply to any ad that interests you. Don't worry that you aren't "25 years old with an MBA" like the ad asks for. Employers will always make compromises in their requirements if they think you're the "best fit" overall.

What about ads that ask for "salary requirements?"

What if the ad you're answering asks for "salary requirements?" The first rule is to avoid committing yourself in writing at that point to a specific salary. You don't want to "lock yourself in."

What if the ad asks for your "salary requirements?"

There are two ways to handle the ad that asks for "salary requirements."

First, you can ignore that part of the ad and accompany your resume with a cover letter that focuses on "selling" you, your abilities, and even some of your philosophy about work or your field. You may include a sentence in your cover letter like this: "I can provide excellent personal and professional references at your request, and I would be delighted to share the private details of my salary history with you in person."

Second, if you feel you must give some kind of number, just state a range in your cover letter that includes your medical, dental, other benefits, and expected bonuses. You might state, for example, "My current compensation, including benefits and bonuses, is in the range of $30,000-$40,000."

Analyze the ad and "tailor" yourself to it.

When you're replying to ads, a finely tailored cover letter is an important tool in getting your resume noticed and read. On the next page is a cover letter which has been "tailored to fit" a specific ad. Notice the "art" used by PREP writers of analyzing the ad's main requirements and then writing the letter so that the person's background, work habits, and interests seem "tailor-made" to the company's needs. Use this cover letter as a model when you prepare your own reply to ads.

Date

To: Search Committee

In response to the urging of someone familiar with your search for an executive vice president for the Association of Health Underwriters, I am sending you a resume which summarizes my background. I offer a unique combination of knowledge, experience, and abilities which I believe would ideally suit the requirements of the Association of Health Underwriters.

Health industry expertise

You will see from my resume that I offer expertise related to health insurance and underwriting. In my current job I have sought out and negotiated contracts with major insurance companies to provide insurance for the organization. On a $1 million budget, I have developed insurance programs which generated $2 million in net income based on $32 million in premium. These highly regarded programs which I developed have brought 6,000 new members into the organization.

Proven executive ability

I offer proven executive ability. I have earned a reputation as someone who has not only strategic vision and imagination but also the tenacity and persistence to follow through on the "nitty-gritty" details of implementing new projects, programs, and concepts. I know how to delegate, and I know how to "micro manage," and I am skilled at tailoring my management style to particular circumstances while always shouldering full responsibility and accountability for results. My current job has involved the responsibility of recruiting, training, and continuously developing a national sales force of brokers throughout the U.S. which broke with the tradition of passive mail solicitation and led to dramatic growth in sales and profitability. With a strong "bottom-line" orientation, I have streamlined headquarters staff and reduced central office expenses to save at least half a million dollars while continuously supervising the association's five regional offices in the recruitment and training of more than 1,200 insurance agents nationally.

Extensive association experience

You will also see from my resume that I am accustomed to "getting things done" within the unique environment of a trade/membership association. I am well known for my ability to attract and retain a cohesive and productive staff, and I am also respected for my exceptional skills in relating to, inspiring, and supporting key volunteer members. A skilled communicator, I have made countless appearances and speeches.

I am aware of the requirements defined by the search committee, and I would enjoy the opportunity to discuss this position further with the Executive Committee. I feel certain I could contribute significantly to the growth and financial health of the Association of Health Underwriters as its Executive Vice President. Thank you for your time and consideration.

Sincerely,

Shane Malone

Employers are trying to identify the individual who wants the job they are filling. Don't be afraid to express your enthusiasm in the cover letter!

2. Talk to friends and relatives.

Don't be shy about telling your friends and relatives the kind of job you're looking for. Looking for the job you want involves using your network of contacts, so tell people what you're looking for. They may be able to make introductions and help set up interviews.

About 25% of all interviews are set up through "who you know," so don't ignore this approach.

3. Finally, and most importantly, use the "direct approach."

More than 50% of all job interviews are set up by the "direct approach." That means you actually mail, e-mail, or fax a resume and a cover letter to a company you think might be interesting to work for.

The "direct approach" is a strategy in which you choose your next employer.

To whom do you write?

In general, you should write directly to the *exact name* of the person who would be hiring you: say, the vice-president of marketing or data processing. If you're in doubt about to whom to address the letter, address it to the president by name and he or she will make sure it gets forwarded to the right person within the company who has hiring authority in your area.

How do you find the names of potential employers?

You're not alone if you feel that the biggest problem in your job search is finding the right names at the companies you want to contact. But you can usually figure out the names of companies you want to approach by deciding first if your job hunt is primarily geography-driven or industry-driven.

In a **geography-driven job hunt,** you could select a list of, say, 50 companies you want to contact **by location** from the lists that the U.S. Chambers of Commerce publish yearly of their "major area employers." There are hundreds of local Chambers of Commerce across America, and most of them will have an 800 number which you can find through 1-800-555-1212. If you and your family think Atlanta, Dallas, Ft. Lauderdale, and Virginia Beach might be nice places to live, for example, you could contact the Chamber of Commerce in those cities and ask how you can obtain a copy of their list of major employers. Your nearest library will have the book which lists the addresses of all chambers.

In an **industry-driven job hunt,** and if you are willing to relocate, you will be identifying the companies which you find most attractive in the industry in which you want to work. When you select a list of companies to contact **by industry,** you can find the right person to write and the address of firms by industrial category in *Standard and Poor's, Moody's,* and other excellent books in public libraries. Many Web sites also provide contact information.

Many people feel it's a good investment to actually call the company to either find out or double-check the name of the person to whom they want to send a resume and cover letter. It's important to do as much as you feasibly can to assure that the letter gets to the right person in the company.

On-line research will be the best way for many people to locate organizations to which they wish to send their resume. It is outside the scope of this book to teach Internet research skills, but librarians are often useful in this area.

What's the correct way to follow up on a resume you send?

There is a polite way to be aggressively interested in a company during your job hunt. It is ideal to end the cover letter accompanying your resume by saying, "I hope you'll welcome my call next week when I try to arrange a brief meeting at your convenience to discuss your current and future needs and how I might serve them." Keep it low key, and just ask for a "brief meeting," not an interview. Employers want people who show a determined interest in working with them, so don't be shy about following up on the resume and cover letter you've mailed.

It pays to be aware of the 14 most common pitfalls for job hunters.

STEP THREE: Preparing for Interviews

But a resume and cover letter by themselves can't get you the job you want. You need to "prep" yourself before the interview. Step Three in your job campaign is "Preparing for Interviews." First, let's look at interviewing from the hiring organization's point of view.

What are the biggest "turnoffs" for potential employers?

One of the ways to help yourself perform well at an interview is to look at the main reasons why organizations *don't* hire the people they interview, according to those who do the interviewing.

Notice that "lack of appropriate background" (or lack of experience) is the *last* reason for not being offered the job.

The 14 Most Common Reasons Job Hunters Are Not Offered Jobs (*according to the companies who do the interviewing and hiring*):

1. Low level of accomplishment
2. Poor attitude, lack of self-confidence
3. Lack of goals/objectives
4. Lack of enthusiasm
5. Lack of interest in the company's business
6. Inability to sell or express yourself
7. Unrealistic salary demands
8. Poor appearance
9. Lack of maturity, no leadership potential
10. Lack of extracurricular activities
11. Lack of preparation for the interview, no knowledge about company
12. Objecting to travel
13. Excessive interest in security and benefits
14. Inappropriate background

Department of Labor studies have proven that smart, "prepared" job hunters can increase their beginning salary while getting a job in *half* the time it normally takes. (4½ months is the average national length of a job search.) Here, from PREP, are some questions that can prepare you to find a job faster.

Are you in the "right" frame of mind?

It seems unfair that we have to look for a job just when we're lowest in morale. Don't worry *too* much if you're nervous before interviews. You're supposed to be a little nervous, especially if the job means a lot to you. But the best way to kill unnecessary fears about job hunting is through 1) making sure you have a great resume and 2) preparing yourself for the interview. Here are three main areas you need to think about before each interview.

Do you know what the company does?
Don't walk into an interview giving the impression that, "If this is Tuesday, this must be General Motors."

Research the company before you go to interviews.

Find out before the interview what the company's main product or service is. Where is the company heading? Is it in a "growth" or declining industry? (Answers to these questions may influence whether or not you want to work there!)

Information about what the company does is in annual reports, in newspaper and magazine articles, and on the Internet. If you're not yet skilled at Internet research, just visit your nearest library and ask the reference librarian to guide you to printed materials on the company.

Do you know what you want to do for the company?
Before the interview, try to decide how you see yourself fitting into the company. Remember, "lack of exact background" the company wants is usually the last reason people are not offered jobs.

Understand before you go to each interview that the burden will be on you to "sell" the interviewer on why you're the best person for the job and the company.

How will you answer the critical interview questions?
Put yourself in the interviewer's position and think about the questions you're most likely to be asked. Here are some of the most commonly asked interview questions:

Anticipate the questions you will be asked at the interview, and prepare your responses in advance.

Q: "What are your greatest strengths?"
A: Don't say you've never thought about it! Go into an interview knowing the three main impressions you want to leave about yourself, such as "I'm hard-working, loyal, and an imaginative cost-cutter."

Q: "What are your greatest weaknesses?"
A: Don't confess that you're lazy or have trouble meeting deadlines! Confessing that you tend to be a "workaholic" or "tend to be a perfectionist and sometimes get frustrated when others don't share my high standards" will make your prospective employer see a "weakness" that he likes. Name a weakness that your interviewer will perceive as a strength.

Q: "What are your long-range goals?"
A: If you're interviewing with Microsoft, don't say you want to work for IBM in five years! Say your long-range goal is to be *with* the company, contributing to its goals and success.

Q: "What motivates you to do your best work?"
A: Don't get dollar signs in your eyes here! "A challenge" is not a bad answer, but it's a little cliched. Saying something like "troubleshooting" or "solving a tough problem" is more interesting and specific. Give an example if you can.

Q: "What do you know about this organization?"

A: Don't say you never heard of it until they asked you to the interview! Name an interesting, positive thing you learned about the company recently from your research. Remember, company executives can sometimes feel rather "maternal" about the company they serve. Don't get onto a negative area of the company if you can think of positive facts you can bring up. Of course, if you learned in your research that the company's sales seem to be taking a nose-dive, or that the company president is being prosecuted for taking bribes, you might politely ask your interviewer to tell you something that could help you better understand what you've been reading. Those are the kinds of company facts that can help you determine whether or not you want to work there.

> Go to an interview prepared to tell the company why it should hire you.

Q: "Why should I hire you?"

A: "I'm unemployed and available" is the wrong answer here! Get back to your strengths and say that you believe the organization could benefit by a loyal, hard-working cost-cutter like yourself.

In conclusion, you should decide in advance, before you go to the interview, how you will answer each of these commonly asked questions. Have some practice interviews with a friend to role-play and build your confidence.

STEP FOUR: Handling the Interview and Negotiating Salary

Now you're ready for Step Four: actually handling the interview successfully and effectively. Remember, the purpose of an interview is to get a job offer.

> A smile at an interview makes the employer perceive of you as intelligent!

Eight "do's" for the interview

According to leading U.S. companies, there are eight key areas in interviewing success. You can fail at an interview if you mishandle just one area.

1. Do wear appropriate clothes.

You can never go wrong by wearing a suit to an interview.

2. Do be well groomed.

Don't overlook the obvious things like having clean hair, clothes, and fingernails for the interview.

3. Do give a firm handshake.

You'll have to shake hands twice in most interviews: first, before you sit down, and second, when you leave the interview. Limp handshakes turn most people off.

4. Do smile and show a sense of humor.

Interviewers are looking for people who would be nice to work with, so don't be so somber that you don't smile. In fact, research shows that people who smile at interviews are perceived as more intelligent. So, smile!

5. Do be enthusiastic.

Employers say they are "turned off" by lifeless, unenthusiastic job hunters who show no special interest in that company. The best way to show some enthusiasm for the employer's operation is to find out about the business beforehand.

6. Do show you are flexible and adaptable.

An employer is looking for someone who can contribute to his organization in a flexible, adaptable way. No matter what skills and training you have, employers know every new employee must go through initiation and training on the company's turf. Certainly show pride in your past accomplishments in a specific, factual way ("I saved my last employer $50.00 a week by a new cost-cutting measure I developed"). But don't come across as though there's nothing about the job you couldn't easily handle.

7. Do ask intelligent questions about the employer's business.

An employer is hiring someone because of certain business needs. Show interest in those needs. Asking questions to get a better idea of the employer's needs will help you "stand out" from other candidates interviewing for the job.

8. Do "take charge" when the interviewer "falls down" on the job.

Go into every interview knowing the three or four points about yourself you want the interviewer to remember. And be prepared to take an active part in leading the discussion if the interviewer's "canned approach" does not permit you to display your "strong suit." You can't always depend on the interviewer's asking you the "right" questions so you can stress your strengths and accomplishments.

> Employers are seeking people with good attitudes whom they can train and coach to do things their way.

An important "don't": Don't ask questions about salary or benefits at the first interview. Employers don't take warmly to people who look at their organization as just a place to satisfy salary and benefit needs. Don't risk making a negative impression by appearing greedy or self-serving. The place to discuss salary and benefits is normally at the second interview, and the employer will bring it up. Then you can ask questions without appearing excessively interested in what the organization can do for you.

Now...negotiating your salary

Even if an ad requests that you communicate your "salary requirement" or "salary history," you should avoid providing those numbers in your initial cover letter. You can usually say something like this: "I would be delighted to discuss the private details of my salary history with you in person."

Once you're at the interview, you must avoid even appearing *interested* in salary before you are offered the job. Make sure you've "sold" yourself before talking salary. First show you're the "best fit" for the employer and then you'll be in a stronger position from which to negotiate salary. **Never** bring up the subject of salary yourself. Employers say there's no way you can avoid looking greedy if you bring up the issue of salary and benefits before the company has identified you as its "best fit."

> Don't appear excessively interested in salary and benefits at the interview.

Interviewers sometimes throw out a salary figure at the first interview to see if you'll accept it. You may not want to commit yourself if you think you will be able to negotiate a better deal later on. Get back to finding out more about the job. This lets the interviewer know you're interested primarily in the job and not the salary.

When the organization brings up salary, it may say something like this: "Well, Mary, we think you'd make a good candidate for this job. What kind of salary are we talking about?" You may not want to name a number here, either. Give the ball back to the interviewer. Act as though you hadn't given the subject of salary much thought and respond something like this: "Ah, Mr. Jones, I wonder if you'd be kind enough to tell me what salary you had in mind when you advertised the job?" Or ... "What is the range you have in mind?"

Don't worry, if the interviewer names a figure that you think is too low, you can say so without turning down the job or locking yourself into a rigid position. The point here is to negotiate for yourself as well as you can. You might reply to a number named by the interviewer that you think is low by saying something like this: "Well, Mr. Lee, the job interests me very much, and I think I'd certainly enjoy working with you. But, frankly, I was thinking of something a little higher than that." That leaves the ball in your interviewer's court again, and you haven't turned down the job either, in case it turns out that the interviewer can't increase the offer and you still want the job.

Last, send a follow-up letter.

Mail, e-mail, or fax a letter right after the interview telling your interviewer you enjoyed the meeting and are certain (if you are) that you are the "best fit" for the job. The people interviewing you will probably have an attitude described as either "professionally loyal" to their companies, or "maternal and proprietary" if the interviewer also owns the company. In either case, they are looking for people who want to work for *that* company in particular. The follow-up letter you send might be just the deciding factor in your favor if the employer is trying to choose between you and someone else. You will see an example of a follow-up letter on page 16.

A cover letter is an essential part of a job hunt or career change.

Many people are aware of the importance of having a great resume, but most people in a job hunt don't realize just how important a cover letter can be. The purpose of the cover letter, sometimes called a **"letter of interest,"** is to introduce your resume to prospective employers. The cover letter is often the critical ingredient in a job hunt because the cover letter allows you to say a lot of things that just don't "fit" on the resume. For example, you can emphasize your commitment to a new field and stress your related talents. The cover letter also gives you a chance to stress outstanding character and personal values. On the next two pages you will see examples of very effective cover letters.

Special help for those in career change

We want to emphasize again that, especially in a career change, the cover letter is very important and can help you "build a bridge" to a new career. A creative and appealing cover letter can begin the process of encouraging the potential employer to imagine you in an industry other than the one in which you have worked.

As a special help to those in career change, there are resumes and cover letters included in this book which show valuable techniques and tips you should use when changing fields or industries. The resumes and cover letters of career changers are identified in the table of contents as "Career Change" and you will see the "Career Change" label on cover letters in Part Two where the individuals are changing careers.

Salary negotiation can be tricky.

A follow-up letter can help the employer choose between you and another qualified candidate.

A cover letter is an essential part of a career change.

Please do not attempt to implement a career change without a cover letter. A cover letter is the first impression of you, and you can influence the way an employer views you by the language and style of your letter.

Date

Exact Name of Person
Title or Position
Name of Company
Address (no., street)
Address (city, state, zip)

**Addressing the Cover
Letter:** Get the exact
name of the person to
whom you are writing. This
makes your approach
personal.

Dear Exact Name of Person: (or Dear Sir or Madam if answering a blind ad.)

With the enclosed resume, I would like to make you aware of my interest in exploring employment opportunities with your organization.

As you will see from my resume, I am currently excelling as Assistant Executive Director of Habitat for Humanity. My major responsibilities include preparing annual operating budgets, budgets for new projects, and budgets for construction while monitoring funds expensed in multiple simultaneous projects. I supervise three staff persons and assure compliance with regulations, including HUD and VA, related to housing ownership. In addition to determining eligibility of applicants and verifying family income as well as criminal records, I approve payment agreements and audit homeowners' compliance with HUD regulations.

Second Paragraph: You
have a chance to talk
about whatever you feel is
your most distinguishing
feature.

You will notice that I have excelled in a track record of promotion with Habitat for Humanity. After graduating with a B.S. in Finance from the University of North Carolina at Chapel Hill, I began employment with Habitat as a Project Manager, was promoted to Acting Executive Director and then to Director of Occupancy, and subsequently to Assistant Executive Director.

Third Paragraph: You
bring up your next most
distinguishing qualities and
try to
sell yourself.

I am comfortable operating within the unique financial constraints of a nonprofit organization, and I offer a proven ability to manage financial resources for maximum effectiveness. I am respected as a professional who deals effectively with people at all levels, from the top-level HUD official and sophisticated bankers, to relatively unsophisticated applicants for housing.

Fourth Paragraph: Here
you have another
opportunity to reveal
qualities or achievements
which will impress your
future employer.

I hope you will call or write me soon to suggest a time convenient for us to meet to discuss your current and future needs. Thank you in advance for your time.

Final Paragraph: She
asks the employer to
contact her. Make sure
your reader knows what
the "next step" is.

Sincerely yours,

Cecelia McCormick

**Alternate Final
Paragraph:** It's more
aggressive (but not too
aggressive) to let the
employer know that you
will be calling him or her.
Don't be afraid to be
persistent. Employers are
looking for people who
know what they want to
do.

Alternate last paragraph:
I hope you will welcome my call soon to arrange a brief meeting when we might meet to discuss your needs and goals and how my background might serve them. I can provide outstanding references at the appropriate time.

Date

Exact Name of Person
Exact Title
Exact Name of Company
Address
City, State, Zip

Dear Exact Name of Person (or Dear Sir or Madam if answering a blind ad):

With the enclosed resume, I would like to make you aware of my interest in exploring employment opportunities with your organization. I am responding to your recent advertisement for an Executive Director.

As you will see from my resume, I have worked for the Shawnee County Health Department since 1995, and I have excelled in a track record of promotion to my current position as Supervisor of the Women's and Children's Health Program. While working within the county's health department, I have become accustomed to interacting with multiple clinics and multiple programs. In my current position, I hire, train, and manage up to 25 individuals while planning and administering multiple budgets totaling more than $2.5 million. I have earned a reputation as a caring individual who is skilled at building consensus and inspiring others to work toward common goals.

An outgoing and energetic individual, I take great pride in the multiple accomplishments of the county's health department, and I have played a key role in many important programs. I co-developed the Shawnee County Healthy Living Program which provided preventive health screening services to the county's 2,000 employees. I have also played a key role in the Pregnant Living Program which has reduced the incidence of teen pregnancies. In addition to organizing numerous projects related to breast cancer awareness and other areas, I developed the Childhood Poison Prevention Program and the Heart Control Program.

While serving the health care needs of the county's indigent population, my main "hobby" has been gaining advanced knowledge through earning additional academic credentials. In addition to earning my L.P.N. and R.N. credentials, I received a Bachelor of Science in Nursing and a Master's in Public Health degree. I am proficient with numerous software programs which I have utilized in my job in order to prepare budgets, track expenditures, and control the funding of multiple programs.

I can provide outstanding personal and professional references at the appropriate time, but I would ask that you not contact the Shawnee County Health Department until after we have a chance to discuss your needs. Since I am in a key management role, I wish my interest in your organization to remain confidential at this time. Thank you in advance for your consideration and professional courtesies.

Yours sincerely,

Lavina Cleveland

This accomplished professional is responding to an advertisement. She analyzed the job vacancy opening very closely and she has made sure that she has tailored her letter of interest to the areas mentioned in the vacancy announcement.

Date

Exact Name of Person
Title or Position
Name of Company
Address (number and street)
Address (city, state, and zip)

Follow-up Letter

A great follow-up letter
can motivate the
employer
to make the job offer,
and the salary offer may
be influenced by the
style and tone of your
follow-up
letter, too!

Dear Exact Name:

I am writing to express my appreciation for the time you spent with me on December 9, and I want to let you know that I am sincerely interested in the position of Executive Director of Adoption Services which we discussed.

I feel confident that I could skillfully interact with your staff, and I would cheerfully relocate to Tennessee, as we discussed.

As you described to me what you are looking for in the person who fills this position, I had a sense of "déjà vu" because my current employer was in a similar position when I went to work for the Salvation Army. The general manager needed someone to come in and be his "right arm" and take on an increasing amount of his management responsibilities so that he could be freed up to do other things. I have played a key role in the growth and success of the organization, and my supervisor has come to depend on my sound advice as much as well as my proven ability to "cut through" huge volumes of work efficiently and accurately. Since this is one of the busiest times of the year for the Salvation Army, I feel that I could not leave during that time. I could certainly make myself available by mid-January.

It would be a pleasure to work for your Adoption Services organization, and I am confident that I could contribute significantly through my strong qualities of loyalty, reliability, and trustworthiness. I am confident that I could quickly learn your style and procedures, and I would welcome being trained to do things your way.

Yours sincerely,

Jacob Evangelisto

In this section, you will find resumes and cover letters of professionals seeking employment, or already employed, in the nonprofit world. How do these individuals differ from other job hunters? Why should there be a book dedicated to people seeking jobs in nonprofit organizations? Based on more than 20 years of experience in working with job hunters, this editor is convinced that resumes and cover letters which "speak the lingo" of the field you wish to enter will communicate more effectively than language which is not industry-specific. This book is designed to help people (1) who are seeking to prepare their own resumes and (2) who wish to use as models "real" resumes of individuals who have successfully launched careers in nonprofit organizations or advanced in those organizations. You will see a wide range of experience levels reflected in the resumes in this book. Some of the resumes and cover letters were used by individuals seeking to enter the field; others were used successfully by senior professionals to advance in the field.

Newcomers to an industry sometimes have advantages over more experienced professionals. In a job hunt, junior professionals can have an advantage over their more experienced counterparts. Prospective employers often view the less experienced workers as "more trainable" and "more coachable" than their seniors. This means that the mature professional who has already excelled in a first career can, with credibility, "change careers" and transfer skills to other industries.

Newcomers to the field may have disadvantages compared to their seniors. Almost by definition, the inexperienced professional—the young person who has recently entered the job market, or the individual who has recently received respected certifications—is less tested and less experienced than senior managers, so the resume and cover letter of the inexperienced professional may often have to "sell" his or her potential to do something he or she has never done before. Lack of experience in the field she wants to enter can be a stumbling block to the junior employee, but remember that many employers believe that someone who has excelled in anything—academics, for example—can excel in many other fields.

Some advice to inexperienced professionals...
If senior professionals could give junior professionals a piece of advice about careers, here's what they would say: Manage your career and don't stumble from job to job in an incoherent pattern. Try to find work that interests you, and then identify prosperous industries which need work performed of the type you want to do. Learn early in your working life that a great resume and cover letter can blow doors open for you and help you maximize your salary.

Special help for career changers...
For those changing careers, you will find useful the resumes and cover letters marked "Career Change" on the following pages. Consult the Table of Contents for page numbers showing career changers.

Date

Exact Name of Person
Title or Position
Name of Company
Address (number and street)
Address (city, state, and zip)

ABUSE CRISIS CENTER EXECUTIVE DIRECTOR

Dear Exact Name of Person: (or Sir or Madam if answering a blind ad.)

With the enclosed resume, I would like to introduce myself and my desire to explore employment opportunities. I believe my extensive background in nonprofit management may be of interest to you.

As you will see from my resume, I currently serve as Executive Director of an organization in Rapid City, where I have managed recruitment and training of a 65-person volunteer staff while supervising three professionals. I have developed cooperation among community organizations while identifying gaps in community services and developing programs to fill those needs. With extensive involvement in financial planning and budgeting, I have resourcefully managed a $200,000 budget for a program providing counseling, support, advocacy, and referral for victims of abuse 24 hours a day, 7 days a week.

In my previous position in Minnehaha County, I was promoted from Community Services Coordinator to Assistant Director and then to Director of a community shelter with a staff of 30 human services professionals and paraprofessionals. In addition to developing and maintaining the $800,000 budget, I was active in grant writing and in numerous community activities which raised the shelter's profile.

The recipient of numerous awards and honors for my contributions and service, I have enjoyed the respect of my colleagues in being elected to leadership positions in professional organizations and high-profile committees. I am widely respected for my ability to develop and maintain effective working relationships, organizational partnerships, and collaborative efforts.

If you can use my considerable leadership abilities and team-building skills, I hope you will contact me to suggest a time when we might meet to discuss your needs and goals and how I might meet them. Thank you in advance for your time.

Sincerely,

Diana Rogers

DIANA ROGERS

1110½ Hay Street, Fayetteville, NC 28305   •   preppub@aol.com   •   (910) 483-6611

OBJECTIVE	To offer my strong management skills and proven track record in fundraising, community relations, and program development to an organization that can use an experienced, motivated professional with a solid background in the directing of nonprofit programs, crisis intervention services, and volunteer activities.
EXPERIENCE	**EXECUTIVE DIRECTOR**. Abuse Crisis Volunteers of Pennington County, Rapid City, SD (2003-present). When I relocated back to Rapid City, was immediately rehired by Abuse Crisis Volunteers of Pennington County as Direct Services Coordinator.

- Gained widespread respect for my leadership and ability to build collaborative coalitions and viable partnerships, and was promoted to Executive Director in 2004.
- As Executive Director, have monitored and directed all aspects of a major crisis intervention agency: implementing policies, determining budgetary requirements, guiding various programs and functions, and managing an organizational budget of $200,000 for a program providing counseling, support groups, advocacy, and referral for victims of abuse 24 hours a day, 7 days a week.
- Identified gaps in community services; and created new programs to fill those gaps.
- Develop ongoing training programs for law enforcement officers; implement prevention programs while overseeing recruitment and training of a staff of 65 volunteers.

Volunteers of St. Mary's Shelter, Minnehaha County, SD (1995-03). *Was promoted in the following "track record" of advancement by a county-wide community shelter with an annual budget of $800,000.*

2000-03: DIRECTOR. While managing the St. Mary's Shelter, directed a staff of 30 human services professionals and paraprofessionals. Acted as liaison between the shelter and the community, establishing relationships with the voluntary Advisory Council, local organizations, and the business community. Developed and maintained an $800,000 budget.
- Conducted effective fundraising through grant writing, solicitations, and special events generated ten percent of the shelter's annual budget.

1997-00: ASSISTANT DIRECTOR. Effectively managed existing services and developed new services for the homeless, maintaining compliance with the shelter program and funding requirements. Supervised and conducted employee evaluations for seven social workers.
- Coordinated the development of new programs, conducted the volunteer recruitment program, determined funding requirements, and served as a liaison to the advisory council and local government agencies.

1995-97: COMMUNITY SERVICES COORDINATOR. Directed and supervised a program with more than 150 volunteers, providing preventive, restorative, and aftercare services to the homeless. Organized fundraising and special events and served as liaison to the Public Affairs committee.

EDUCATION	Enrolled in Black Hills State University's Nonprofit Management Program, Spearfish, SD.

- This is a program of executive education for leading professionals in the nonprofit organizational management field.

Earned **Bachelor of Arts, Sociology,** Black Hills State University, Spearfish, SD, 1993.

HONORS & AFFILIATIONS	Numerous awards for effectiveness as a volunteer including the Mary Teele Jackson Award. Pennington County Delegation to the Governor's Summit on Volunteerism; South Dakota Association for Volunteer Administration; Pennington Children's Advisory Committee.

Date

Exact Name of Person
Title or Position
Exact Name of Company
Address (no., street)
Address (city, state, zip)

Dear Exact Name of Person: (or Dear Sir or Madam if answering a blind ad.):

Enclosed is a resume describing the professional skills and experience I could put to work for you. Please consider my resume as a formal expression of my interest in the job of Director of Addictions Counseling.

A Certified Substance Abuse Counselor and National Certified Addiction Counselor, I offer expertise in managing treatment centers and dependency units. In my current position as an Addictions Consultant for the Illinois Prison System, I have led the state to make major strides forward in its efforts to provide addictions counseling to inmates in the state's overcrowded prison system. In previous positions, I served as Director of Counseling and as Director of a treatment center which served adults and adolescents.

I offer extensive insight into how personality and environment influence individuals to embark upon a lifetime of addictions, and the addendum I am providing to my resume shows the numerous publications I have authored. I understand that the prevailing view in Illinois is that substance abuse should be primarily considered to be a health problem rather than a law enforcement problem, and I have been proud to be associated with "the solution" to this endemic healthcare problem.

With outstanding personal and professional references, I am confident that you would find me in person to be a congenial individual who is skilled in dealing with people. I offer a proven ability to establish rapport with patients and their families as well as with the wide range of professionals at all levels involved in chemical dependency treatment.

I would enjoy an opportunity to meet with you in person to discuss your needs and my background. I hope to hear from you at your earliest convenience.

Sincerely,

Phillip Leslie

PHILLIP LESLIE

1110½ Hay Street, Fayetteville, NC 28305   •   preppub@aol.com   •   (910) 483-6611

2002 to present   ***Addictions Consultant.*** Illinois State Prison, Chicago, IL. Involved in designing a program for a federal grant to provide information about addictions to inmates who do not have the opportunity to attend a formal inpatient program due to overcrowding of the prison system. Train personnel to deliver the orientation and intervention of drug/alcohol rehabilitation treatment. Train and assist counselors in presenting aftercare program. Inform and train DOC personnel at the corrections facility about addictions and treatment.

2000-02   ***Director of Windy City Treatment Center.*** Chicago, IL. Designed and delivered all chemical dependency services at Windy City Treatment Center, including screening for hire, training, and supervision of chemical dependency personnel. Responsible to the Chief of Psychiatry or Medical Director for the quality and delivery of program service. Responsible to Assistant Administrator of Psychiatry Services for all administrative duties executed at Windy City Treatment Center. Provided chemical dependency resources for prevention and education within the medical center as well as in the community.

1996-00   ***Director of Counseling, Chemical Dependency Unit.*** Windy City Medical Center, Chicago, IL. Served as supervisor of all chemical dependency clinical services including chemical dependency counselors, interns-in-training, and DWI counselors. Coordinated with the Program Director for maintenance of patient rights and compliance with the Chemical Dependence Quality Assurance Plan. Also served as a primary counselor for patients assigned by the Program Director. As Primary Counselor, performed intakes and assessments, conducted individual counseling sessions, and conducted educational orientation sessions. Was responsible for all components of patients' charts. Worked closely with family members of the chemically dependent patient to ensure quality care for the family unit.

1985-95   ***Program Coordinator.*** Illinois State Hospital, Chicago, IL. Developed and maintained therapeutic patient program for assigned unit(s) based on patient and community needs, recommendations by hospital administrator and hospital medical staff, and input from the multidisciplinary team. Ensured the delivery of quality patient care.

1983-85   ***Director of Adolescent Substance Abuse Program & Substance Abuse Counselor.*** Chicago Mental Health, Chicago, IL. Responsible for individual as well as group counseling. Directed substance abuse treatment for all adolescents. Licensed ADETS instructor emergency answering service. Responsible for development of school programs in reference to substance abuse. Evaluated and treated the dual diagnosed patient. Performed assessments of DWI offender's court consultations, hospital consultations, and admission screenings for inpatient as well as outpatient facilities. Established workshops/lectures, supervised substance abuse workers. Performed family intervention and referrals.

1980-83   ***Clinical Director/Alcoholism Counselor.*** State of Illinois, Chicago, IL. Conducted individual and group counseling, didactic lectures, admission assessments, admission screenings, patient files, and patient care. Established family and aftercare programs.

1978-80   ***Alcoholism/Drug Counselor.*** Life Center of Chicago, Chicago, IL. Responsible for individual and group counseling, didactic lectures, and participation in adolescent program group facilitation. Was active in family programs as lecturer and counselor.

EDUCATION   **M.A. degree in Public Health,** Georgetown University, Washington, DC, 1978.
B.S. in Nursing, University of North Carolina at Chapel Hill, NC, 1975.

Date

Exact Name of Person
Exact Title
Exact Name of Company
Address
City, State, Zip

ADMINISTRATIVE ASSISTANT,

currently supporting the
administrative needs of
two nonprofit
organizations

Dear Exact Name of Person (or Dear Sir or Madam if answering a blind ad):

With the enclosed resume, I would like to make you aware of the administrative and customer service skills which I could put to work for your organization.

As you will see from my resume, I provide administrative support for both the Wisconsin Association for Latin People and the Fond Du Lac Better Health Alternative. One of my main responsibilities is financial recordkeeping, which includes maintaining daily files containing names of charity fundraising bingo winners and amounts won, along with amounts paid to charity. I was specially recruited for my current position by the organization's chief executive, whom I met when we both worked at the Salvation Army. When he decided to accept the position as the operating chief of the Wisconsin Association for Latin People and the Fond Du Lac Better Health Alternative, he asked me to make the transition with him and become his Administrative Assistant. I am held in high regard and can provide outstanding references at the appropriate time.

Experienced in the use of a variety of software packages, I am proficient with Microsoft Word, Excel and Access. I offer an extensive background in general bookkeeping along with excellent typing skills. I possess excellent customer service as well as oral and written communication skills.

If you can use a hardworking professional who thrives on meeting ambitious goals, I hope you will contact me to suggest a time when we might meet to discuss your goals and how my background might serve your needs. I can provide outstanding references at the appropriate time.

Sincerely,

Lynn Evans

Alternate Last Paragraph:
I hope you will welcome my call soon to arrange a brief meeting when we might meet to discuss your needs and goals and how my background might serve them. I can provide outstanding references at the appropriate time.

LYNN EVANS

1110½ Hay Street, Fayetteville, NC 28305   •   preppub@aol.com   •   (910) 483-6611

OBJECTIVE   To benefit an organization that can use a detail-oriented professional who offers excellent customer-service skills along with a knack for troubleshooting and problem solving.

EDUCATION   Pursuing **Associate of Science degree in Computer Technology,** Fond Du Lac Technical Community College, Fond Du Lac, 2001-present; am completing this degree in my spare time while excelling in my full-time job.
Graduated from Fond Du Lac Senior High School, 1998. Graduated in the top 20% of my class and played varsity women's basketball.

LANGUAGE   Fluently speak, write, and read Spanish

EXPERIENCE   **ADMINISTRATIVE ASSISTANT.** *Wisconsin Association for Latin People* and *Fond Du Lac Better Health Alternative,* Fond Du Lac, WI (2001-present). Provide administrative support for these two nonprofit charity organizations which receive the majority of their funds from the City of Fond Du Lac.
- Perform financial recordkeeping of large amounts of money; maintain files of charity fundraising bingo winners and amounts won, along with amounts paid to charity.
- Help calculate funds based on percentage necessary to maintain the organization. In frequent field conditions on fundraising projects, have been told that I am a "human calculator" with the ability to quickly and accurately process large sums of money.
- Utilize a computer daily in order to compose letters and input statistical data related to individuals served and expenditures made.
- Have become known for my ability to interact gracefully with the customer base of these two organizations.
- Fluent in Spanish, frequently act as a translator for non English speaking constituents.

CASHIER. *Salvation Army,* Fond Du Lac, WI (2000). Refined customer-relations and communication skills while providing quick and courteous service to customers.
- Served as the "right arm" of the chief operating officer, and was trusted with the responsibility of handling large amounts of cash while making daily deposits.
- Was aggressively recruited for the job above when the head of the Salvation Army (my boss) accepted the position of General Manager of the Wisconsin Association for Latin People and Fond Du Lac Better Health Alternative and wanted me to move with him to be his Administrative Assistant.

Highlights of earlier experience: As a volunteer crisis "hot line" counselor, gained problem-solving and troubleshooting skills while providing an empathetic ear to individuals in distress.

SPECIAL SKILLS
- Experienced in the use of a variety of software packages which include PowerPoint, Excel, Word, and Access.
- Am an experienced general bookkeeper with typing skills.
- Have extensively used cash registers and adding machines.
- Offer excellent customer-service as well as oral and written communication skills.

PERSONAL   Have a "knack" for numbers and money-handling. Am an energetic and cheerful professional who subscribes to the philosophy of "treating others as I would like to be treated." Have the proven ability to deal calmly and tactfully with even the most irate customers.

Date

Exact Name of Person
Title or Position
Name of Company
Address (no., street)
Address (city, state, zip)

AFFILIATE MANAGER,
American Cancer Society

Dear Exact Name of Person: (or Dear Sir or Madam if answering a blind ad.)

I would appreciate an opportunity to talk with you soon about how I could contribute to your organization through my background in marketing, public relations, and management.

As you will see from my resume, I am excelling as an Affiliate Manager for the American Cancer Society in Northfield. On a part-time basis, I serve as a continuing advocacy presence for the affiliate office of a state nonprofit organization. I offer a proven ability to develop and implement community support programs which include educational development, presentations, public relations, advocacy, and fund development. Currently I work closely with local business and industry, local government, and health care institutions in the areas of fund acquisition, volunteer recruitment and training, and the development of educational programs, and I have made numerous contributions.

In my spare time, I am pursuing a Masters degree in Theological Studies at the University of Vermont in Burlington. Previously I earned a Master of Arts degree from Dartmouth College and a Bachelor of Arts degree from the Indiana State University. Although much of my early career was spent in land use planning and economic development, I transitioned to the nonprofit sector several years ago, and I derive great satisfaction from being involved in the process of helping the less fortunate in our society.

With strong management and communication skills, I am confident that I could make significant contributions to your organization. I excel in finding ways to develop consensus among disputing parties. I hope you will welcome my call soon to arrange a brief meeting at your convenience to discuss your current and future needs and how I might serve them. Thank you in advance for your time.

Sincerely,

Roy Curtis

ROY CURTIS

1110½ Hay Street, Fayetteville, NC 28305   •   preppub@aol.com   •   (910) 483-6611

OBJECTIVE   I want to contribute to an organization that can use an astute problem solver and strategic thinker who offers a proven ability to resourcefully and cost-effectively manage programs which serve the indigent, elderly, and needy.

EDUCATION   Pursuing **Master's in Theological Studies,** University of Vermont, Burlington, VT.
Earned **Master of Arts** degree in **Marketing/Geography and Land Use Analysis,** Dartmouth College, Hanover, NH, 1992.
Received **Bachelor of Arts** degree in **Geography** (with a minor in Psychology), Indiana State University, Terre Haute, IN, 1990.

EXPERIENCE   **AFFILIATE MANAGER.** American Cancer Society, Northfield, VT (2004-present). While excelling in this full-time position, also serve part-time as a continuing advocacy presence for the affiliate office of a state nonprofit organization.
- Develop and implement community support programs which include educational presentations, public relations, advocacy, and fund development.
- Work closely with local business and industry, local government, and health care institutions in the areas of fund acquisition, volunteer recruitment and training, and the development of educational programs.

DIRECTOR. St. Francis Homeless Shelter, Northfield, VT (2002-03). Oversaw all aspects of the operation of this 44-bed nonprofit facility, including budgeting, recruiting, grant writing, and management of human and fiscal resources.
- Managed yearly operational budget of $183,000; interviewed/hired center personnel.
- Planned and directed the recruitment of a volunteer staff that served lunches to an average of 120 people each day.
- Provided case management and counseling to clients while processing assessment forms, statistical and fiscal reports, and other operational paperwork.
- Acted as liaison between clients and other service providers such as local and state social services, mental health organizations, churches, and philanthropic agencies.

ASSOCIATE DIRECTOR. Northfield Area Economic Development Corporation, Northfield, VT (1993-2002). Began as a Chief Planner in 1993, and was promoted to Associate Director in 1999. Represented the interests of the NAEDC in meetings with industry and business representatives as well as with industrial properties committees; provided managerial oversight in the absence of the Director.
- Oversaw all efforts to recruit new industry while encouraging retention and expansion of existing industry; acted as liaison with industry, local colleges and universities, public works, and government agencies on the state and local level.
- Worked closely with business and industry while coordinating with community colleges in promoting the industry training program.
- Served on the Private Industry Council and the Workforce Development Board.
- Submitted proposals and applications for state financial assistance for companies interested in locating in Northfield; met with clients/representatives of state agencies.
- Reviewed all site location, subdivision, and zoning cases and assisted developers in site selection; managed an operational budget of $50,000 for the section. Drafted unified City of Northfield zoning/subdivision ordinance. Created land use development policy for the county and performed land use plan analyses.

PERSONAL   Served four years as a YMCA volunteer and Boys Wrestling Coach.

CAREER CHANGE

Date

Exact Name of Person
Title or Position
Name of Company
Address (no., street)
Address (city, state, zip)

AREA EXECUTIVE DIRECTOR,

Breast Cancer Society

Dear Exact Name of Person: (or Dear Sir or Madam if answering a blind ad)

With the enclosed resume, I would like to make you aware of the considerable skills and sales abilities I could put to work for you in the position as Pharmaceutical Sales Consultant which you recently advertised.

As you will see from my resume, I am currently excelling in a job which requires a dynamic recruiter, manager, and motivator. As Area Executive Director for the Breast Cancer Society, I manage more than 170 volunteers in seven counties. Since taking over the position in 2002, I have nearly tripled the number of volunteers while increasing income by 170%. I have developed a strong network of contacts throughout those seven counties while working with hospitals, health departments, and other health agencies to communicate the mission of BCS.

In a part-time job for two years while earning my college degree in Marketing at Gannon University (where I was on scholarship and a member of the Honors Program), I excelled in my first sales job while working as a Sales Associate at Burlington Coat Factory.

You would find me in person to be a poised individual with outstanding leadership ability and a high level of personal initiative. Known for creativity and resourcefulness, I am respected for my attention to detail and follow-through. I would welcome the opportunity to work with a fine company that challenges its employees to adopt an attitude of "what if?"

Thanks for your time and consideration.

Sincerely,

Vanessa Carter

VANESSA CARTER

1110½ Hay Street, Fayetteville, NC 28305   •   preppub@aol.com   •   (910) 483-6611

OBJECTIVE

To make a contribution as a resourceful and dynamic hard worker with proven marketing abilities, outstanding time management skills, as well as the personal initiative and motivation to succeed in assignments that require persistence, creativity, and follow through.

EDUCATION

B.S. in Marketing, Gannon University, Ogden, UT, 2000.
- Received a four-year academic scholarship based on my SAT/ACT scores.
- Member, Honors Program, for four years. Major GPA 3.57/4.0; Dean's list three semesters.
- Named to Student Advisory Board, Honors Program, 1999.
- Received President's Youth Service Award.

EXPERIENCE

AREA EXECUTIVE DIRECTOR. Breast Cancer Society, Salt Lake City, UT (2002-present). Have utilized my marketing, recruiting, motivational, and training skills to make significant contributions to this organization while managing 170 volunteers in seven counties.
- Under my strong leadership, income increased 179% in 2002-03 and showed another 69% increase in the last fiscal year; total income for last fiscal year was $417,235 of which $399,339 was Hand-in-Hand Walk income. In one county, boosted total annual income from $186 in 2002 to $53,000 in 2003 and to $101,000 in 2004.
- Recruit, train, manage, and motivate volunteers for both patient services and fund raising; have succeeded in nearly tripling the number of volunteers to 170 individuals.
- Work with hospitals, health departments, and health agencies to communicate the mission of the BCS; have developed a network of contacts within the medical community.
- Plan, organize, and manage fundraising events including the Relay for Life activities.
- Have developed and maintained partnerships with appropriate organizations; for example, developed a partnership between the Breast Cancer Society and the Utah Family Medical Center to facilitate services for cancer patients and boost fundraising.

MEMBER ACCOUNTS MANAGER. Northwest Fitness Center, Utah Family Medical Center, Salt Lake City, UT (2001-02). Created, organized, and implemented marketing and promotional campaigns and events; presented corporate membership plan to companies.
- Maintained all accounting records, supervised receptionists and enrollment process, handled member billing and inquiries, and developed departmental procedures.
- Prepared daily deposits, trained new staff, ordered/displayed items for sale in athletic pro shop. Implemented a computer system to implement sales transactions.

CUSTOMER SERVICE REPRESENTATIVE. Electric Heating Company, Salt Lake City, UT (2000). Assisted with administering Low Income Assistance Program. Contacted eligible customers and informed them of program requirements and benefits. Utilized computer software to enter data and notified customers of due payments.

Other experience:
HEAD ADMINISTRATIVE COORDINATOR. Gannon University, Ogden, UT (1999-2000). Was part of a three-member team working to coordinate tutoring for the Honors Program.
SALES ASSOCIATE. Burlington Coat Factory, Salt Lake City, UT (1997-99). Trained new staff, maintained the store, and provided customer service.

PERSONAL

Outstanding personal and professional references available on request. Active member of the community with affiliations which include the Salt Lake City Chamber of Commerce, Toastmasters Club, and others. Highly creative problem solver.

Date

To: Mr. Malcolm Stepford, Executive Director, Friends of Cancer Center
From: Kathleen Williams

Dear Mr. Stepford:

With the enclosed resume, I would like to make you aware of my interest in the position of Regional Cancer Control Director for the Friends of Cancer Center.

Currently I am excelling as Area Executive Director in Nashville. When I took over this area, community organization had deteriorated to the point that there was no working relationship at all between the Friends of Cancer Center and Nashville Regional Hospital System, one of the largest hospitals in the area. Through revitalization of existing programs, development of new programs, as well as the recruiting, training, and management of volunteers, I was able to restore Nashville Regional Hospital's confidence in the Friends of Cancer Center and we now have a successful partnership. To increase community awareness of the Friends of Cancer Center, I have initiated a number of new programs, including a highly successful **"New Beginning"** program at Nashville, in which 30 program facilitators served the needs of 400 participants in the last year. Through my efforts, revenues from the annual Friends for Life increased from $36,000 in 1997 to $114,000 in 2004. In the rest of Davidson County, the Friends of Cancer Center previously had little presence. I now manage the activities of a team of 30 volunteers whom I recruited and trained to handle fundraising and patient service programs. I established Davidson County's Friends for Life event, raising $40,000 in a county with a population of only 29,000. The **"Road to Recovery"** programs are scheduled to be launched in early 2005.

In addition to my expert knowledge of Friends of Cancer Center programs, I offer the strong management and supervisory skills which this position requires. In a previous management position with a profit-making company subcontracted by municipalities to handle appraisal functions, I handled key management responsibilities and played a significant role in creating, implementing, and executing the company's business plan. A major responsibility of mine involved traveling throughout Tennessee to establish "from scratch" and then manage offices performing the tax appraisals. I hired, trained, and provided oversight for all satellite office employees as I performed liaison with local and state officials.

It is my sincere desire to be of service to the Friends of Cancer Center as Regional Cancer Control Director. Please give me the opportunity to talk with you in person about this position, as I feel certain that I could significantly contribute to the Friends of Cancer Center in this capacity. Thank you in advance for your consideration of my deep desire to serve in a management role.

Sincerely,

Kathleen Williams

KATHLEEN WILLIAMS

1110½ Hay Street, Fayetteville, NC 28305 • preppub@aol.com • (910) 483-6611

OBJECTIVE To offer my experience in program and project management, my proven leadership and motivational skills, as well as my background in planning and development of Cancer Control programs, fundraising, community organization, and volunteer management.

EDUCATION **B.S. in Merchandising,** East Tennessee State University, Johnson City, TN, 1995. Through training, have become a Certified Appraiser, Tennessee Department of Revenue.

COMPUTERS Proficient with Windows XP, HBOC hospital software, and Optika Imaging System.

EXPERIENCE **AREA EXECUTIVE DIRECTOR.** Friends of Cancer Center, Nashville, TN (2002-present). Took over as Executive Director for this area at a time when many activities and tasks were in disarray; through careful management of programs and services, was able to quickly revitalize and restore confidence in the local Friends of Cancer Center. Direct activities of over 150 volunteers in this three-county area, aggressively directing fundraising efforts and handling staffing for patient services, projects, and events.
- Raised nearly $218,000 in 2004, an increase of almost $80,000 over 2003; increased **Friends for Life** income in Nashville dramatically, from $36,000 in 2003 to $114,000 in 2004; rebuilt the Friends of Cancer Center's relationship with Nashville Regional Hospital System which had broken down completely before I took over.
- Established the Friends of Cancer Center presence in Davidson County, developing relationships with the local health department; recruited, trained, and currently manage 30 volunteers; organized within the community to build a solid, capable team in a county with little previous Friends of Cancer Center representation; through my initiative, contributions skyrocketed to 100 times the previous year's level; raised $40,000 in the county.
- Retrained volunteers and am working to rebuild relationships with Nashville Providence Hospital and the medical community; am finalizing plans to implement the following new programs in Nashville: **Lung Cancer Support Group**, **Road to Recovery.**
- Strengthened existing patient services programs and implemented new ones.
- Completed "**Make Yours a New Beginning Family**" Facilitator Training, 2004.

PATIENT ACCOUNTS REPRESENTATIVE. Nashville Regional Hospital, Nashville, TN (2002). Performed a variety of financial, administrative, and clerical services for patients at this busy medical center; performed follow-up and collections on all self-pay accounts.
- Handled patient complaints, collected past due accounts, filed insurance claims.

MANAGER & COMPUTER SPECIALIST. Copland Services, Nashville, TN (1997-2001). For a company which was subcontracted by counties and municipalities to perform property appraisals, handled key management responsibilities which involved establishing and managing offices throughout Tennessee to perform subcontracted appraisal functions.
- Hired and trained all office employees and functioned as the liaison with corporate officers, computer programmers, as well as officials from state and local governments.
- Interviewed, hired, trained, and supervised as many as 25 data entry clerks.

AFFILIATIONS Member of Tennessee Association of Volunteer Administrators, Nashville Chamber of Commerce, Cancer Committee at Tennessee Regional Hospital, and Cancer Campaign Committee of the Davidson County Health Department.

PERSONAL Excellent personal/professional references available. Known for strong personal initiative.

Exact Name of Person
Title or Position
Name of Company
Address (no., street)
Address (city, state, zip)

ASSISTANT EXECUTIVE DIRECTOR,

Habitat for Humanity

Dear Exact Name of Person: (or Dear Sir or Madam if answering a blind ad.)

With the enclosed resume, I would like to make you aware of my interest in exploring employment opportunities with your organization.

As you will see from my resume, I am currently excelling as Assistant Executive Director of Habitat for Humanity. My major responsibilities include preparing annual operating budgets, budgets for new projects, and budgets for construction while monitoring funds expensed in multiple simultaneous projects. I supervise three staff persons and assure compliance with regulations, including HUD and VA, related to housing ownership. In addition to determining eligibility of applicants and verifying family income as well as criminal records, I approve payment agreements and audit homeowners' compliance with HUD regulations.

You will notice that I have excelled in a track record of promotion with Habitat for Humanity. After graduating with a B.S. in Finance from the University of North Carolina at Chapel Hill, I began employment with Habitat as a Project Manager, was promoted to Acting Executive Director and then to Director of Occupancy, and subsequently to Assistant Executive Director.

I am comfortable operating within the unique financial constraints of a nonprofit organization, and I offer a proven ability to manage financial resources for maximum effectiveness. I am respected as a professional who deals effectively with people at all levels, from the top-level HUD official and sophisticated bankers, to relatively uneducated applicants for housing.

I hope you will call or write me soon to suggest a time convenient for us to meet to discuss your current and future needs. Thank you in advance for your time.

Sincerely yours,

Cecelia McCormick

Alternate last paragraph:
I hope you will welcome my call soon to arrange a brief meeting when we might meet to discuss your needs and goals and how my background might serve them. I can provide outstanding references at the appropriate time.

CECILIA McCORMICK

1110½ Hay Street, Fayetteville, NC 28305 • preppub@aol.com • (910) 483-6611

OBJECTIVE

To obtain a challenging administrative position in the human services field which will utilize my knowledge of housing services, especially in low-cost housing.

EXPERIENCE

Advanced through this track record of promotion with Habitat for Humanity, Newton, PA, 1993-present:

2003-present: ASSISTANT EXECUTIVE DIRECTOR. As Assistant Executive Director, prepare operational budgets, development budgets for new projects, and budgets for construction; monitor budgets for adequate funds to complete projects and prepare requests for additional funds as needed.

- Monitor bank accounts, project cash flow needed to operate; assure funds are correctly charged between development and operations. Monitor operational, development, and TAR accounts; review maintenance charges.
- Supervise three staff persons; assure compliance with regulation for occupancy, rent computation, annual reexamination, and interim-rent adjustment; monitor waiting list; approve payment agreements and rent extensions; audit tenant files for compliance with HUD regulations and Housing Authority policies and procedures.
- Assist with financial compliance audit, construction costs payments, and close out documents for EIOP. Monitor monthly financial statements to assure budget line items are not exceeded and prepare modifications if needed.
- Interpret federal, state, and local regulations necessary to operate and administer programs of Habitat for Humanity. Attend Commissioner's regular and annual meetings.
- Obtained an additional $100,000 for Mutual Help Program and negotiated the purchase of a 60-acre tract of land for the project.

1998-2003: DIRECTOR OF OCCUPANCY. Determined eligibility of applicants; collected and verified income, family composition, and criminal record history. Computed rent, giving adequate deductions in accordance with HUD regulations.

- Resolved complaints, counseled residents on delinquent rent, and investigated fire and damage reports; assisted with annual inspection of units for compliance with housekeeping and assisted in annual inventory inspection of 204 units.
- Supervised three staff persons.

1998: ACTING EXECUTIVE DIRECTOR. Served as Executive Director to the Housing Authority; conducted planning meetings; made recommendations on policy.

- Began construction on a $1.1 million dollar new construction project for 30 units; managed all personnel functions. Prepared all reports and documents to amend requirements; reviewed monthly budget reports from fee accountant.
- Managed 204 housing units.
- Supervised five administrative and three maintenance staff employees.

1993-97: PROJECT MANAGER. Conducted orientation, determined eligibility, and conducted move-in inspections for 92 units in Luzerne County. Assisted maintenance staff with inventory and inspections.

- Conducted annual recertification of all residents.

EDUCATION

Graduated with a **Bachelor of Science in Finance,** University of North Carolina at Chapel Hill, NC, 1993.

Graduated from Newtown High School, Newtown, PA, 1989.

CAREER CHANGE

Date

Exact Name of Person
Title or Position
Address (no., street)
Address (city, state, zip)

ASSISTANT MANAGER

employed in the financial services field is seeking a transition into the nonprofit world

Dear Exact Name of Person: (or Dear Sir or Madam if answering a blind ad.)

With the enclosed resume, I would like to make you aware of my strong interest in the position as Community Employment Specialist which you recently advertised.

As you will see from my resume, I am excelling in my current job in the profit-making private sector, but it is my desire to make a career change into the human services field. I am confident that my high-energy personality and sincere desire to help others could be of great benefit in the job you advertised. After reading your advertisement, I believe I satisfy all of the requirements you are seeking in this position serving the developmentally disabled population.

In my current job, I am highly respected for my ability to establish and maintain smooth working relationships. I am certain I could excel in identifying and developing job training and placement opportunities in local businesses, and I believe my business experience would be an asset in that regard.

My first experience with nonprofit organizations was immediately after college graduation, when I served with distinction as a Community Service Coordinator. In that capacity, I was involved in interviewing clients and placing them in appropriate community work programs. I enjoyed the opportunity to be of service to others, and I am confident that I now possess even more skills and abilities which could be of value.

I can provide excellent personal and professional references at the appropriate time, but I would prefer that you not contact my current employer until after we have a chance to talk. I hope my versatile talents and experience will interest you, and I am confident I could become a productive and caring member of your professional team. Thank you in advance for your time.

Yours sincerely,

Alicia Walter

ALICIA WALTER

1110½ Hay Street, Fayetteville, NC 28305 • preppub@aol.com • (910) 483-6611

OBJECTIVE

To benefit an organization through my highly refined communication and customer service skills as well as my desire to utilize my talents and abilities in a way that contributes to the lives of others.

EDUCATION

B.S., Criminal Justice, Regents College, Albany, NY, 1997.
A.A.S., Criminal Justice, Onondaga Community College, Syracuse, NY, 1995.

EXPERIENCE

Have excelled in this track record of progression with Hudson Financial Services, Albany, NY (2002-present).
2004-present: ASSISTANT MANAGER. Was promoted to assistant manager based on my exceptional communication, problem-solving, and customer service skills; negotiate with car dealers and financial decision makers while achieving or exceeding my quota of $250,000 a month in loans.
- Call on past due accounts; handle all personal loans; assist real estate specialist.
- Have become respected for my outgoing nature and ability to develop outstanding relationships.

2002-04: LOAN PROCESSOR. Pulled credit bureau reports to process indirect car loans and conduct monthly monitoring of insurance policies to ensure customers are maintaining continuous coverage.
- Verified loan contracts with customers; provide assistance with real estate lending.
- Assisted in collections work and in accepting loan payments.

Previous experience:
CREDIT REPRESENTATIVE & ADMINISTRATIVE ASSISTANT. Alliance Corporation, Albany, NY (2001-02). Supervised the funding and management of revolving accounts.
- Pulled credit bureau reports and made decisions on whether to grant loans.
- Provided assistance to customers as well as employees in our office and other offices.
- Monitored the payment of bills and office supply orders.

SENIOR CUSTOMER SERVICE REPRESENTATIVE. Alliance Corporation, Troy, NY (2000-01). Credited customers' accounts when payments were made in cash or through the mail. Handled purchases of sales finance accounts.
- Developed highly refined collections skills and techniques.
- Provided customer service and responded to customer inquiries and problems.

COMMUNITY SERVICE COORDINATOR. Albany Employment Commission Service, Albany, NY (1997-99). Interviewed clients and placed them in appropriate community service work programs.

Other experience:
SECURITY JOB. Onondaga Lake Mall, Syracuse, NY (1995-96). Demonstrated attention-to-detail skills and my reliability in this part-time job to finance my college education.
ENGLISH & ALGEBRA TUTOR. Onondaga Community College, Syracuse, NY (1994). Due to my excellent academic achievements in the areas of math and English, was selected to provide assistance to students who were struggling in these courses.

PERSONAL

Proficient in using a variety of software used in the finance industry. Experienced in working with credit bureaus. Am a skillful communicator.

Date

Exact Name of Person
Title or Position
Name of Company
Address (number and street)
Address (city, state, and zip)

ASSISTANT MANAGER, RECREATION CENTER

Dear Exact Name of Person: (or Sir or Madam if answering a blind ad.)

With the enclosed resume, I would like to introduce myself and the experience I offer related to project management, operations management, and service operations management.

As you will see from my resume, I have excelled as an Assistant Manager in a nonprofit organization which provides food service and recreational programs as part of an effort to enhance employee morale. With my current employer, I began in an entry-level position and was promoted to handle a variety of management responsibilities. I have been involved in employee hiring, training, and evaluation for a seven-day-a-week snack bar as well as a bowling alley. In addition to controlling inventory, I play a key role in budget preparation and budget management, and I have earned respect for my resourcefulness and bottom-line orientation.

On my own initiative, I have organized a variety of special projects and events which included birthday parties, anniversary celebrations, history celebrations and events, Christmas and Hanukkah parties, and other such projects. The emphasis throughout each project was on careful planning, preparation, and follow through while providing outstanding customer service.

The organization I work for conducts continuous customer evaluations of the services we provide, and I have been singled out by name on numerous evaluations because of my gracious style of interacting with the public. I can provide excellent personal and professional references.

Please be assured that I am ready to travel or work whatever hours your needs require. I hope you will contact me if my considerable skills and talents interest you.

Sincerely,

John O'Sullivan

JOHN O'SULLIVAN

1110½ Hay Street, Fayetteville, NC 28305 • preppub@aol.com • (910) 483-6611

OBJECTIVE

I want to contribute to an organization that can use a skilled operations manager who is known for my attention to detail in inventory control and budgeting as well as for my dedication to the highest standards of quality control, customer service, and profitability.

EDUCATION

Pursuing **Bachelor's degree in Business** in my spare time; have completed courses at Jefferson Community College, Watertown, NY; degree anticipated 2006.

Completed courses sponsored by my employers in these and other areas:

Operations Management	Quality Control	Customer Service
Restaurant Management	Catering	Snack Bar Management

EXPERIENCE

ASSISTANT MANAGER. Recreation Center, Fort Drum, NY (2001-present). Manage popular services sponsored by the Department of the Army; act as the Assistant Manager of two key operations and routinely manage them with little to no supervision.

- **Employee training and hiring**: In charge of interviewing, training, and supervising new employees.
- **Operations management**: Manage operations of a bowling alley and a seven-day-a-week snack bar.
- **Financial control:** Provide vital input into budgets for both the bowling alley and the snack bar; play a key role in raising profits, reducing expenses, and establishing new controls for inventory in both service operations.
- **Food service management:** Operate a popular facility which maintains operating hours of 11 am-11 pm; I personally arrive at the facility at 7 am in order to examine inventory, determine which items needed to be ordered, and handle the bookkeeping and other paperwork. The snack bar serves pizzas, burgers, hot dogs, chicken, turkey, and other items to as many as 1,000 customers daily.
- **Bowling center management**: Manage all aspects of a 10-lane bowling alley which is a chief form of entertainment for residents of this 5,000-person military community.
- **Events management:** Organize and manage a wide variety of special projects and events which include:

Birthday parties	Anniversary parties	Black history celebrations
Christmas parties	Hanukkah parties	Native American history events

- **Computer operations:** Utilize a computer to input data and maintain records; use software including Microsoft Word, Excel, and Access.
- **Performance evaluations:** Always receive the highest evaluations of my performance in every measured area. Was commended as a very hard worker who set the standard for others and cited for my strong communication skills and ability to relate effectively to customers, employees, and supervisors. Received many citations and awards for outstanding performance.

Experience in high school:

WAREHOUSEMAN. Commissary, Fort Drum, NY (1999-01). Worked up to 30 hours a week after school and on weekends during my junior and senior year of high school.

- Learned to perform nearly every job in a warehouse, and was the only man who worked in the facility; performed a variety of heavy lifting of products such as televisions.
- Became knowledgeable of the basics of stock control and warehouse management.

PERSONAL

Have a strong work ethic and thrive on helping an activity reach its full potential in terms of customer service and profitability. Am known for my reliability and punctuality. Can provide excellent personal and professional references.

Date

Exact Name of Person
Exact Title
Exact Name of Company
Address
City, State, Zip

Dear Exact Name of Person (or Dear Sir or Madam if answering a blind ad):

With the enclosed resume, I would like to make you aware of my interest in exploring employment opportunities with your organization.

As you will see, I will receive a B.S. degree in Communications from Dartmouth College in 2005. In a recent internship--which became a part-time job--with the Grafton County Public Information Office, I have assisted the county's Public Information Officer in administering the county's media relations, community relations, and internal relations program. On a formal evaluation of my work, I was praised for my "ability to grasp unfamiliar concepts quickly, eagerness to learn new skills, and dependability."

Proficient with several software programs, I had an opportunity to gain experience with PageMaker, Photoshop, and Illustrator. I offer a proven ability to rapidly master new software programs and applications.

You will notice from my resume that I took time off from college before returning for my senior year at Dartmouth. In addition to earning money to partially finance my college degree, I gained valuable experience in management during that year. I was successful in managing a small retail store while handling responsibility for cash flow, inventory control, merchandising, personnel management, and bottom-line results.

As I approach college graduation, I am confident that my strong communication skills and ability to establish effective working relationships can be of value to an organization that can use a dedicated hard worker. I can provide excellent references.

Yours sincerely,

Caleb Smith

CALEB SMITH

1110½ Hay Street, Fayetteville, NC 28305   •   preppub@aol.com   •   (910) 483-6611

OBJECTIVE   I want to contribute to the growth and profitability of a company that can use a talented organizer, manager, and communicator who offers a proven ability to establish effective working relationships through my natural sales abilities and strong problem-solving skills.

EDUCATION   **Bachelor of Science (B.S.) Degree in Communications,** Dartmouth College, Hanover, NH, 2005. Totally financed my college education through work and scholarships.
Graduated from Porter Senior High School, Manchester, NH, 1998.
- Was a member of the Junior Varsity and Varsity Basketball teams.

COMPUTERS   Experienced with numerous software programs including Adobe PageMaker, Photoshop, Illustrator, Word, and other programs.

EXPERIENCE   **ASSISTANT TO THE PUBLIC INFORMATION DIRECTOR.** Grafton County Public Information Office, Hanover, NH (2004-present). Was specially selected for this internship which became a part-time job. Assisted the Grafton County Public Information Officer in administering Grafton County's community relations, media relations, and internal relations program.
- Handle responsibilities related to external communications and media relations; am in charge of a full-page layout which appears in the Saturday newspaper weekly. Develop the weekly theme for the ad after consulting with department heads. Then utilize Adobe PageMaker, Photoshop, and Illustrator to develop the full page piece.
- Handle responsibilities for financial accounting; control inventory.
- Manage a small office; answer phones and provide customer service.
- Play a key role in writing, publishing, and distributing the *Grafton Bulletin*, which serves as the internal communication medium for 900 county employees. Participate in government meetings; gain insight into the workings of government.
- Became skilled in writing and editing under tight deadlines as I responded to citizen inquiries and drafted press releases. Developed a *Guide to Services* brochure for public distribution. Received written praise for my ability to grasp unfamiliar concepts quickly, eagerness to learn new skills, and dependability.

ASSISTANT DIRECTOR. Junior Basketball Camp, Manchester, NH (2000-02). Refined my management and motivational skills while organizing a basketball camp for more than 350 children, whom I coached and supervised in their drills and play activities.
- Strengthened my public speaking skills through speaking to large groups. Refined my motivational skills working one-on-one with individuals with different learning styles.

MANAGER. Abercrombie & Fitch, Manchester, NH (2000-01). Began as an Assistant Manager and was promoted to manager of a retail store in a prominent mall; was personally accountable for cash deposits, merchandising, inventory, personnel management, and the achievement of bottom-line goals. Took a year off from college and worked in this job and the one above in order to earn money for college.

Other experience: WAREHOUSE WORKER. Sam's Club, Manchester, NH. In this summer job, was promoted into management after my first 30 days of employment; learned how to work with others in shipping/receiving activities.

PERSONAL   Volunteer Junior Olympic Basketball Coach. Highly motivated individual who desires to make a difference. Excellent references.

CAREER CHANGE

Date

Exact Name of Person
Title or Position
Exact Name of Company
Address (no., street)
Address (city, state, zip)

BUYER & FINANCIAL PLANNER

in a retail organization seeks to transition skills to a nonprofit organization

Dear Exact Name of Person: (or Dear Sir or Madam if answering a blind ad.)

With the enclosed resume, I would like to introduce you to the considerable financial planning skills which I would like to utilize for the benefit of your organization. I am making a career change from financial management in the retail world to financial management in the human services field, and I can assure you that I have much to offer. I am responding to your recent advertisement for a Financial Manager for the New York Community Resources Cooperative.

After earning my college degree in Communications, I began working for the Nordstrom organization and have excelled in an unusually rapid track record of advancement to Buyer. In my current position, I am responsible for a $10 million sales volume, and much of what I do is similar to managing a portfolio of commercial accounts. In 2003, I increased volume by over 4% while also increasing profit margin dollars, and in 2004 so far, I am showing a 26% increase in sales compared to 2003.

While handling multimillion-dollar responsibility related to 14 departments in 22 stores, I have conducted extensive negotiations with vendors in San Francisco and Billings while also performing liaison with store managers throughout western MT. I work extensively with financial software and am highly proficient with Excel, which I use on a daily basis to analyze data for stores, vendors, and product lines.

I believe the primary reason for my success has been my communication skills as well as my ability to establish and maintain excellent working relationships. Each time I have been reassigned responsibility for a new area within Nordstrom, my reputation has preceded me and I have been enthusiastically welcomed by store managers who had heard "through the grapevine" that I am a true professional who can be counted on to help them achieve outstanding bottom-line results.

Although I could remain with the Nordstrom organization and am held in high regard, I have decided that I wish to make a change into the human services field. With my strong communication and financial management skills, I feel certain I could make valuable contributions, and I would hope to rise into the ranks of management based on my accomplishments.

I hope you will contact me to suggest a time when we might meet to discuss your needs and how I might meet them. Thank you in advance for your time.

Sincerely,

Kaylee Charlie

KAYLEE CHARLIE

1110½ Hay Street, Fayetteville, NC 28305   •   preppub@aol.com   •   (910) 483-6611

OBJECTIVE

I want to contribute to an organization that can use a skilled financial manager and planner who thrives on meeting ambitious sales goals and financial objectives in a fast-paced, competitive environment where building strong relationships is essential to success.

EDUCATION

Earned **Bachelor of Science in Communications with a Minor in Public Relations,** The University of Montana, Missoula, MT, 1995.
Excelled in extensive training sponsored by the Nordstrom organization related to financial accounting, inventory control, and financial planning as well as sales and customer service.

EXPERIENCE

Have advanced in a track record of promotion with the Nordstrom organization:
2001-present: BUYER & FINANCIAL PLANNER. Missoula, MT. Was promoted in an unusually short time frame from Associate Buyer to Buyer, and then received in 2002 the prestigious **Gold Employee Award;** have excelled in managing an annual volume of $10 million while directing the planning, development, presentation, and profitability for the Women's Sportswear Departments in 22 stores.
- In 2003, increased volume by over 4% while also increasing profit margin dollars; in 2004 so far, am showing a 26% increase in sales over 2003.
- As a buyer, travel to San Francisco 15 times a year; to the corporate office in Billings six times a year; and to stores throughout western Montana in order to re-merchandise stores, retrain sales personnel, and consult with store managers.
- Negotiate prices with vendors from companies including Nine West, Ralph Lauren, Tommy Hilfiger, and Kenneth Cole; am known for my skill in negotiating the best price to ensure an optimal markup and gross margin.
- Aggressively manage my financial plan for 14 departments in 22 stores.
- Extensively communicate with vendors and store managers.
- Have earned an excellent reputation among vendors and store managers; each of the three times I was reassigned to a new buying area, my reputation as a vibrant communicator and strong manager preceded me and I was enthusiastically welcomed by the store management for whom I was assigned to perform buying.
- Am highly creative and resourceful by nature, and am continuously engaged in a process of developing new projects and contests to increase sales; have sponsored numerous sales contests.
- Extensively consult with store managers on sales and margin; provide them with expert guidance related to inventory and product line.

2000-01: ASSOCIATE BUYER. Missoula, MT (2000-01). Assisted four buyers.

1996-00: AREA SALES MANAGER. Missoula, MT (1998-00). Was responsible for sales associates' schedules; responded to customer inquiries and concerns. Conducted monthly department meetings; interviewed new sales associates. Increased volume by 1.5%; exceeded personal sales goal by 61%.

1995-96: SALES ASSOCIATE. Bozeman, MT. Was recruited after college graduation.

COMPUTERS

Highly proficient in utilizing computers in order to analyze financial data; on a daily basis use Excel to analyze sales, vendor, and store data.

PERSONAL

Can provide outstanding references. Offer a reputation as an outgoing communicator with an ability to establish and maintain excellent working relationships.

Date

Exact Name of Person
Title or Position
Name of Company
Address (no., street)
Address (city, state, zip)

CASE MANAGER,
Department of Social
Services

Dear Exact Name of Person: (or Dear Sir or Madam if answering a blind ad.)

With the enclosed resume, I would like to make you aware of my interest in exploring employment opportunities with your organization.

As you will see from my resume, I excelled academically while obtaining my B.S. in Social Work. Inducted into the National Association of Social Workers, I was also accepted into the Social Work Honor Society because of my excellent grades and demonstrated potential for leadership.

Currently a Case Manager at the Department of Social Services, I work with the Community Program for Disabled Adults and have been evaluated as "one of the brightest interns participating in this program." I excel in assessing and coordinating all care for nine patients including home health, mental health, housing, economic, and social needs.

On my own initiative, I established new community resources including "HEAR NOW" which provides hearing aids to people who cannot afford them. I also developed a new information resource for the elderly, handicapped, and disabled seeking housing. In my spare time, I assist the Adult Services Unit in conducting adult protective services investigations of abuse and neglect. I have been recognized as an exemplary advocate with outstanding "networking" ability, and I have gained an excellent understanding of how community social services organizations interrelate.

I hope you will call or write me soon to suggest a time convenient for us to meet to discuss your current and future needs. Thank you in advance for your time.

Sincerely yours,

Lucy Jones

Alternate last paragraph:
I hope you will welcome my call soon to arrange a brief meeting when we might meet to discuss your needs and goals and how my background might serve them. I can provide outstanding references at the appropriate time.

LUCY JONES

1110½ Hay Street, Fayetteville, NC 28305 • preppub@aol.com • (910) 483-6611

OBJECTIVE

I am eager to contribute to an organization that can use an enthusiastic self starter who offers an excellent education in social work along with hands-on experience in dealing with people of all age groups, ethnic, cultural, and socioeconomic backgrounds.

EDUCATION

Bachelor of Science degree in Social Work (B.S.W.), Baker College, Flint, MI, 2004.
- Was inducted into the **Social Work Honor Society, Beta Phi Chi**, because of excellent grades and demonstrated potential for leadership in this field.
- Was selected to the **Golden Key National Honor Society** honoring the top 15% of juniors and seniors among Michigan universities. Was accepted for membership into the **National Association of Social Workers.**
- Achieved a GPA of 3.82 overall and 3.9 in my major.

EXPERIENCE

CASE MANAGER (STUDENT INTERN). Genesee County Department of Social Services, Flint, MI (2004-present). Work with the Community Program for Disabled Adults, and was evaluated as one of the brightest interns participating in this program; excel in assessing and coordinating all care for nine patients including home health, mental health, housing, economic, and social needs.
- On my own initiative, established new community resources including "HEAR NOW" which provides hearing aids to people who cannot afford them; developed a new information resource for the elderly and disabled seeking housing.
- Plan goals and objectives with CAP patients; order medical supplies/equipment.
- Assist Adult Services Unit in conducting adult protective services investigations of abuse and neglect. Perform extensive documentation related to all interviews, correspondence, and contact with clients; became skilled in preparing paperwork used in social work.
- Prepare written correspondence/business letters to clients and outside contacts.
- Attend Advisory Board meetings and staff meetings.
- Recognized as an outstanding advocate with superb "networking" ability; network successfully with other community resource professionals and have gained an excellent understanding of how the community social services organizations interrelate.

Held the following positions while financing my education:
RECEPTIONIST. Cingular Wireless, Flint, MI (2002-04). Operated a switchboard and paging system for three Cingular Wireless sales offices; because of my excellent public relations skills, was selected to assist in scheduling workshops.
- Was commended for my effective interaction with high-level executives.

DEPARTMENTAL ASSISTANT. Genesee County Memorial Hospital, Community Relations Department, Flint, MI (2001). While working in the hospital's Community Relations Department and Employee Wellness Center, assisted in planning and coordinating events while making reservations for hospital functions.
- Gathered data from hospital employees through conducting interviews to compile data related to the hospital's Employee Fitness Program; attended hospital board meetings.

SENIOR CITIZENS TELEMARKETER. Michigan Senior Citizens Center, Lansing, MI (1999-00). Initiated telephone contact with senior citizens/prospective clients; produced a significant increase in visits by retirees.

PERSONAL

Am a creative and dynamic "opportunity finder" who excels in discovering new resources. Adapt easily to new environments. Excel at working independently or as a part of a team.

Exact Name of Person
Title or Position
Name of Company
Address (no., street)
Address (city, state, zip)

CASEWORKER II,
Department of Social
Services, is seeking a
position as Adoption
Services Coordinator

Dear Exact Name of Person: (or Dear Sir or Madam if answering a blind ad.)

I would appreciate an opportunity to talk with you soon about how I could contribute to your organization through my experience in the social services field as well as my strong personal qualities of reliability, dedication, and compassion.

As you will see from my resume, I have enjoyed a track record of promotion with the Department of Social Services since 1995. I began in an entry-level position as a Clerk in Administration and have advanced to a management position handling more than 200 cases simultaneously. I am highly regarded and provide excellent references at the appropriate time.

I am particularly interested in the position of Adoption Services Coordinator which you described in your advertisement. As an adopted child myself, I believe I could relate well to the range of emotions and issues experienced by adopted children, although I have no "personal agenda" and believe that each situation is unique.

I hope you will call or write me soon to arrange a brief meeting at your convenience to discuss your current and future needs and how I might serve them. Thank you in advance for your time.

Sincerely yours,

Ashley Cooper

ASHLEY COOPER

1110½ Hay Street, Fayetteville, NC 28305   •   preppub@aol.com   •   (910) 483-6611

OBJECTIVE

To contribute to an organization that can use my strong management skills as well as my experience in human services work.

EXPERIENCE

Have excelled in the following track record of promotion with the Maine Department of Social Services, Portland, ME (1995-present).
2003-present: CASEWORKER II. Evaluate applicants for all types of public assistance, figuring household budgets for amounts of assistance to be granted and making sure assistance received is within federal mandated time frames.
- Assist in training new employees and covering other caseloads when vacancies arose.
- Was promoted into this position from Caseworker I.

2000-03: CASEWORKER I. With the Assistance Program, was responsible for processing applications to see if they met federal regulations, figuring household budgets to determine food stamp allotments, making all revisions in the cases, and keeping all cases in current status. Assisted in training new personnel.

1997-2000: CLERICAL SUPERVISOR IV, ADMINISTRATION. Supervised a staff of six people responsible for daily maintenance of all department records.
- Was essential in establishing work flow between departments and incorporating new changes into agency policy.
- Assisted in the establishment of a microfilming program and an intra-agency computer system.
- Trained new personnel. Performed general office management including filing, bookkeeping, and filing. Demonstrated my skill in establishing efficient office procedures and systems that benefit the entire operating system.

1996-97: CLERK III, ADMINISTRATION. Handled recordkeeping and research while serving as the Assistant Supervisor.

1995-96: CLERK II, ADMINISTRATION. Handled filing of agency correspondence and computer-generated forms; researched records to provide assistance to county agencies.

Other experience:
EXECUTIVE SECRETARY. Casco Bay Gift Shop, Portland, ME (1993-95). Handled accounts receivable/payable; acted as store manager in owner's absence.
- Accompanied owner on buying trips to throughout Maine for new merchandise.
- Prepared weekly employee work schedules, assisted with sales, and processed and confirmed all special requests for merchandise.

EDUCATION

Completed **B.S. in Psychology,** University of Maine, Augusta, ME, 1994.
Previously studied Business and Merchandising for three years at Delaware State University, Dover, DE.

ACTIVITIES

Board of Advisors, Maine Volunteer Program, Portland, ME
Hospice Volunteer, Portland, ME
Deacon, Highland Presbyterian Church, Portland, ME
Cubmaster, Boy Scout Troop 747, Portland, ME

Date

Exact Name of Person
Title or Position
Name of Company
Address
City, State, Zip

Dear Exact Name of Person: (or Dear Sir or Madam if answering a blind ad.)

With the enclosed resume, I would like to make you aware of my interest in exploring employment opportunities with your organization.

As you will see from my resume, I earned an M.S.W. with a concentration in Child Welfare and a B.A. in Sociology and Social Services. I am a member of the American Association of Social Workers. In my earliest experience as a Social Work Intern, I gained experience in working with emotionally disturbed children both in groups and individually.

In my current employment as an Investigator with the Child Protective Services, my responsibilities include intervention and stabilization of families in crisis as the result of child abuse and neglect investigations. I am required to document case findings, conduct family assessments, write court petitions and court reports, and I routinely make on-the-spot decisions based on my understanding of family dynamics and community resources.

In prior employment with the Family and Children's Services, I excelled as the Crisis Social Worker where I was responsible for providing service to families with acute problems.

I hope you will call or write me soon to suggest a time convenient for us to meet to discuss your current and future needs. Thank you in advance for your time.

Sincerely yours,

Leah Porter

Alternate last paragraph:
I hope you will welcome my call soon to arrange a brief meeting when we might meet to discuss your needs and goals and how my background might serve them. I can provide outstanding references at the appropriate time.

LEAH PORTER

1110½ Hay Street, Fayetteville, NC 28305   •   preppub@aol.com   •   (910) 483-6611

OBJECTIVE

I want to contribute to an organization that can use an astute problem solver who offers a genuinely compassionate style of relating to others along with an ability to manage programs, projects, people, and finances.

EDUCATION

Master of Science in Social Work (M.S.W.), concentration in Child Welfare, University of Idaho, Moscow, ID, 1994.
B.A., Sociology and Social Sciences, Boise State University, Boise, ID, 1992.
Internships:
Residential Social Work Intern. Latah Family Group Center, Moscow, ID. Individual and group therapy for emotionally disturbed children.
School Social Work Intern. Latah Area School, Moscow, ID. Elementary, Jr. High, and psychiatric population.

EXPERIENCE

INVESTIGATOR. Child Protective Services, Latah County, Moscow, ID (2000-present). Am involved in activities related to intervention and stabilization of families in crisis as the result of child abuse and neglect investigations. Document case findings, conduct family assessments, and write court petitions and court reports. Perform on-the-spot decision making while utilizing my knowledge of family dynamics and available community resources.

CRISIS SOCIAL WORKER. Family and Children's Services, Latah County, Moscow, ID (1998-00). Responsible for providing service to families with acute problems. Assessed situations; developed and initiated appropriate short-term goals. Allocated resources from other community agencies in order to stabilize the family.

GROUP FACILITATOR. Moscow Family Center, Moscow, ID (1996-98). Facilitated mandated parenting group for parents of teens. Goals focused on adoption of good parenting techniques.

CLINIC SUPERVISOR. Family Education, Boise State University, Boise, ID (1994-1996). Responsible for training and supervising volunteers, inventory, medical records, statistics, and policies. Provided information and counseling in the areas of birth control, pregnancy, sexual orientation and other areas of human sexuality. Promoted to this position from a volunteer.

VOLUNTEER EXPERIENCE

Choice Living. (1993). Provided companionship to para and quadriplegics and worked to improve their ability to be less dependent on others.
Drug Rehabilitation Program. (1992). Co-facilitated the first component of the rehabilitation program which consisted of group education of drugs with an emphasis on personal growth. Promoted drug abuse awareness in the community by publicizing in local papers and displaying banners at community events.
Boise Youth Home. (1990-91). Worked with adolescents dealing with issues of child abuse and neglect, drugs, and delinquency. Coordinated shelter activities within the community.

PROFESSIONAL TRAINING

David Rosetta - "Domestic Violence"
Corey Silver - "Independent Family"
Jonathan Frank - "Helping the Family"

MEMBERSHIPS

American Association of Social Workers

Exact Name of Person
Title or Position
Name of Company
Address (no., street)
Address (city, state, zip)

Dear Exact Name of Person: (or Dear Sir or Madam if answering a blind ad.)

With the enclosed resume, I would like to make you aware of my interest in exploring employment opportunities with your organization. My husband and I have recently relocated to the Los Angeles area, and I am seeking an organization which can utilize my vast experience in treatment programs management.

As you will see from my resume, I received an M.Ed. in Learning and Behavior Disorders and a B.A. in Mental and Emotional Disturbances. In my most recent position as Day Treatment Programs Supervisor, I directed all educational aspects of three-day treatment programs serving grades K-12. On my own initiative, I developed an implementation plan and acquired Colorado State Department of Public Instruction and Non-Public certifications for three-day treatment programs.

In previous employment with the Santa Barbara school system, I provided educational and therapeutic consultation while writing successful grants and developing innovative new programs for students.

I thoroughly enjoy the daily challenges associated with helping the less fortunate, and I can point to numerous contributions I have made to my field and to needy individuals.

I hope you will call or write me soon to suggest a time convenient for us to meet to discuss your current and future needs. I can provide outstanding personal and professional references. Thank you in advance for your time.

Sincerely yours,

Stacey Franklin

Alternate last paragraph:
I hope you will welcome my call soon to arrange a brief meeting when we might meet to discuss your needs and goals and how my background might serve them. I can provide outstanding references at the appropriate time.

STACEY FRANKLIN

1110½ Hay Street, Fayetteville, NC 28305 • preppub@aol.com • (910) 483-6611

EXPERIENCE

DAY TREATMENT PROGRAMS SUPERVISOR. Seattle Mental Health Center, Seattle, WA (2000-2004). Within a mental health setting, directed all educational aspects of three day treatment programs serving grades K-12.

- Initiated and implemented the development, startup, and overall management of the educational components within three Day Treatment Programs.
- Researched requirements, developed implementation plan and acquired Washington State Department of Public Instruction and Non-Public certifications for treatment programs.
- Supervised and developed professional and paraprofessional staff responsible for the implementation of specialized instructional curriculum.
- Acted as a liaison with other mental health and public school personnel to maintain effective communication and consultation for the educational programs.
- Supervised, coordinated, and assisted in the educational evaluation, placement, and transition process of clients into and out of the established system.
- Provided behavioral, academic, and instructional resources and methods information for educational staff, outside agencies, parents, clinical staff, and clients.
- Reviewed screening information, diagnostic assessments, and ongoing educational progress of clients.

EDUCATIONAL COORDINATOR & EDUCATIONAL THERAPIST. Santa Barbara School System, Santa Barbara, CA (1995-00). Developed academic programs serving special population youth (K-12).

- Consulted with teachers in regards to specific instructional and curriculum needs.
- Evaluated and tracked students, determining their educational placements and monitoring their progress.
- Developed and presented staff inservice training.
- Coordinated meetings between various professionals regarding student progress.
- Developed and executed a comprehensive cognitive retraining program for a young adult with a head injury.
- Provided educational and therapeutic consultation to clients' parents and teachers on various educational methods and therapeutic concerns.

Program Development: Developed a tutoring and support program for learning disabled college students, emphasizing expressive writing, study skills, time management, organization, and self-awareness.

Grant Writing: Wrote a grant to establish the Learning Disabilities Resource Center.

EDUCATION

- Received **M.Ed. in Learning and Behavior Disorders,** University of Colorado, Denver, CO, 1995.
- Received a **B.A. in Mental and Emotional Disturbances,** University of Colorado, Denver, CO, 1992.
- Received the Emma Jordan Award for academic achievement and leadership, 1992.

ORGANIZATIONS

- Council for Exceptional Children
- Council for Administrative Services
- Division of Learning Disabilities
- Division of Behavior Disorders
- Division of Teacher Education

REFERENCES

Outstanding references available upon request.

Date

Exact Name of Person
Title or Position
Name of Company
Address (no., street)
Address (city, state, zip)

DEMOCRATIC PARTY EXECUTIVE DIRECTOR

Dear Exact Name of Person: (or Dear Sir or Madam if answering a blind ad.)

With the enclosed resume, I would like to make you aware of my interest in exploring employment opportunities with your organization.

As you will see from my resume, I am utilizing my B.A. in Government while serving as Executive Director for the Washington Democratic Party. I was specially recruited for this job which involves overseeing a staff of three and directing fundraising activities because of the reputation I earned while working for Congressman Timmons of the U.S. House of Representatives. I began working for Congressman Timmons in an entry-level role and was rapidly promoted to Campaign Director. Subsequently I was promoted to District Representative and then to District Director. In my current job with the Democratic Party, I routinely work with members of the legislature while supervising the internship program and handling multiple other responsibilities.

While pursuing my degree, I worked in demanding part-time jobs in lawyers' offices in order to finance my college education. Through my strong work ethic and time management skills, I was able to excel academically.

If you are seeking a highly motivated individual known for unlimited personal initiative and persistence, I hope you will call or write me soon to suggest a time convenient for us to meet to discuss your current and future needs. Thank you in advance for your time.

Sincerely yours,

Tracy Bartlett

Alternate last paragraph:
I hope you will welcome my call soon to arrange a brief meeting when we might meet to discuss your needs and goals and how my background might serve them. I can provide outstanding references at the appropriate time.

TRACY BARTLETT

1110½ Hay Street, Fayetteville, NC 28305   •   preppub@aol.com   •   (910) 483-6611

_____

EDUCATION   **Bachelor of Arts degree in Government,** Gonzaga University, Spokane, WA, 1998.
- Graduated with a 3.3 GPA.

Associates degree in Criminal Justice, Walla Walla Community College, Walla Walla, WA, 1995. As a Tutor, assisted students having trouble with math and sociology.

EXPERIENCE   **EXECUTIVE DIRECTOR.** WA Democratic Party's '96, Olympia, WA (2003-present). Was specially recruited for this job which involves overseeing a staff of three while directing fundraising activities and providing support for the campaigns of WA Democratic Party; play a key role in making decisions regarding which candidates receive contributions.
- Supervise the internship program for college interns. Manage office expenses.
- Work with Washington's U.S. Senatorial and Congressional delegations' campaigns to assist them in obtaining information or assistance they need; also work with House of Representative and Senate candidates who request help.
- Assist with the Voter Registration Program and massive direct mail efforts.

DISTRICT DIRECTOR. Congressman Michael Timmons, U.S. House of Representatives, Seattle, WA (1999-03). Excelled in the following track record of promotion:
2001-03: DISTRICT DIRECTOR. Supervised a staff of seven people and four offices throughout the 2nd Congressional District while assisting with the Congressman's schedule.
- Attended meetings on behalf of the Congressman; spoke on behalf of the Congressman before organizations such as White House Conference on Small Business, Chambers of Commerce, and civic groups.
- Supervised the internship program for college interns.
- Accompanied the Congressman when he traveled in the district; met with constituents.
- Was in charge of military academy nominations for the district.
- Was a direct link between the Congressman and his district.

2000-01: DISTRICT REPRESENTATIVE. Represented the Congressman at various meetings and events throughout the district; accompanied the Congressman throughout the district and assisted with the Congressman's schedule.
- Supervised internship program for college interns.
- Met with constituents on behalf of the Congressman; composed letters to constituents.
- Assisted constituents with obtaining passports and securing help from federal agencies.

1999-00: CAMPAIGN DIRECTOR, TIMMONS FOR CONGRESS. Directed the successful campaign of Michael Timmons; planned the candidate's daily schedule and appointments. Accompanied the candidate to campaign functions in all counties.
- Attended meetings and spoke on behalf of the candidate.
- Organized volunteers and groups throughout the counties; telephoned registered voters; organized rallies; organized and planned highly successful fund raisers while assisting with fundraising from individuals and Political Action Committees.

Other experience: Financed my college education by working in these jobs during college.
OFFICE ASSISTANT. Jacks, Hailey, & Jacks, Spokane, WA. Assisted with loan closings, prepared documents for court, assisted with title searches, and provided office support.
OFFICE ASSISTANT. Richard Williams, Attorney at Law, Spokane, WA. Responsible for file preparation of all legal documents for child support cases; accompanied attorney to court and communicated with child support clients.

PERSONAL   Offer proven ability to excel in stressful and demanding situations. Self-motivated.

Date

Exact Name of Person
Title or Position
Exact Name of Company
Address (no., street)
Address (city, state, zip)

DEPUTY COUNTY MANAGER

is seeking the County Manager position in another county.

Dear Exact Name of Person: (or Dear Sir or Madam if answering a blind ad.)

With the enclosed resume, I would like to confidentially express my interest in the position of County Manager.

Since earning my Master of Public Administration degree and my Bachelor of Arts in Political Science, I have completed extensive training at the Institute of Government at Des Moines including a Budget and Finance Course as well as a Municipal Administration Course. While earning my Master's degree, I was selected for a prestigious internship with the City Attorney's Office. In prior experience, I excelled as Assistant to the City Manager in Iowa City, and I worked full-time while earning my Master's degree.

In my current position as a Deputy County Manager with Des Moines, I assist the manager with all daily operations and have played a key role in annual budget preparation for the $25 million budget. Known for my strong personal initiative, I am currently coordinating a $6 million expansion of the Des Moines Water District and have recently negotiated 10-year solid waste disposal and transportation agreements. In previous experience, I played a key role in preparing and administering a $2 million budget while coordinating land-use planning activities and implementing a Community Development Grant project which created dozens of new jobs. Much of my job has involved economic development initiatives, and I have enthusiastically embraced the challenge of helping Des Moines increase its jobs base.

The position of County Manager is the next logical step in my career, and I would be honored to discuss the position of County Manager of Delaware City with you. My wife and I have travelled extensively throughout the areas surrounding Delaware City, and we think it is a place of great beauty and wholesome charm.

I would appreciate an opportunity to meet with you at your convenience, and I hope you will contact me to suggest a time convenient for you when we might talk. Although I can provide outstanding references at the appropriate time, I would appreciate your holding my expression of interest in Delaware City in confidence until we speak. Thank you in advance for your time and professional courtesies.

Sincerely,

Jimmie West

JIMMIE WEST

1110½ Hay Street, Fayetteville, NC 28305   •   preppub@aol.com   •   (910) 483-6611

OBJECTIVE
I am seeking to contribute to a community that needs an experienced local government administrator known for a high-energy approach to economic development as well as a fiscally prudent style of managing public resources.

EDUCATION
Master of Public Administration, The University of Iowa, Iowa City, IA, 2002.
Bachelor of Arts in Political Science, The University of Iowa, Iowa City, IA, 2000.
Professional training: Institute of Government, Des Moines, IA. Completed the Budget and Finance Course, 2004. Completed the Municipal Administration Course, 2003.

EXPERIENCE
DEPUTY COUNTY MANAGER. Des Moines, IA (2003-present). Assist the county manager with all aspects of daily operations.
- Prepare budgeting data and assist with annual budget preparation for a $25 million budget.
- Currently coordinating a $6 million expansion of the Des Moines Water District.
- Recently negotiated 10-year solid waste disposal and transportation agreements.
- Chair meetings of the county's Safety Committee; recently led an investigation into an oil spill which led to the development of tough new standards for hazardous material handling by county officials and our associated vendors.
- Played a key role in creating the new Employee Handbook for the county's 550 employees; negotiated with union officials and continuously provide liaison.

ASSISTANT ADMINISTRATOR. Iowa City, IA (2002-03). Directed the preparation and administration of the town's annual $2 million budget.
- Planned and coordinated water and sewer system expansions.
- Coordinated land-use planning activities for the town, including zoning annexation.
- Interfaced with all department heads and established excellent working relationships.
- Directed the administration and implementation of the Community Development Grant project which created dozens of new jobs in Iowa City while establishing new programs for senior citizens.

INTERN. Iowa City Attorney's Office, Iowa City, IA (2002). Was handpicked for this prestigious internship while completing my Master's degree. Assisted county attorney with property acquisition project. Served as liaison between the county and residents concerning purchase and relocation efforts.

ASSISTANT TO THE CITY MANAGER. Iowa City, IA (2000-01). In my first job after earning my college degree, was handpicked for an entry-level position and then rapidly promoted to Assistant to the City Manager. Was entrusted with numerous responsibilities normally handled by more experienced personnel because of the City Manager's confidence in my leadership ability and strong personal initiative. Prepared the town's first Comprehensive Annual Financial Report.
- Coordinated Independence Day 2001.
- Assisted with Fiscal Year 2001 budget preparation. Coordinated with the Town Engineer in construction of wastewater treatment plant improvements.

REFERENCES
Outstanding references provided upon request.

CAREER CHANGE

Date

Exact Name of Person
Title or Position
Exact Name of Company
Address (no., street)
Address (city, state, zip)

DIRECT CARE WORKER,
Family Care, Inc.

Dear Exact Name of Person: (or Dear Sir or Madam if answering a blind ad.)

I would appreciate an opportunity to talk with you soon about how I could benefit your organization as a Pharmaceutical Sales Representative through my expertise in a wide range of medical specialties, procedures, terminology, and pharmacology. I offer strong communication, planning, and organizational abilities.

Most recently, I served as a Direct Care Worker for an innovative total care medical facility for mentally and physically handicapped women. While providing primary medical care, I refined my knowledge of medication and medical specialties. In previous positions as Program Coordinator for the Little League of Georgia and as a CNA for Family Respect, I discovered my knack for presenting and communicating information to groups of people. I am knowledgeable of the use, dosage, effectiveness, and side effects of many types of medication, including oral and other contraceptives and gynecological medication and treatments.

You would find me to be a caring, dedicated professional who has the ability to quickly establish rapport with medical professionals. With strong communication skills, I am at ease in the medical community and have an excellent reputation. I am confident that doctors and other decision makers would welcome me "with open arms" as a Pharmaceutical Sales Representative, and it would be an honor to represent your outstanding product line.

I hope you will call or write me soon to suggest a time convenient for us to meet and discuss your current and future needs and how I might serve them. Thank you in advance for your time.

Sincerely,

Julie Green

JULIE GREEN

1110½ Hay Street, Fayetteville, NC 28305 • preppub@aol.com • (910) 483-6611

OBJECTIVE
To offer my expertise to an organization in need of a well-trained medical professional experienced in a wide range of medical specialties, procedures, terminology, and pharmacology who possesses excellent communication, planning, and organizational skills.

LICENSURES
Certified Nurse's Aide; CPR and First Aid certified

EXPERIENCE
DIRECT CARE WORKER. Family Care, Inc., Savannah, GA (2003-present). Am refining my knowledge of pharmacology and medical procedures while providing primary care to six mentally and physically handicapped women of various ages residing in an innovative total-care facility.
- Liaise with a staff of 18 doctors representing a wide range of disciplines including cardiology, psychology, ENT, and urology.
- Provide for each patient's personal, recreational, and medical needs while keeping within a strict state-mandated budget.
- Perform admission interviews, medication distribution, and charting of patient status.
- Act as staff liaison with physicians, coordinating schedules and rounds.
- Utilize charts to determine patient needs.
- Conduct a variety of tests, including blood tests.
- Proficient with the care of catheters and orogastric/nasogastric tubes.

PROGRAM COORDINATOR. Little League of Georgia, Atlanta, GA (2000-03). Polished planning skills and pediatric knowledge while organizing and directing classes in breastfeeding, child care, and early childhood development.

FAMILY SUPPORT COUNSELOR. Fort Stewart, GA (1998-00). Worked in a volunteer capacity organizing a wide range of counseling sessions, fundraisers, and recreational activities for over 150 military families.
- Planned and conducted counseling sessions for spouses of military personnel.
- Accessed community and organizational social service agencies for assistance to needy families. Planned, organized, and directed a variety of fundraisers for needy families and academic scholarships.

CNA. Family Respect, Atlanta, GA (1995-98). Handled a wide range of counseling, medical, and administrative functions working for this nationwide nonprofit organization.
- Conducted pregnancy, birth control, sexually transmitted diseases, and general health and hygiene counseling, including lectures at area high schools and community centers.
- Managed pre-op and post-op patient care and room preparation.
- Assisted other medical personnel in male and female physicals, OB/GYN care, outpatient surgery, and TAB procedures.
- Gained knowledge of the use, dosage, side effects, and effectiveness of a wide range of contraceptives and gynecological medication and treatments.

EDUCATION
Completed three semesters towards an R.N. degree, Armstrong Atlantic State University, Savannah, GA. Areas of study included microbiology, medical terminology, anatomy and physiology, and anthropology.
Graduated from a Certified Nursing Aide training course, Savannah, GA, 1995.

PERSONAL
Am a caring, dedicated professional who can quickly establish a rapport with both patients and medical professionals. Received written commendations for medical care excellence.

Exact Name of Person
Title or Position
Name of Company
Address (no., street)
Address (city, state, zip)

**DIRECTOR OF
VOLUNTEER SERVICES,**
Princeton University

Dear Exact Name of Person: (or Dear Sir or Madam if answering a blind ad.)

    With the enclosed resume, I would like to make you aware of my interest in exploring employment opportunities with your organization. I am interested in the position of Director of Volunteer Services for the Mayo Clinic which you recently advertised online through the VolunteerAdministrators.com website. I have read the position description and I am confident that I am the individual you are seeking.

    As Director of Volunteer Services for the hospital affiliated with Princeton University, I serve as the Administrative Liaison for two 501(c)3 corporations. On my own initiative, I established a $1 million endowment, and I developed the certification program for the Hospital Directors of Volunteer Services statewide. I arrived at my current position with extensive experience as a Director of Volunteer Services, as I had previously served the Jersey City Medical Center in the same capacity. While at Jersey City, I developed numerous new programs including the Interpreters Program which facilitated the comfort of nonEnglish-speaking patients.

    Respected for my expertise in the area of volunteer services management, I serve on numerous boards, committees, and task forces in various organizations. Even in my spare time, I am involved in volunteer services; for example, I have chaired the Publication Committee for the National Society of Volunteer Services of the National Hospital Association (NSVS/NHA).

    I hope you will call or write me soon to suggest a time convenient for us to meet to discuss your current and future needs. Thank you in advance for your time.

Sincerely yours,

Linda Mallory

Alternate last paragraph:
    I hope you will welcome my call soon to arrange a brief meeting when we might meet to discuss your needs and goals and how my background might serve them. I can provide outstanding references at the appropriate time.

LINDA MALLORY

1110½ Hay Street, Fayetteville, NC 28305 • preppub@aol.com • (910) 483-6611

EXPERIENCE

2000-present. Director of Volunteer Services. Princeton Hospital/Princeton University,
- Established a $1 million endowment.
- Documented $17.5 million impact on hospital's "bottom line" my final fiscal year.
- Served as the administrative liaison for two 501(c)3 corporations.
- Member, Employee Recognition Task Force and the Employee Literacy Advisory Council.
- Chaired the Publication Committee, National Society of Volunteer Services of the National Hospital Association (NSVS/NHA).
- Secured corporate sponsors to underwrite the entire 2001 Annual Conference of the NSVS/NHA. Developed the Certification Program for the Hospital Directors of Volunteer Services statewide.
- Secured corporate sponsors to underwrite the annual conference of the Hospital Directors of Volunteer Services.

1993-99. Director of Volunteer Services. Jersey City Medical Center.
- Developed Life Light event. Developed the Interpreters Program..
- Was a member of the Employee Activities Committee.
- Served on the Editorial Advisory Board "Center Scope."
- Developed highly successful annual fundraising events. Active Speaker's Bureau member.

CREATIVE WORKS
- Developer, Hospital Directors of Volunteer Services Certification Conference, 2001.
- Presenter, "Easy Living," National Society of Volunteer Services, Baltimore, MD, 2000.
- Trainer, Association of Volunteer Services, 2000.
- Presenter, " Fun-Raising Fund-Raising," Hospital Conference, 1998.
- Developer, Recruiting/Rewarding/Retention of Volunteers for the Department of the Army, Fort Dix, New Jersey, 1996.
- Author, Why Volunteer? Family Support Services, Department of the Army, Fort Dix, New Jersey, 1996.
- Author, Motivational Paper, "Three Ways to Make It," 1996.
- Editor, Newsletter for New Jersey Society of Volunteer Services, 1996.
- Panelist, New Jersey Association of Volunteer Services, 1995.

MEMBERSHIPS
- New Jersey Society of Volunteer Services.
- Coast Council (New Jersey) Directors of Volunteer Services.
- New Jersey Association of Volunteer Administrators.
- Hospital Conference Volunteer Services Association.
- National Society of Volunteer Services of the National Hospital Association: Board of Directors (2001-04); Education Committee (2001).
- Hospital Conference - Directors of Volunteer Services: Chair, Certification Committee (2000-02); President (1998-00).

HONORS
- Who's Who Among Human Services Professionals, 2002.
- Who's Who Among Americans, 1999; Who's Who in the East, 1998.
- New Jersey Governor's Award for Volunteer Program Excellence, 1994, 1995.

EDUCATION

Bachelor of Arts degree in Public Administration, University of North Carolina at Chapel Hill, Chapel Hill, NC, 1993.

PERSONAL

Outstanding personal and professional references available on request.

Date

To: Search Committee

In response to the urging of someone familiar with your search for an executive vice president for the Association of Health Underwriters, I am sending you a resume which summarizes my background. I offer a unique combination of knowledge, experience, and abilities which I believe would ideally suit the requirements of the Association of Health Underwriters.

Health industry expertise

You will see from my resume that I offer expertise related to health insurance and underwriting. In my current job I have sought out and negotiated contracts with major insurance companies to provide insurance for the organization. On a $1 million budget, I have developed insurance programs which generated $2 million in net income based on $32 million in premium. These highly regarded programs which I developed have brought 6,000 new members into the organization.

Proven executive ability

I offer proven executive ability. I have earned a reputation as someone who has not only strategic vision and imagination but also the tenacity and persistence to follow through on the "nitty-gritty" details of implementing new projects, programs, and concepts. I know how to delegate, and I know how to "micro manage," and I am skilled at tailoring my management style to particular circumstances while always shouldering full responsibility and accountability for results. My current job has involved the responsibility of recruiting, training, and continuously developing a national sales force of brokers throughout the U.S. which broke with the tradition of passive mail solicitation and led to dramatic growth in sales and profitability. With a strong "bottom-line" orientation, I have streamlined headquarters staff and reduced central office expenses to save at least half a million dollars while continuously supervising the association's five regional offices in the recruitment and training of more than 1,200 insurance agents nationally.

Extensive association experience

You will also see from my resume that I am accustomed to "getting things done" within the unique environment of a trade/membership association. I am well known for my ability to attract and retain a cohesive and productive staff, and I am also respected for my exceptional skills in relating to, inspiring, and supporting key volunteer members. A skilled communicator, I have made countless appearances and speeches.

I am aware of the requirements defined by the search committee, and I would enjoy the opportunity to discuss this position further with the Executive Committee. I feel certain I could contribute significantly to the growth and financial health of the Association of Health Underwriters as its Executive Vice President. Thank you for your time and consideration.

Sincerely,

Shane Malone

SHANE MALONE

1110½ Hay Street, Fayetteville, NC 28305 • preppub@aol.com • (910) 483-6611

OBJECTIVE

To contribute to the growth and financial health of an organization that needs a savvy, creative executive with expert knowledge of the health insurance/underwriting industry along with a proven ability to innovate, manage, motivate, coordinate, communicate, and troubleshoot within the unique environment of a membership association.

EXPERIENCE

DIRECTOR, MEMBERS INSURANCE. National Home Builders Association, Washington, DC (2003-present). Have excelled in originating insurance programs for the members of NHBA: developed highly regarded insurance programs which brought 6,000 new members into the organization while producing millions of dollars in net income.

- Sought out and negotiated contracts with major insurance companies to provide insurance for the organization.
- On a $1 million operating budget, developed insurance programs which generated $2 million in net income based on $32 million in premium.
- Recruited, trained, and continuously developed a national sales force of NHBA brokers throughout the U.S. which first, arrested declining sales that were the result of passive mail solicitations and second, dramatically boosted sales and profitability.
- Streamlined headquarters staff and reduced central office expenses, resulting in a $500,000 savings; developed annual programs of work and budgets.
- Supervise five regional offices in the recruitment and training of more than 1,200 insurance agents nationally.
- Closely monitor government affairs related to health insurance; maintain excellent relationships with governmental regulatory bodies and state departments of insurance.
- Maintain liaison with association personnel in charge of operations, legislation, education, public relations, and communications as well as with the executive committee.
- Am known for my extraordinary ability to attract, develop, and retain a cohesive and productive staff and for my talent in motivating and inspiring key volunteer leadership.

Other experience:
NATIONAL MEMBERSHIP FIELD DIRECTOR. National Home Builders Association, Washington, DC. Was promoted to this position after excelling as **Membership Director for Mideastern and Eastern U.S.**; formulated and implemented national membership programs and campaigns that led to the development of new units in the U.S.

VICE PRESIDENT OF MARKETING. Schultz & Co., Newark, DE. Developed marketing programs for the manufacturing and marketing companies owned by this conglomerate.

LIFE AND HEALTH INSURANCE BROKER. American Insurance Agency, Newark, DE. Was a property and casualty underwriter as well as a life and health insurance broker.

EDUCATION & TRAINING

Hold a **Bachelor of Arts (B.A.) degree,** Delaware State University, Dover, DE.
Complete annually 15 hours of continuing education to maintain Life and Health Insurance Broker's license.
Took numerous courses to comply with life and health insurance industry requirements.

PERSONAL

Have given numerous speeches and made hundreds of personal appearances. Am known for my ability to ensure optimum utilization of personnel. Offer a reputation for integrity.

Date

Exact Name of Person
Title or Position
Name of Company
Address (no., street)
Address (city, state, zip)

Dear Exact Name of Person: (or Dear Sir or Madam if answering a blind ad.)

With the enclosed resume, I would like to make you aware of my desire to contribute to your organization in a management capacity. I am particularly drawn to rural areas which are underserved by the medical and social services community.

My commitment to working in rural areas has been reinforced by the many diverse professional and personal experiences I have had with different people in various locations. Of these experiences there are two which best illustrate my interests.

The first experience involves a village in the bush of Nigeria, where I spent two years learning about and living in a culture diametrically opposed to my own. As a American Red Cross Volunteer, my job was to offer technical assistance with food and shelter by developing programs within the context of their culture.

The second experience involved my work as a Wilderness Instructor. In setting up wilderness courses targeting dysfunctional adolescents, I learned firsthand that the beauty of nature can make its way into troubled hearts and soothe them. I am a strong believer in the power of nature to influence human behavior in positive ways.

I will be available to interview and visit with you at your convenience. I hope you will call or write me soon to suggest a time convenient for us to meet to discuss your current and future needs and how I might serve them. Thank you in advance for your time and consideration.

Sincerely yours,

Jane Culver

JANE CULVER

1110½ Hay Street, Fayetteville, NC 28305   •   preppub@aol.com   •   (910) 483-6611

OBJECTIVE I want to contribute to an organization that can use a versatile and highly motivated individual who offers exceptional creativity along with outstanding programming skills.

EDUCATION **Master of Health Science,** University of Notre Dame, Notre Dame, IN, 1998.
Bachelor of Social Work, University of North Carolina at Asheville, Asheville, NC, 1995.
Associate of Arts in Liberal Arts, Indiana State University, Terre Haute, IN, 1990.

EXPERIENCE **DIRECTOR.** Fire Safety Program, Indianapolis, IN (2001-present). Organized the camp phase of a fire safety program for nine through eleven-year-olds and was responsible for the efforts of four interns.
- Provided instruction on fire safety, cooperative living, and camp craft skills.

AGRICULTURE EXTENSION AGENT. American Red Cross, Nigeria (1998-00). Provided technical help to subsistence level farmers in food and shelter.
- Initiated secondary projects addressing local health and environmental concerns.
- Trained farmers and would-be farmers in techniques related to crop rotation.

SOCIAL WORK INTERN. Indianapolis Memorial Medical Center, Indianapolis, IN (1998). Planned and organized the disposition of hospitalized veterans in need of comprehensive and extended care.
- Conducted indepth patient interviews and utilized community and government resources.

WILDERNESS INSTRUCTOR. America the Beautiful Project, Columbus, IN (1997-98). Co-instructed 5, 7, and 30-day wilderness courses targeting behavior disordered adolescents.
- Conducted challenge activities and outdoor workshops for mainstream populations.
- Became convinced that outdoor wilderness experiences can contribute significantly to the mental health and mental well being of human beings.

STUDENT RESIDENT ASSISTANT. Indiana State University, Terre Haute, IN (1997). Monitored and directed the activities of 150 university housing residents and was responsible for student conduct and norms. Planned and implemented 40+ programs in education, recreation, and social concerns.

CRISIS COUNSELOR. Indiana Mental Health Hospital, Terre Haute, IN (1996-97). Monitored telephone lines serving four counties. De-escalated highly distressed individuals and contacted local support services.

COMPUTERS Proficient with a wide range of computer software including Word, Excel, Access.

LANGUAGES Fluent in Spanish; have traveled extensively throughout Central America.

PERSONAL Outstanding references upon request. Highly athletic individual who enjoys nearly all sports including soccer, rugby, and football. Have volunteered my time as a Little League coach to children in numerous age groups.

Exact Name of Person
Title or Position
Exact Name of Company
Address (no., street)
Address (city, state, zip)

DISTRICT EXECUTIVE,
Boy Scouts of America

Dear Exact Name of Person: (or Dear Sir or Madam if answering a blind ad.)

   With the enclosed resume, I would like to express my interest in your organization and acquaint you with my skills and experience related to your needs.

   As you will see from my resume, I hold a B.A. in Human Relations degree which I have put to good use while serving for 11 years as a District Executive with the Boy Scouts of America. In that capacity, I managed districts in Nebraska, Colorado, South Dakota, and North Dakota and was responsible for recruiting, training, financial administration, program planning and management, and community liaison. Since Boys Scouts of America is an organization devoted to shaping youth in moral, ethical, and spiritual ways while teaching leadership ability as well as a variety of skills useful throughout life, I was continually involved in training and counseling young people. I acted as Director of Summer Camp operations during the summers, which involved planning and managing summer camp experiences for thousands of boys trying to earn Merit Badges and acquire skills in areas ranging from carpentry to first aid. I am a skilled counselor and program manager.

   During my involvement with the Boy Scouts, I utilized numerous technical and mechanical skills which I gained in earlier experience in production and manufacturing environments.

   Although I was held in the highest regard by the Boy Scouts organization, I have relocated to your area with my wife, and I am seeking employment outside the Boy Scouts organization. I am confident that I could become a valuable asset to any organization that can use a talented organizer and programmer.

   If you can use a dependable and experienced individual who offers a proven ability to adapt easily to new situations and rapidly master new tasks, I hope you will contact me. I enjoy being in a position in which I can help others, and I offer highly refined skills in dealing with the public. I can provide excellent personal and professional references at the appropriate time, and I hope I will have the pleasure of talking with you soon in person.

Yours sincerely,

Robert Harrington

ROBERT HARRINGTON

1110½ Hay Street, Fayetteville, NC 28305 • preppub@aol.com • (910) 483-6611

OBJECTIVE

I want to benefit an organization that can use a versatile professional who offers excellent counseling, training, administrative, and human resources skills along with extensive technical knowledge which I have applied in manufacturing and production environments.

EDUCATION

Graduated with a **B.A. in Human Relations**, University of North Dakota, Grand Forks, ND, 1984. Previously completed courses at Creighton University before transferring to University of North Dakota.
Completed extensive executive training sponsored by the Boy Scouts of America.
- As a youth, achieved the rank of **Eagle Scout.**

EXPERIENCE

DISTRICT EXECUTIVE, BOY SCOUTS OF AMERICA. Boy Scout Units in Nebraska, Colorado, South Dakota, and North Dakota (1995-05). Completed training to become an executive in this unique organization dedicated to helping youth grow morally as well as in numerous skill areas.
- In an essentially entrepreneurial role, was in charge of starting new units, recruiting and training volunteer leaders, and providing leadership to units in the district.
- Was a frequent public speaker at scouting events.
- Handled extensive financial management responsibility; assisted in planning and administering a budget, and implemented aggressive fundraising campaigns to achieve ambitious budgetary goals.
- Was constantly involved in training and retraining adult leaders and youth leaders.
- Counseled adults and youth in personal, financial, and organizational areas; was known for my approachable manner and ability to relate to others easily.
- Acted as Director of Summer Camp operations which were week-long experiences in which boys earned Merit Badges; formulated the programs designed to help boys achieve those Merit Badges, hired and trained counselors, ordered supplies, and was responsible for a vast amount of property and equipment at each camp serving hundreds of boys each summer.

SERVICE & MAINTENANCE TECHNICIAN. Wilson Sportswear, Inc., Grand Forks, ND (1992-94). Played a key role in helping this plant achieve record levels of efficiency and productivity; ultimately the decision was made to close the plant and move manufacturing operations to Mexico.
- Received the highest-possible evaluations of my performance. Applied my wide-ranging technical knowledge and skills in resolving numerous service problems.

DESIGNER & SALES REPRESENTATIVE. Bright Ideas, Fargo, ND (1990-92). For this popular lamp supplier, was involved in product design as well as customer sales and service.
- Assisted in training other employees; was entrusted with numerous managerial responsibilities by the owner because of my sound judgment and common sense.

RESTAURANT MANAGER. Restaurants in Grand Forks and Fargo, ND (1984-90). Gained extensive experience in food service while working as Kitchen Manager and Manager at popular restaurants including Denny's and Olive Garden.

PERSONAL

Can provide outstanding personal and professional references.

Exact Name of Person
Title or Position
Name of Company
Address (no., street)
Address (city, state, zip)

DOMESTIC VIOLENCE CRISIS VOLUNTEER, DOMESTIC VIOLENCE AGENCY

Dear Exact Name of Person: (or Dear Sir or Madam if answering a blind ad.)

I would appreciate an opportunity to talk with you soon about how I could benefit your organization through my experience related to social work, family and individual counseling, case management, and professional networking.

As you will see from my resume, I offer a Bachelor of Science degree in Social Work from the University of South Carolina. During my recent fieldwork, I gained excellent case management experience while providing foster home supervision and determining removal of children to foster homes. I am considered an expert at accessing school, community, and allied health agency resources and programs. Through aggressive and effective liaison with health agencies, I have obtained access to vital resources for abuse victims, and I have been praised as "an ingenious networker."

My organizational and time-management abilities are excellent, as I was a full-time student while also working full-time to pay for my college expenses. You would find me to be an honest, versatile professional dedicated to improving the quality of life for troubled children and families.

I hope you will call or write me soon to suggest a time convenient for us to meet and discuss your current and future needs and how I might serve them. Thank you in advance for your time.

Sincerely,

Rachel Hoffman

Alternate last paragraph:
I hope you will welcome my call soon to arrange a brief meeting at your convenience to discuss your current and future needs and how I might serve them. Thank you in advance for your time.

RACHEL HOFFMAN

1110½ Hay Street, Fayetteville, NC 28305 • preppub@aol.com • (910) 483-6611

OBJECTIVE
To benefit an organization seeking a hardworking professional with excellent communication, planning, and organizational skills who possesses knowledge related to social work, case management, and professional networking.

EDUCATION
Bachelor of Science degree in Social Work, concentration in Community Services, University of South Carolina, Columbia, SC, 2000; earned Dean's List honors.
Related courses include Process of Social Work Intervention, Organizational Management, Interviewing Fundamentals, Social Legislation/Case Law, Social Research Methods, Human Behavior, Crisis Intervention, Developmental Psychology, Gerontology, Introduction to the Exceptional Child, Police & the Community, and Social Environment.

EXPERIENCE
DOMESTIC VIOLENCE CRISIS VOLUNTEER. Richland County Domestic Violence Agency, Columbia, SC (2003-present). Serve as companion and victim advocate while providing emotional support, information, and encouragement to victims of domestic violence and their family members.
- Help maintain a 24-hour telephone service and meet with victims in the emergency room, law enforcement center, and domestic violence office.
- Actively participate in fundraising events and health fairs; attend volunteer meetings.
- Respect confidentiality at all times. Refined essential intervention skills including active listening, communication, and the ability to interact with a broad variety of people.
- Through aggressive and effective liaison with health agencies, I obtain access to resources for abuse victims.

SOCIAL WORKER. Kershaw County Foster Care Services, Camden, SC (2000-03). Gained valuable case management and social work experience while performing field work as a foster care intern; became familiar with local, state, and federal regulations pertaining to foster homes.
- Determined relicensing of foster homes by observing child-foster parent interaction, interviewing children and foster parents, and documenting summaries of visits with the proper agencies.
- Assisted social team workers and court authorities in removal of children from parents for placement in foster homes.
- Conducted supervisory visits between children and biological parents.
- Provided a wide range of administrative functions, including compiling and writing quarterly reports, reviewing professional manuals, participating in group discussions, and attending staff meetings.
- Liaised with schools and community allied health agencies; made applicable referrals.
- Assisted in deciding on-site child removal to foster homes during inspections.

Worked in a variety of jobs while attending college full-time:
SUPERVISOR. Talbots, Columbia, SC. Refined my ability for easily establishing a rapport with people from diverse cultural and socioeconomic backgrounds while assisting in the daily operations of this clothing store.
ADMINISTRATIVE ASSISTANT. University of South Carolina Bookstore, Columbia, SC. Provided book inventory, recordkeeping, shelving, customer service, and data entry.

PERSONAL
Am a caring, dedicated professional sincerely aspiring to help improve both an individual's and a family's quality of life. Enjoy challenges, problem-solving, and decision-making.

Date

Exact Name of Person
Title or Position
Name of Company
Address (no., street)
Address (city, state, zip)

Dear Exact Name of Person: (or Dear Sir or Madam if answering a blind ad.)

I would appreciate an opportunity to talk with you soon about how I could contribute to your organization through my background in public relations, marketing, and management.

As you will see from my resume, I am serving as the Area Director of Educational Services provided to military professionals at a busy military base. While establishing and supervising educational services at 20 field sites which serve the needs of thousands of people annually, I manage more than 30 individuals who include field representatives, a senior field advisor, secretary, test administrators, and lab monitors. Known for my ability to interact effectively with others, I coordinate with faculty and supervise administrative field personnel, and I also handle the responsibility of interviewing, hiring, and training field employees. While managing multiple budgets, I oversee the operation of educational services which enable students to earn one of 35 different degrees from 40 academic institutions.

My management and problem-solving skills are highly refined. When I assumed my current position, the organization was in a severe budget crisis. Through intelligent planning and effective utilization of scarce resources, I have been able to push enrollment in our education programs to an all-time high while assuring a balanced budget and quality services.

I can provide outstanding references at the appropriate time, and I hope you will welcome my call soon to arrange a brief meeting at your convenience to discuss your current and future needs and how I might serve them. Thank you in advance for your time.

Sincerely,

Molly Clement

MOLLY CLEMENT

1110½ Hay Street, Fayetteville, NC 28305   •   preppub@aol.com   •   (910) 483-6611

OBJECTIVE

To contribute to an organization that can use a dynamic communicator and analytical thinker with exceptional communication and counseling skills, proven management and administrative ability, along with extensive familiarity with the adjunct educational system.

EDUCATION

Completed 12 semester hours, **Ed.M. Program in Counselor Education**, Jefferson Community College, Watertown, NY, 1997-98.

Received **Bachelor of Science (B.S.) degree in Recreation Administration**, Richland Technical Community College, Richland, VA, 1995.

Earned **Associate of Arts (A.A.) degree in General Education**, Jefferson Community College, Watertown, NY, 1993.

EXPERIENCE

AREA DIRECTOR. Educational Services, Ft. Drum, NY (2004-present). As the Area Director for programs serving military professionals, supervise field representatives, a senior field advisor, secretary, test administrators, and lab monitors at 20 field sites.
- Recruit, interview, and assign qualified instructors and tutors to all classes.
- Coordinate with Education Service Officers in daily supervision of field personnel.
- Interview, hire, and ensure training of 23 field employees annually.

SENIOR FIELD ADVISOR. Ft. Drum, NY (2000-04). As Senior Field Advisor for programs serving military programs, assisted the area director in hiring and training field personnel.
- Coordinated course schedules for 35 different degree programs offered by 40 academic institutions. Assisted students in the selection and registration of courses and SOCAD evaluation of military credit.
- Prepared and balanced enrollment and financial reports.
- Assisted students in applying for Pell Grants, VA Benefits, and tuition assistance.
- Prepared publicity; ordered and maintained an inventory of academic materials.
- Recruited and assigned qualified instructors.

COORDINATOR FOR GRADUATE SCHOOL/SCHOOL OF EDUCATION & REGISTRATION RECORDER. Ft. Drum, NY (1997-99). Excelled in two different positions within the Office of the Registrar.
- From 1998-99, as Coordinator for Graduate School/School of Education, established student files, distributed grades, and prepared minutes for admission meetings.
- From 1997-98, as Registration Registrar, maintained all registration information, organized all grades, and prepared enrollment reports.

YOUTH SPORTS DIRECTOR. Ft. Drum, NY (1996-97). Organized youth sports teams while training and certifying volunteer coaches; maintained sports equipment and facilities; assisted in community activities and in the administration of the Youth Activities Center.

RECREATION ASSISTANT. Recreation Center, Richland, VA (1993-96). Assisted in scheduling and administering organized activities for a busy recreation center.

TITLE I - ADVENTURE CAMP DIRECTOR. Camp Snowy River, Watertown, NY (1992-93). Established a therapeutic multi-activity day camp program for multiple handicapped facility residents.

PERSONAL

Speak, read, and write German. Knowledgeable of software using Microsoft.

Date

Exact Name of Person
Title or Position
Exact Name of Company
Address (no., street)
Address (city, state, zip)

EMERGENCY ASSISTANCE COORDINATOR,

Phoenix Community Center, is responding to an internal opening within the organization for which she works

Dear Exact Name of Person: (or Dear Sir or Madam if answering a blind ad.)

With the enclosed resume, I would like to formally request that you consider me for another position with the Phoenix Community Services Agency. I am responding to your recent ad for a Social Worker for the Senior Citizens Case Assistance Program.

As you are aware, I have served the Phoenix Community Center since 2001 as its Emergency Assistance Coordinator. I truly enjoy working with the aging population, and I have developed an excellent reputation within the human services community. After reading the ad you placed, I am certain that I have all the qualifications you are seeking. In addition, I offer the advantage of thoroughly understanding the internal operations of the Phoenix Community Services Agency as a proud member of its team since 2001.

You may not be aware that, prior to becoming your Emergency Assistance Coordinator, I worked with the elderly as Activities Director of the Canyon Retirement Home. I realized from that job that I had "found my calling" in working with senior citizens, and I truly thrived on bringing laughter and structure to their lives through the creative activities I planned and implemented.

With a reputation as a highly competent and conscientious individual, you will also see that I previously excelled in a track record of promotion with two convenience store chains, where I was promoted to District Manager over nine stores and then to Regional Sales Manager over 76 stores. Although I excelled as a manager in profit-making organizations, I have found that my take-charge, "make-it-happen" personality is well suited to the complex environment of nonprofit services organizations. As Emergency Assistance Coordinator, I have enjoyed the satisfaction of being able to make a difference in people's lives, and I am confident that I could continue to serve with distinction in this new position.

Please give me every consideration for this position, and also please give me the opportunity to formally interview for the position so that I demonstrate that I am the person you are seeking.

Yours sincerely,

Kate Easton

KATE EASTON

1110½ Hay Street, Fayetteville, NC 28305 • preppub@aol.com • (910) 483-6611

OBJECTIVE

To benefit the Phoenix Community Services Agency through my love and admiration for senior citizens, my outstanding reputation within the human services community, and my indepth knowledge of community resources and services suited to this population.

AFFILIATION

Was named "Woman of the Year" in 2004 by the Arizona Business and Professional Women's Organization. Served as President, 2003 and 2004.
Served on the Board of Directors of Rape Crisis in Phoenix, 1998-03.

EXPERIENCE

EMERGENCY ASSISTANCE COORDINATOR. Phoenix Community Services Agency, Phoenix, AZ (2001-present). Continuously interface with the aging population while handling casework for those seeking emergency assistance through the Center; work closely with the executive director and casework committee in developing guidelines for the quantity and quality of assistance provided to clients.

- Work closely with Department of Social Services social workers and maintain cooperative relationships with organizations providing essential human services; have earned respect for my professionalism and compassionate style.
- Had input into the creation of the center's database in my department, and maintain files.
- Inform people including senior citizens about programs and services which could be of assistance to them; provide referral, follow-up, and advocacy activities on behalf of older adults and others.
- Personally approach the service delivery system on the client's behalf, especially in the case of the frail or aging, when the inquirer is unable to investigate the resources available.
- Increase community awareness of information and case assistance services.
- Provide training for other staff who perform casework.
- Established an extensive network of contacts involved in providing emergency assistance within the community; develop and maintain a notebook for staff on resources and key contact individuals within professional helping organizations and volunteer operations.

ACTIVITIES DIRECTOR. Canyon Retirement Home, Phoenix, AZ (2000-01). Excelled in working with the elderly and enjoyed the process of bringing laughter and structure to the lives of senior citizens.

Other experience (1984-00): Excelled in a track record of promotion with Circle K and Convenience Food Marts, Inc.; earned a reputation as an excellent manager.

- Began as a Cashier-Clerk with Convenience Food Marts, Inc., then was promoted to Assistant Manager and Store Manager, then to District Manager.
- Was recruited by Circle K to be District Manager of nine stores in Tucson; promoted to Regional Sales Manager over 76 stores.

EDUCATION

Arizona State University, Tempe, AZ. Completed courses in archaeology, Bible, business education, and computer science.
University of Phoenix, Phoenix, AZ. A.S. degree in Nursery Crops Technology, 1985.

PERSONAL

Am a high energy, take-charge individual who enjoys the challenge of solving problems and finding solutions to human resources dilemmas. Outstanding references. Solid speaking, writing, and computer skills.

Date

Exact Name of Person
Title or Position
Name of Company
Address (no., street)
Address (city, state, zip)

Dear Exact Name of Person: (or Dear Sir or Madam if answering a blind ad.)

I would appreciate an opportunity to talk with you about how I could contribute to your organization through my experience and personal qualities.

In my current position as an Employment Interviewer with the Employment Security Commission of Alabama, I work with individuals claiming unemployment benefits as I help them identify potential new opportunities for employment.

In my previous position with a private organization, I set up a new Jobs Center "from scratch" after I was recruited for the job by a former college instructor who was on the board of directors. In an essentially entrepreneurial role, I cultivated the support of business leaders in Tuscaloosa as I secured their commitment to working with a new public employment agency. Utilizing my strong computer knowledge, I set up a website which allows prospective job hunters to search online for openings, and the city of Tuscaloosa has become very proud of its new employment "baby." The program I developed has become a model statewide, and I received a special award from the Mayor recognizing my accomplishments.

I hope you will call or write me to suggest a time convenient for us to meet and discuss your current and future needs and how I might serve them. Thank you for your time.

Sincerely yours,

Carol Cummings

CAROL CUMMINGS

1110½ Hay Street, Fayetteville, NC 28305 • preppub@aol.com • (910) 483-6611

OBJECTIVE

To benefit an organization that can use an experienced professional who offers excellent planning and organizational skills as well as a strong track record in client relations.

EXPERIENCE

EMPLOYMENT INTERVIEWER. Employment Security Commission of Alabama, Tuscaloosa, AL (2004-present). Counsel unemployed individuals filing unemployment compensation claims, seeking employment, and entering retraining programs; screen individuals for claims requirements and match eligible candidates to specific jobs throughout Tuscaloosa County.
* Enroll/screen applicants for programs for economically disadvantaged persons and dislocated workers.
* Interact with local community college to enroll applicants in an educational program to enhance employability.

JOB PROGRAMS COORDINATOR. Tuscaloosa Business Coalition, Tuscaloosa, AL (2002-04). Was aggressively recruited for this position by a former college instructor who taught me at the University of Alabama. Took on the challenge of a newly created position which involved the development and implementation of a new public employment agency in Tuscaloosa.
* Prospected for new job opportunities in the community by calling on business and community leaders to secure their participation in the program. Succeeded in recruiting the top ten largest employers, who allowed all of their job vacancies to be posted through the Tuscaloosa Jobs Center which we set up.
* On my own initiative, developed a website for the Jobs Center and turned it into a popular site where potential applicants could search for viable job openings.
* Received a special award from the Mayor of Tuscaloosa for my efforts in enriching the jobs base of the city. The program I developed has been touted as a model and is being implemented in a dozen cities throughout the U.S.

PHYSICAL EDUCATION TEACHER. Lakewood Elementary School, Tuscaloosa, AL (2000-02). Taught fundamentals of various sports and recreational activities to different physical education classes.
* Assisted in the coordination of the annual field day.

ASSISTANT DEN LEADER. Girl Scouts of America, Tuscaloosa, AL (1996-2000). Assisted in all aspects of administrative functions.
* Planned den meetings and corresponding activities.
* Created programs to increase cognitive and social skills while earning badges and awards.
* Gathered supplies and equipment needed for major camping events.

Highlights of other experience: Honed client relations skills while acting as the "front line" of a busy law office; refined bookkeeping skills, including accounts payable and accounts receivable, while working as a secretary/office manager; processed legal documents.

EDUCATION

Bachelor of Arts degree in Sociology, The University of Alabama, Tuscaloosa, AL, 2000.

PERSONAL

Experienced in many areas of office management. Type 70 wpm, and offer proficiency in Microsoft Word. Outstanding references on request.

CAREER CHANGE

Date

Exact Name of Person
Title or Position
Name of Company
Address (no., street)
Address (city, state, zip)

Dear Exact Name of Person: (or Dear Sir or Madam if answering a blind ad.)

With the enclosed resume, I would like to make you aware of my interest in exploring employment opportunities with your organization. I am responding to your advertisement for an Events Coordinator for the City of Charlotte Coliseum.

As you will see from my resume, I am currently the Events Coordinator for the Golden Knights, the U.S. Army's famed parachute demonstration team. For this world-famous organization, it is my responsibility to plan, coordinate, and execute day-to-day international parachuting demonstrations and competitions for 80 personnel organized into five units.

In previous employment as a Researcher and Development Test Supervisor, I planned, conducted, and reported data on field experiments involving airborne equipment. My analytical and problem-solving skills are highly refined.

Although I have been encouraged to remain with the Golden Knights in my current role, I have decided to leave the military and enter the civilian work force. It is my desire to benefit the city of Charlotte as the Events Coordinator for your coliseum. I understand the financial importance of aggressively recruiting bookings for the coliseum, and I am confident that I could positively impact the city's bottom line through my ability to sell and coordinate. I am accustomed to working hard to achieve ambitious goals, and I would welcome the opportunity to apply those skills as well as my natural persistence for the benefit of the City of Charlotte.

You would find me in person to be a congenial individual with outstanding public relations skills. I can provide excellent personal and profession references.

I hope you will call or write me soon to suggest a time convenient for us to meet to discuss your current and future needs. Thank you in advance for your time.

Sincerely yours,

Charles Glenn

Alternate last paragraph:
I hope you will welcome my call soon to arrange a brief meeting when we might meet to discuss your needs and goals and how my background might serve them. I can provide outstanding references at the appropriate time.

CHARLES GLENN

1110½ Hay Street, Fayetteville, NC 28305   •   preppub@aol.com   •   (910) 483-6611

OBJECTIVE

To benefit an organization that can use a young dedicated professional who offers abilities in operations management and program development along with outstanding public relations skills in dealing with public officials to coordinate major events.

EXPERIENCE

EVENTS COORDINATOR. Golden Knights, U.S. Army, U.S. and overseas locations (1999-present). Plan, coordinate, and execute day-to-day international parachuting demonstrations and competitions for 80 personnel organized into five units.

- Integrate five team aircraft into daily training and public parachuting demonstrations; the Golden Knights have performed 475 demonstrations before nine million spectators.
- Coordinate directly with U.S. military and national-level public affairs administrators.
- Plan travel and accommodations for 80 personnel traveling 250 days annually to 45 states and seven countries. Contributed to the team's success in winning every U.S. men's national event and the European Championship.

RESEARCH AND DEVELOPMENT TEST SUPERVISOR. U.S. Army, Ft. Campbell, KY (1996-99). Planned, conducted, and reported data on user-tests and field experiments involving airborne equipment, procedures, and systems related to aerial delivery and transportation products used in air movement operations.

- Oversaw air movement in both U.S. Army and Air Force aircraft conducting special operations in the areas of airdrop, low altitude parachute extraction, as well as external and internal air transport.
- Received respected medals and was praised for my outstanding analytical and problem-solving skills.

QUALITY CONTROL INSPECTOR. U.S. Army, Ft. Campbell, KY (1993-95). Supervised up to 350 employees overseeing logistical maintenance and training support for daily operations and deployment for a 400-person parachute battalion.

FIRST-LINE SUPERVISOR. U.S. Army, Benning, GA (1990-92). Was promoted ahead of my peers to train and manage a team of 14 individuals.

EDUCATION & TRAINING

B. S. degree in Mathematical Science & Operations Research, University of Kentucky, adjunct campus at Ft. Campbell, 1998. Completed degree while working full-time in the military. Attended courses through military schools including: Jump Master, Halo Jump Master, Parachute Rigger, Airdrop Inspector, and Leadership Courses.

HONORS & AWARDS

Made the elite U.S. Army Parachute Team; only 4% of all applicants actually make the team which has a 97% drop out rate.
Received medals and awards for excellent contributions and superior accomplishments:

Master Parachutist Badge	Parachute Rigger Badge
Expert Infantryman's Badge	Expert Rifleman's Badge
Army Commendation Medal	Army Achievement Medal
Overseas Ribbon	Army Service Ribbon
British Parachute Wings	Canadian Parachute Wings

PERSONAL

Am a hardworking dedicated professional with the ability to get projects done under "pressure deadlines." Have the ability to work effectively and efficiently under stressful situations. Pride myself in a job well done. Willing to relocate.

Exact Name of Person
Title or Position
Name of Company
Address (no., street)
Address (city, state, zip)

EXECUTIVE DIRECTOR,
Diabetic Consortium, is
seeking a new position as
Director of Fundraising

Dear Exact Name of Person: (or Dear Sir or Madam if answering a blind ad.)

With the enclosed resume, I would like to make you aware of my interest in exploring employment opportunities with your organization. I am responding to your advertisement for a Director of Fundraising.

As you will see from my resume, I am currently the Executive Director for the Richmond Diabetic Consortium. In that capacity I manage daily operations of a federally funded regional service agency that plans, develops, and ensures the availability of essential health and support services to diabetic patients and their loved ones.

Prior to this employment, I served as the Diabetic Program Director for the Eastern Diabetic Care Consortium. In that position, I coordinated and conducted diabetic education, orientation, and training to encourage awareness, cooperation, and participation with the Consortium. I also liaised with related agencies, councils, and task forces while aggressively coordinating grant funding, fundraisers, and other funding projects.

You will notice from my resume that I worked full-time in a corporate setting while completing my undergraduate degree in health care administration. In a track record of promotion with a leading financial institution, I refined my financial management skills and gained a wealth of experience related to the "customer care" concept as implemented in business. Although I excelled in the business world, I greatly enjoy utilizing my management skills in a human services organization where I have the opportunity to render practical help to my fellow man on a daily basis.

I hope you will call or write me soon to suggest a time convenient for us to meet to discuss your current and future needs. Thank you in advance for your time.

Sincerely yours,

James Cooke

Alternate last paragraph:
I hope you will welcome my call soon to arrange a brief meeting when we might meet to discuss your needs and goals and how my background might serve them. I can provide outstanding references at the appropriate time.

JAMES COOKE

1110½ Hay Street, Fayetteville, NC 28305 • preppub@aol.com • (910) 483-6611

OBJECTIVE

I want to contribute to an organization that can use an enthusiastic young professional with outstanding managerial and customer relations skills.

EDUCATION

B.S., Health Care Administration, Virginia Commonwealth University, Richmond, VA. 1992.
Associate of Science in Business Administration, Baylor University, Waco, TX, 1985.
In my spare time, am pursuing Master's degree in **Health Care Services,** Virginia Commonwealth University, Richmond, VA.

EXPERIENCE

EXECUTIVE DIRECTOR. Richmond Diabetic Consortium, Richmond, VA (2001-present). Manage the daily operations of a federally-funded regional service agency that plans, develops, and ensures the availability of essential health and support services to diabetic patients and their loved ones.
- Coordinate with the Consortium Board and allied health agencies.
- Supervise four full-time case workers, one full-time housing manager, three part-time community health advisers, and one full-time clerical employee.
- Negotiate, monitor, renew, and terminate all service contracts in addition to managing all consortium service billing and reimbursement; handle client and provider disputes.
- Maintain all financial and legal records, develop and keep an annual budget, account for all monies spent, and complete all necessary reports required by the state.
- Direct all fund development activities and grant writing. Oversee preparation of newsletters and brochures.

DIABETIC PROGRAM DIRECTOR. Eastern Diabetic Care Consortium, Richmond, VA (1992-2000). Coordinated and conducted diabetic education, orientation, and training in the area to encourage awareness, cooperation, and participation with the Consortium.
- Prepared records, documents, correspondence, and other paperwork concerning Consortium activities while also developing annual fundraising activities.
- Implemented programs in accordance with all federal and state guidelines while also monitoring the activities of and negotiating agreements with service providers. Arbitrate problems between clients and service providers and approve care invoices.
- Liaised with related agencies, councils, and task forces while actively coordinating grant funding, fundraisers, and other funding projects. Provided outreach, early intervention, and public relations to all area print and broadcast media.

Worked full-time while completing my college degree; gained excellent financial skills in different positions with Alamo Health Services, Houston, TX:
INSURANCE BILLING SUPERVISOR. (1990-92). Rapidly promoted from Credit Service Representative to provide and maintain management and statistical billing reports while overseeing the centralized billing of all AHS offices within the United States, including recruiting, training, supervising, and evaluating a staff of billing clerks.

CREDIT SERVICE REPRESENTATIVE. (1987-90). Supervised and assisted branch offices in collection of insurance, commercial, and private pay accounts.

INSURANCE COLLECTION SPECIALIST. (1986-87). Monitored, researched, and resolved all insurance receivables with emphasis on accounts in excess of $10,000.

AFFILIATIONS

Past President, Virginia Association of Consortium. Excellent references on request.

TWO-PAGE RESUME

HEIDI COLE

1110½ Hay Street, Fayetteville, NC 28305   •   preppub@aol.com   •   (910) 483-6611

OBJECTIVE

To offer a track record of distinguished performance as a dedicated, innovative professional with proven analytical, motivational, and planning skills along with a reputation for excellence in program development, research, technical writing, and public speaking.

EXECUTIVE DIRECTOR, Crisis Center. Here is an example of a two-page resume.

EXPERIENCE

EXECUTIVE DIRECTOR. Center of Portland, Inc., Portland, OR, (2003-present). Manage two full-time professional staff employees and one part-time bookkeeping employee. Oversee the entire business operation and the Crisis Center for this nonprofit organization which provides 24-hour-a-day telephone crisis intervention/support and information/referral services.

- Have improved and reorganized internal management; developed mission statement and strategic plan.
- Introduced creative fundraising strategies, grant acquisitions, and provided the leadership needed to take the organization from a financial deficit situation to a positive operating balance.

DIRECTOR, OREGON DIVISION OF SOCIAL SERVICES, Portland, OR (1996-03). Supervised the administration of 100 county social services departments through a staff of 1,150 employees and a billion-dollar-plus budget. Developed changes which allowed the 100 county departments to operate more efficiently and productively.

- Provided guidance for a wide range of programs including child protective, adult, child support enforcement, food stamp, foster care and adoption, and employment programs.
- Guided the Job and Basic Skills Program to recognition as one of the country's most outstanding models.
- Was the first to secure funding from the General Assembly for the state's child protective services program.
- Prepared documentation which convinced a private foundation to provide funding used for a massive reorganization of the entire child welfare system: devoted 18 months to planning which resulted in Oregon's becoming one of eight states to receive this assistance which totaled $3.3 million in the program's first year.
- Applied my diplomatic skills working with the governments of each of the 100 counties to ensure their programs met federal and state regulations while also dealing regularly with administrators of other state agencies (health, commerce, and the court system).
- Developed a program which saved more than $200 million over five fiscal years through a unique state, local, and federal initiative to reduce erroneous benefit payments.
- Created and presented to the General Assembly a comprehensive social service reform plan which introduced fairer standards.
- Acted as legislative liaison for the division by lobbying for bills which were advantageous for the Division of Social Services.
- Was the only person to hold this appointed position under two governors (from different political parties) and the only person to "come up through the ranks" to this level.

REGIONAL DIRECTOR, OREGON DEPT. OF HUMAN RESOURCES, Portland, OR (1993-96). Was recruited and handpicked for the state director's position on the basis of my performance in this capacity. Provided a 33-person staff and a 17-county region with leadership in child welfare, public assistance, child support and other related programs.
- Managed a child welfare program recognized as the best from among the four regions.
- Created an Assist to Families Program recognized for the lowest error rates.

ASSISTANT CHIEF, PREVENTATIVE AND SUPPORT SERVICES. Portland, OR (1992-93). In the Department of Human Resources, streamlined procedures and developed policies while supervising 12 employees.
- Created and implemented a model program to prevent repeat adolescent pregnancies.
- Oversaw the monitoring, evaluation, and certification of 400 contracts.

CONSULTANT, OR DEPT. OF HUMAN RESOURCES, Portland, OR (1984-92). Developed a model training plan and peer supervision program as a technical advisor and consultant for a ten-county region's Assist to Dependent Children programs.
- Designed and administered successful marketing strategies that increased multidisciplinary approaches to Child Welfare Service delivery in the 17 regional counties.
- Guided 34 county Departments of Social Services in the creation and implementation of a new employment and training program for public assistance recipients.

Highlights of other experience: Multnomah County, Portland, OR, 1980-84.
- As a Child Welfare Worker, earned recognition for my success in taking a backlog of 42 children who had been in foster care for five, ten, or more years and placing them either with relatives or for adoption. Developed a model program for the county which earned praise from state and federal officials and led to my advancement.

EDUCATION

Master of Social Work (MSW) degree, Portland State University, Portland, OR, 1992. Certificate of completion, Public Management Program (PMP), The State of OR. **B.S., Secondary Education,** University of Washington, Seattle, WA, 1980.

AFFILIATIONS

Have held membership in professional and civic organizations including the following: National Welfare Association (NWA); National Child Welfare Administration

HONORS & AWARDS

Chosen to serve on numerous national task forces, honored in 2002 by National Welfare Association (NWA) as an outstanding contributor to efforts to simplify welfare programs.
- Was appointed to the National Welfare Simplification and Advisory Committee by the U.S. Department of Agriculture in 2001 – the committee included eleven members throughout the country.
- Was appointed to The Presidential Commission on Childhood and Youth Deaths.
- Received a U.S. Department of Agriculture Award for Distinguished Service for superb efforts in implementing a unique cooperative federal, state, and local initiative to reduce erroneous benefit payments: saved nearly $200 million over five fiscal years (2002).
- Was honored with the NWA Leadership Award in recognition of outstanding leadership on behalf of program simplification and coordination (2002).
- Received the Social Security Administration Commissioners' Award for delivering high quality disability benefits and service to the citizens of Oregon (2002).
- Won recognition from the Governor's Center at Portland State University and the National Child Welfare Center in Portland for strategic planning, executive leadership, innovative organizational development, and management in the public sector.

PERSONAL

Possess strong mediation skills and the ability to remain diplomatic yet get my point across. Well-developed talents in instructing, teaching, and briefing others in a concise manner.

Date

Exact Name of Person
Title or Position
Name of Company
Address (no., street)
Address (city, state, zip)

**FAMILY ADVOCACY
SPECIALIST,**
United Methodist Church

Dear Exact Name of Person: (or Dear Sir or Madam if answering a blind ad.)

I am responding to your advertisement in the newspaper for a Program Coordinator. I was quite excited when I read the ad in the newspaper because I offer all the skills and abilities you seek. Fluent in Spanish, I have counseled clients in Spanish while providing case management services to individuals with a wide range of problems and impairments.

In my most recent job as a Family Advocacy Specialist, I served as the "subject matter expert" on family advocacy issues for the United Methodist Church. Utilizing programming and fundraising techniques which have been hailed as "ingenious" and "unique," I led a small staff in developing the Foster Care & Shelter Programs now used in 23 states. It has been one of the biggest thrills of my life to be involved in designing and implementing programs which I know will positively impact the lives of young children for many years to come.

What my resume does not reveal is my affable nature and warm personality that is well suited to the social services field, which I truly enjoy. Although my chosen profession is one in which case workers encounter tragic and sad human realities on a daily basis, I am confident of my ability, refined through experience, to help anyone improve his or her situation. I also offer highly refined skills in budget planning and administration.

I am an experienced social services professional who would enjoy contributing to your needs and goals, and I hope you will favorably review my application and call me to set up an interview at your convenience. Thank you in advance for your time.

Sincerely yours,

Stephanie Taylor

STEPHANIE TAYLOR

1110½ Hay Street, Fayetteville, NC 28305　　•　preppub@aol.com　　•　　(910) 483-6611

OBJECTIVE

To contribute to an organization that can use a skilled social worker who offers experience in handling problems related to child abuse, mental illness, and family violence as well as problems associated with poverty, illiteracy, and joblessness.

LANGUAGE

Fluent in Spanish

EXPERIENCE

FAMILY ADVOCACY SPECIALIST. United Methodist Church Family Support Center, New York, NY (2003-present). Play a key role in implementing and coordinating the Family Advocacy Program throughout the US for this major Christian church.
- Conduct surveys to identify deficiencies in services for abused spouses or children.
- Implemented an innovative community education program which included training programs for individuals; publicized information describing the grounds for reporting suspected abuse.
- Train social services representatives, youth services staff, and social services volunteers as well as personnel in other organizations and agencies in the procedures for identifying and referring suspected child abuse.
- Serve as the "subject matter expert" on family advocacy issues as a member of the Family Advocacy Case Team. Developed the Foster Care & Shelter Programs now used in 23 states.

CHILD DEVELOPMENT EDUCATION SPECIALIST. The State of Florida, Miami, FL (2000-03). Worked as Training Coordinator in the Child Development Services Branch; advised and trained those providing day care to preschoolers on age-appropriate activities, and assured that centers/homes were arranged to enhance the physical, emotional, social, and cognitive development of children.
- Completed extensive assessments on each home or center module regularly.
- Planned training modules which were used as instructional guides for caregivers. Completed assessments of children identified as having problems such as developmental delay or behavioral difficulty. Gained insight into the factors that cause stress in caregiving, and counseled workers about how to anticipate and cope with such problems.
- Provided both individual training as well as group sessions.
- Became skilled in improving the day care provided in small homes and large centers.

SOCIAL PROGRAMS COORDINATOR. United Methodist Church, Charlotte, NC (1992-99). Worked with nearly every kind of social services problem while counseling individuals and families; dealt with problems associated with unhappy marriages, unwed parenthood, and financial difficulties as well as problems related to caring for the ill and handicapped.
- Developed programs appropriate for mentally challenged and Downs Syndrome children.
- Created educational materials and provided instruction related to First Aid, sex education, nutrition, home management and home economics, and other areas.
- Became extensively involved in delinquency prevention; counseled juveniles.

EDUCATION

Bachelor of Science (B.S.) degree in Social Services Administration, Thomas Edison State College, Trenton, NJ, 1992.
Completed extensive professional training related to family advocacy, parent effectiveness, substance abuse, children's services, and services for the mentally and physically challenged.

PERSONAL

Am considered an experienced public speaker. Have completed extensive training related to preparing and delivering briefings. Truly enjoy the social services field.

Date

Exact Name of Person
Title or Position
Name of Company
Address (no., street)
Address (city, state, zip)

FAMILY RESOURCE SPECIALIST,
Community Service Agency

Dear Exact Name of Person: (or Dear Sir or Madam if answering a blind ad.)

I would enjoy an opportunity to meet with you in person to discuss with you the ways in which I could become a valuable part of your team in the mental health and human services area. I am writing in response to your ad for a Habilitation Specialist.

Since graduating with my B.S. degree from Ohio State University, I have worked in preventive medicine. I have coordinated treatment for the mentally challenged and physically disabled, provided crisis intervention services to children and young adults, and developed "from scratch" a program providing services to at-risk families.

I am proud of the fact that I have made valuable contributions to every organization I have served. Even in my internship, I became the first intern to receive an Achievement Award as a result of my efforts in research and program development. Most recently, I played a key role in developing a new program serving at-risk families, and I taught a highly popular parenting class entitled "Parenting by Heart." In a prior job I worked in a short-term, inpatient crisis intervention hospital for children and won the highly respected "Employee of the Month" award in my first quarter of employment based on a secret election by peers and patients. I have coordinated programs for the mentally and physically challenged.

You would find me in person to be a caring and enthusiastic young professional who genuinely thrives on the challenge of helping others. I can provide exceptionally strong personal and professional references.

I hope you will write or call me soon to suggest a time when we might meet to discuss your current and future needs and how I might serve them. Thank you in advance for your time.

Sincerely yours,

Jennifer White

JENNIFER WHITE

1110½ Hay Street, Fayetteville, NC 28305 • preppub@aol.com • (910) 483-6611

OBJECTIVE

To benefit an organization that can use a human services and mental health professional who has earned a reputation as an innovative, compassionate hard worker while serving the needs of at-risk families, performing crisis intervention for children and young adults, and coordinating programs for the physically disabled and mentally challenged.

EDUCATION

B.S., Community Health Education, The Ohio State University, Columbus, OH, 2000.

EXPERIENCE

FAMILY RESOURCE SPECIALIST. Franklin County Community Service, Columbus, OH (2002-present). In an essentially "entrepreneurial" role after being hired for one of two newly created positions, utilize my resourcefulness and enthusiasm in establishing a network throughout the community; developed a clientele of "at-risk" families and provided support services and education for over 100 families while personally handling a normal caseload of 20 families at any one time.

- Effective at earning the trust and respect of others, in numerous situations I am the only professional in the community who can gain access to a home when problems arise.
- Make home visits to families at risk for spouse abuse or child neglect/abuse for the Family Advocacy Program; prepare home studies for prospective adoptive parents.
- Represent families' interests as an "expert" on the Family Advocacy Case Team.
- Maintain confidential case files while working closely with agencies or personnel including the schools, hospital staff/medical personnel, chaplains, and social workers.
- Along with the other resource specialist, give unselfishly of my personal time in order to organize morale-booster socials and professional support programs for the staff.
- Teach a highly effective parenting class entitled *"Parenting by Heart."*

MENTAL HEALTH ASSISTANT. Park Medical Center, Columbus, OH (2000-01). In a short-term, inpatient crisis intervention hospital for children and young adults, provided one-on-one care to children and adolescents while organizing activities and guiding informal group sessions.

- Was highly respected for my skills: in my first quarter of employment, was nominated for and won the "Employee of the Month" in a secret ballot by peers and patients.

TREATMENT COORDINATOR. Hamilton County Hospital, Cincinnati, OH (1996-00). For a client load of 21 mentally and physically challenged adults, developed, oversaw, and evaluated personal programs which would increase their level of independence.

- Coordinated with and instructed professionals at residences, day treatment programs, and sheltered workshops in order to bring every stage together for a successful program. Trained as an investigator, was selected to serve on the Special Review Committee which reviewed and made decisions on cases.

PREVENTIVE MEDICINE INTERN. U.S. Army Medical Department, Ft. Campbell, KY (1996). Excelled in an internship created especially for me, and then became the department's first intern to be awarded an Army Achievement Award as a result of my initiative and accomplishments in research and program development.

- Interviewed 20 preventive medicine professionals, created slides and a script, and then presented the results to the department chief. Produced a comprehensive tool for the Community Health Nursing Department which is still being utilized.

PERSONAL

Use computers with Microsoft Word, Excel, and PowerPoint. CPR and First Aid certified.

Date

Exact Name of Person
Title or Position
Name of Company
Address
City, State, Zip

FAMILY SERVICES PROGRAM COORDINATOR

Dear Exact Name of Person: (or Dear Sir or Madam if answering a blind ad.)

With the enclosed resume, I would like to make you aware of my interest in exploring employment opportunities with your organization.

As you will see from my resume, after obtaining my M.S. degree in Guidance and Counseling/Psychological Counseling, I gained years of experience as a Social Worker and Counselor for several organizations. Currently as Family Services Program Coordinator at a military community, I supervise eight individuals while directing a wide range of human services and outreach programs provided to military professionals and their families. I am considered as the country's leading technical expert in establishing Family Support Groups. I wrote the Family Support Handbook for Ft. Drum which is being adopted for use at all military bases.

My responsibilities include managing programs providing legal and financial advice as well as crisis counseling to individuals experiencing personal problems ranging from marital distress to suicidal feelings. Continuously involved in developing and implementing programs which facilitate people's involvement in life-enriching activities, I have trained hundreds of managers in effective counseling techniques.

You would find me to be a public relations professional who is skilled at coordinating and implementing large-scale events, authoring and publishing materials ranging from handbooks to policy manuals, as well as training and managing teams of dedicated specialists.

I hope you will call or write me soon to suggest a time convenient for us to meet to discuss your current and future needs. Thank you in advance for your time.

Sincerely yours,

Eileen Lincoln

Alternate last paragraph:
I hope you will welcome my call soon to arrange a brief meeting when we might meet to discuss your needs and goals and how my background might serve them. I can provide outstanding references at the appropriate time.

EILEEN LINCOLN

1110½ Hay Street, Fayetteville, NC 28305 • preppub@aol.com • (910) 483-6611

OBJECTIVE

To contribute to an organization that can use a public relations professional skilled at coordinating large-scale events, authoring and publishing materials ranging from handbooks to policy manuals, as well as training and managing teams of dedicated specialists.

EDUCATION

Master of Science in Guidance and Counseling/Psychological Counseling, Jefferson Community College, Watertown, NY, 1987.
Bachelor of Science, majors in Sociology and Political Science and minor in Psychology, Duke University, Durham, NC, 1982.
Completed executive development programs related to human services administration, service program development and management, crisis intervention program management, and outreach program coordination.

EXPERIENCE

PROGRAM COORDINATOR. Community and Family Services, Ft. Drum, NY (2000-present). At the military community, supervise eight individuals while directing a wide range of human services and outreach programs provided to military professionals and their families.

- Am considered the country's leading technical expert in establishing Family Support Groups; wrote the Family Support Handbook for Ft. Drum and have trained hundreds of managers and supervisors.
- Manage programs providing legal and financial advice as well as crisis counseling to individuals experiencing personal problems ranging from marital distress to suicidal feelings; develop and implement programs which facilitated people's involvement in life-enriching activities.
- Supervise a 7-day-a-week Welcome Center; manage a wide range of programs designed to assist individuals and families traumatized by relocation, transition, and other matters. Train hundreds of managers and professional supervisors in effective counseling techniques.
- Plan and implement this military community's annual Family Symposium and train all facilitators; by aggressive promotion, increased participation from 572 in 2003 to 1811 in 2004.
- Have excelled in recruiting, training, and managing dozens of volunteers, many of whom give up to 40 hours a week to the Outreach Programs which I plan and coordinate.
- Handle extensive public speaking responsibilities; conduct briefings for 2,000 people monthly.

FAMILY SUPPORT SPECIALIST. Family Support Center, Ft. Drum, NY (1997-99). Taught numerous classes including Parent Effectiveness Classes, Employment Workshops, and courses in Communication Skills while working at one of the nation's airlift centers.

- Created a new service directory for this community after developing the fact sheets and other data collection tools used in obtaining and compiling information.
- Interviewed and counseled individuals and referred them to social services agencies.

GUIDANCE COUNSELOR. Army Education Center, Ft. Knox, KY (1993-96). Handled extensive administrative duties including preparing quarterly reports, financial reports, and class projections while enrolling individuals in programs including Headstart, High School Completion Program, language programs, job skills training courses, and other courses; was Test Control Officer, Property Book Officer, and Contracting Officer.

PERSONAL

Offer highly refined public speaking skills. Am known as an outstanding communicator.

Date

Exact Name of Person
Title or Position
Name of Company
Address (no., street)
Address (city, state, zip)

**FOSTER FAMILY
SERVICES
COORDINATOR,**
Worcester County
Foster Care
Services

Dear Exact Name of Person: (or Dear Sir or Madam if answering a blind ad.)

With the enclosed resume, I would like to make you aware of my interest in exploring employment opportunities with your organization. I believe I can benefit your organization through my management skills as well as my knowledge of Medicare and Medicaid guidelines.

As you will see from my resume, I hold a B.S. in Nursing and a current Massachusetts Nursing License. In my current position as Foster Family Services Coordinator, I am in charge of making decisions about the ability of families to qualify as foster homes. I also make recommendations regarding the placement of children in foster homes.

In previous experience as a Case Coordinator, I coordinated comprehensive individualized courses of treatment to develop efficient discharge plans while working with patients, families, and a multidisciplinary team. I also monitored and facilitated the appropriate utilization of resources and reviewed cases, determining appropriateness of admission or continued hospitalization.

As a Nurse by training, I feel I have unique competencies which allow me to be of great value in a human services setting.

I hope you will call or write me soon to suggest a time convenient for us to meet to discuss your current and future needs. Thank you in advance for your time.

Sincerely yours,

Felicia Davis

Alternate last paragraph:
I hope you will welcome my call soon to arrange a brief meeting when we might meet to discuss your needs and goals and how my background might serve them. I can provide outstanding references at the appropriate time.

FELICIA DAVIS

1110½ Hay Street, Fayetteville, NC 28305　•　preppub@aol.com　•　(910) 483-6611

OBJECTIVE

To benefit an organization seeking a highly motivated health care professional with experience in coordinating services including foster family service as well as hospital and home health services while applying my thorough knowledge of Medicare/Medicaid guidelines.

EDUCATION

Bachelor of Science in Nursing, University of Massachusetts, Boston, MA, 1992.
Associates Degree in Nursing, Worcester State College, Worcester, MA, 1990.
Completed course work on quality assurance and utilization review including the Critical Care Seminar, a 40-hour seminar in New York, NY 1996.

EXPERIENCE

FOSTER FAMILY SERVICES COORDINATOR. Worcester County Foster Care Service, Worcester, MA (2002-present). Qualify applicants who wish to provide foster care to children of all ages; conduct in-home visits to assess quality of home care. Make recommendations about the placement of children in qualified foster homes.
* Supervise up to 20 family services assistants.

Advanced in the following track record of dedicated service to Bristol County Regional Hospital, a 382-bed facility located in New Bedford, MA:
2002: CASE COORDINATOR. Coordinated comprehensive individualized courses of treatment to develop efficient discharge plans while working with patients, families, and a multidisciplinary team.
* Monitored and facilitated the appropriate utilization of resources.
* Assisted various departments to identify opportunities to streamline operations, avoiding duplication and preventing delays in treatments and services.
* Reviewed cases, determining appropriateness of admission or continued hospitalization.

2000-02: QUALITY REVIEW SPECIALIST SUPERVISOR. Structured daily work flow for the Utilization Review Department. Created written appeals on behalf of the hospital regarding payment denials from federally funded accrediting agencies. Developed strategic planning for hospital resources.

1997-00: UTILIZATION REVIEW COORDINATOR. Prepared concurrent reviews for Medicare and Medicaid to ensure compliance with rules, regulations, and standards established by the federal review program and specific reimbursement agencies; prepared quality reviews. Conferred with physicians, staff nurses, social workers, physical therapists, and new staff members to ensure appropriate documentation.

1996: ASSISTANT NURSE MANAGER SICU. Cared for patients recovering from neurological trauma and other surgeries.
* Assisted with the orientation of health care providers to the Surgical Intensive Care Unit. Supervised a staff of 25 employees, preparing payroll records and schedules.

1992-96: STAFF NURSE. Performed all duties of a staff and charge nurse. Acted as a Staff Liaison with the University of Massachusetts School of Nursing.

AFFILIATIONS

Member, American Nursing Association
Member, Quality Utilization Management Massachusetts Support Group

PERSONAL

Am an organized, efficient, and detail-oriented professional. Pride myself on my ability to communicate with people from a variety of backgrounds. Excellent references.

Date

Exact Name of Person
Title or Position
Name of Company
Address (number and street)
Address (city, state, and zip)

Dear Exact Name of Person: (or Sir or Madam if answering a blind ad.)

With the enclosed resume, I would like to make you aware of my interest in discussing the possibility of employment with your organization.

In my current position as a Program Assistant, I work with nine male juvenile sex offenders in a group home where I have 24-hour-a-day responsibility. I have earned a reputation as an outstanding communicator, and I have found that my communication skills have enabled me to tactfully resolve difficult problems and motivate troubled youth to turn their lives around. I often share my own personal story with youth, as I grew up in a large family in a tough urban environment, and I have watched as many of my friends succumbed to the pressures of others persuading them to adopt drugs and alcohol as a way of life.

You would find me in person to be a congenial, straightforward individual who is skilled in every aspect of public relations and customer service. I can provide outstanding personal and professional references.

If you can use a go-getter with a make-it-happen attitude, I hope you will contact me to suggest a time when we might meet to discuss your goals and how I might help you achieve them.

Yours sincerely,

Norman Harris

NORMAN HARRIS

1110½ Hay Street, Fayetteville, NC 28305   •   preppub@aol.com   •   (910) 483-6611

OBJECTIVE   I want to contribute to an organization that can use a dedicated social worker who is known for my caring manner as well as my belief that the elderly as well as children deserved to be honored and given a helping hand by sincere, empathetic professionals.

EDUCATION   Earned a **Bachelor of Science in Social Work (B.S.W.),** *magna cum laude,* with a 3.83 GPA, Arkansas State University, Jonesboro, AR, 1998.
Throughout my 20 years of service in the U.S. Air Force, completed numerous courses related to these and other areas:

leadership	human resources	personnel management
communication	labor relations	race relations
substance abuse symptoms		counseling techniques

Certified in CPR and First Aid by the American Red Cross.

EXPERIENCE   **PROGRAM ASSISTANT.** Craighead County Mental Health, Jonesboro, AR (2002-present). In a group home for nine male juvenile sex offenders aged 14-18, monitor and assist children on a 24-hour-a-day basis.
- Maintain/administer prescription medicine for charts.
- Transport clients to appointments and to outings in other locations as deemed appropriate by Craighead County Mental Health.
- Have become very knowledgeable of the special needs of this particular client population, and have excelled in handling and diffusing hostile situations with clients.
- Have seen firsthand how important it is to assure the proper administration of prescription medicines to clients.

HOSPICE INTERN. Jonesboro Home Care Center, Jonesboro, AR (2000-02). Derived enormous satisfaction from this four-month internship in a hospice environment.
- It gave me a great feeling of accomplishment to help someone through their last journey in life in a peaceful way; I also learned that the dying still have much to contribute to those around them, and I greatly enjoyed listening and providing a comforting presence to little children and the elderly whom I saw die.
- Learned how gratifying it is for people to die in their own natural surroundings.

SOCIAL WORKER TRAINEE & VOLUNTEER. Craighead County Hospital, Jonesboro, AR (1998-00). While earning my B.S.W. degree, worked 3,000 hours with older people in the Intermediate Ward; became skilled in working with amputees and with older people with AIDS, Hepatitis C, and cancer.
- Functioned as the personal assistant to many elderly people, and took them to doctors appointments, on outings, and to activities. Became a favorite assistant of the nursing staff; often assisted them in various activities.

RECREATIONAL SPECIALIST. U.S. Air Force, various locations (1990-97). Developed a recreational program which was voted "best" in the parent organization while advancing to top management positions in the recreational management field.
- Supervised up to eight recreational assistants while supervising athletic events, overseeing the maintenance of athletic fields, and overseeing a wide range of athletic events, competitions, tournaments, and activities.

PERSONAL   Can provide outstanding personal and professional references. Have a true love of geriatric patients and children and feel that they are often the "throwaway citizens" in society.

Date

Exact Name of Person
Title or Position
Name of Company
Address (no., street)
Address (city, state, zip)

**HEART HEALTHY
ADVOCATE,**
American Heart
Association

Dear Exact Name of Person: (or Dear Sir or Madam if answering a blind ad.)

I would appreciate an opportunity to talk with you soon about how I could contribute to your organization through my formal education in social work as well as my versatile experience in social services, business management, office operations, and transportation management.

In my current position as a "Heart Healthy" Advocate, I am involved in spreading the word about healthy heart activities on behalf of the American Heart Association. In a previous job in the human services/social work field prior to receiving my degree, I worked as an Eligibility Specialist for Wake County and was involved in interviewing clients and assessing their needs. I gained a reputation as a caring counselor and respected coworker, and I was encouraged to apply for a social work position in the county.

From previous work experience in the Air Force, I am accustomed to dealing graciously with the public while working under tight deadlines and solving difficult problems. I offer a naturally compassionate personality along with an ability to handle large volumes of work efficiently and accurately. I can provide outstanding personal and professional references.

I hope you will welcome my call soon to arrange a brief meeting at your convenience to discuss your current and future needs and how I might serve them. Thank you in advance for your time, and I will look forward to meeting you.

Sincerely yours,

Arlene Larson

ARLENE LARSON

1110½ Hay Street, Fayetteville, NC 28305 • preppub@aol.com • (910) 483-6611

OBJECTIVE

To contribute to an organization that can use a cheerful hard worker who offers an education and experience related to social work and human services.

EDUCATION

Bachelor of Arts (B.A.) degree in Social Work, East Carolina University, Durham, NC, 2000. Completed this degree at night while excelling in my full-time job.

EXPERIENCE

Applied my communication and people skills in these simultaneous positions, Raleigh, NC:
HEART HEALTHY ADVOCATE. Wake County American Heart Association (AHA) (2003-present). Fill a high-visibility role as liaison and coordinator for activities of the Wake County American Heart Association, which has the mission of improving the general public's understanding of AHA and assisting AHA patients.

- During this program's first year as a grant recipient, administered funds and refined my public speaking skills representing the organization at numerous meetings and while training staff members and volunteers.
- Developed and maintained relations with county and city housing authorities in order to expand the availability of safe and affordable housing for clients.
- Screened and assessed applicants for the nine subsidized units for homeless AHA patients; maintained the waiting list and made decisions on filling vacancies.

COMMUNITY SUPPORT SPECIALIST. Wake County Mental Health Foundation (2000-03). Assisted case managers in a residential program for mentally challenged adults by providing one-on-one preparation designed to aid in future independent living while regularly assessing and reporting on their progress.

- Provided liaison with community agencies in order to ensure each person received all services available to help them reach their goals.

ELIGIBILITY WORKER. Wake County, Raleigh, NC (1999-00). Performed assessments of clients to determine eligibility for medical assistance in the form of Medicaid or Medicare; became skilled in handling a heavy caseload and became known for my accuracy in preparing large volumes of paperwork.

- Became acquainted with the vast interlocking network of social services organizations, and referred clients to those agencies and organizations.
- Assisted clients in preparing personal budgets and strengthening their ability to manage their finances.
- Earned a reputation as a compassionate counselor and effective motivator while treating people from all walks of life with dignity and respect.

OFFICE MANAGER'S ASSISTANT. Carolina Construction Service, Durham, NC (1997-99). As the "right arm" of a busy office manager in a fast-paced insurance office, excelled in activities ranging from word processing, to invoicing, to customer service.

SHIPPING SPECIALIST. U.S. Air Force, Elmendorf AFB, AK (1994-97). Received two prestigious medals for exceptional performance and exemplary service while specializing in managing the transportation of people and property worldwide.

- Worked with commercial airlines and shipping operations while processing every kind of paperwork and report related to making reservations and coordinating shipments.

PERSONAL

Am a patient, calm person who can handle a heavy work load and not get stressed out by tight deadlines. Have been told many times that I am a gifted counselor and communicator.

Exact Name of Person
Title or Position
Name of Company
Address (no., street)
Address (city, state, zip)

HOME VISITOR, HEAD START PROGRAM.

This individual is applying for a position as Assistant Director for the Rape Crisis Centers of Seattle.

Dear Exact Name of Person: (or Dear Sir or Madam if answering a blind ad):

With the enclosed resume, I would like to make you aware of my interest in exploring employment opportunities with your organization. I am responding to your advertisement for an Assistant Director for the Rape Crisis Centers of Seattle, WA.

In my current position as a Home Visitor for the Head Start Program, I foster a positive environment for effective social, emotional, and physical development while providing in-home and in-class educational experiences for 12 children. I assess each child's needs and progress to formulate individualized programs of activities and work closely with a Parent Involvement Coordinator, Health Coordinator, and Nutritionist to provide the best service for each child.

In earlier employment with Day Care for Adults, I provided services to adults with mental, emotional, or physical challenges. I developed and wrote monthly progress notes and quarterly care plans for participants as a valued member of a multidisciplinary team. I also co-facilitated a support group for the family members of Alzheimer's victims.

My skills in assessment would be excellent fits for the position you are seeking to fill. I also offer strong leadership ability and a knack for establishing warm working relationships. I realize that Seattle is committed to helping rape victims, and it would be an honor to be associated with the fine work you do.

I hope you will call or write me soon to suggest a time convenient for us to meet to discuss your current and future needs. Thank you in advance for your time.

Sincerely yours,

Jaylene Carl

Alternate last paragraph:
I hope you will welcome my call soon to arrange a brief meeting when we might meet to discuss your needs and goals and how my background might serve them. I can provide outstanding references at the appropriate time.

JAYLENE CARL

1110½ Hay Street, Fayetteville, NC 28305 • preppub@aol.com • (910) 483-6611

OBJECTIVE

To benefit an organization in need of a caring human services professional who offers excellent communication skills and experience in counseling people of all ages.

EDUCATION

Bachelor of Arts (B.A.) in Social Work, University of Nebraska, Lincoln, NE, 1987.
- Graduated **summa cum laude** with a GPA of 3.8 overall and 4.0 in my major.
- Completed internships in geriatric, pediatric, and mental health areas.

EXPERIENCE

HOME VISITOR. Head Start Program, Lincoln, NE (2003-present). Foster a positive environment for effective social, emotional, and physical development while providing in-home and in-class educational experiences for 12 children.
- Assess each child's needs and progress to formulate individualized programs of activities.
- Aid each child in many developmental areas including discipline, creativity, and large and small motor skills.
- Utilize parents in planning, teaching, and follow-through of developmental activities during home visit sessions, teaching parents how to teach their children.
- Work closely with a Parent Involvement Coordinator, Health Coordinator, and Nutritionist to provide the best service for each child.

SOCIAL WORKER. Day Care for Adults, Omaha, NE (2000-03). While assisting with administrative tasks, provided counseling, information, and referral services for 30 participants at the center and in the community with an approach to improving quality of life.
- Provided services to adults with mental, emotional, or physical challenges.
- Developed and wrote monthly progress notes and quarterly care plans for participants as a valued member of a multidisciplinary team.
- Interviewed potential participants and processed admissions and discharges.
- Assisted with the preparation of grant proposals.
- Co-facilitated a support group for the family members of Alzheimer's victims.
- Assisted with the care and feeding of patients.

SOCIAL WORKER. Omaha Group Home, Lincoln, NE (1988-00). Provided activities and services in both a residential and day care setting to 167 adults unable to care for themselves.
- Furnished counseling, information, and referral services to participants and their primary caregivers. Kept extensive records on the progress of each adult while formulating individual care plans.
- Processed discharges and collected social histories for new participants in the program.

OTHER EXPERIENCE & TRAINING
- Have attended numerous workshops, seminars, and training sessions to stay abreast of new developments in the field of social work.
- Passed exam to become a licensed Social Work Associate in Nebraska.
- Completed training to become a facilitator of support groups for family members of Alzheimer's disease victims.
- Am certified in CPR and First Aid.

PERSONAL

Enjoy one-on-one communication with people. Am a caring and compassionate person. Have done extensive volunteer work. Excellent references on request.

Date

Exact Name of Person
Title or Position
Name of Company
Address (no., street)
Address (city, state, zip)

Dear Exact Name of Person: (or Dear Sir or Madam if answering a blind ad.)

With the enclosed resume, I would like to make you aware of my interest in exploring employment opportunities with your organization.

As you will see from my resume, I obtained a B.S. in Special Education from the University of Nevada, and I have advanced quickly to my current position as Director of the Community Alternatives Program. With a proven ability to handle multiple simultaneous tasks, I am developing alternative strategies for helping the homeless. While overseeing operations of a network of 10 homeless shelters, I have been commended in writing for my leadership ability while coordinating services with agencies that provide adaptive behavior training, personal care, speech therapy, physical therapy, occupational therapy, medical supplies and durable medical equipment. While managing a small staff of professionals, I am involved in a variety of activities related to quality control and financial control of scarce resources.

In a previous job, I wrote Individual Habilitation Plans, quarterly reviews, behavior assessments, and individual programs as a Residential Programs Director for the Human Service Providers. I also handled all financial aspects of the program.

I have attended many training inservice conferences which I can utilize for the benefit of your organization. I can provide excellent references upon your request.

I hope you will call or write me soon to suggest a time convenient for us to meet to discuss your current and future needs. Thank you in advance for your time.

Sincerely yours,

Kimberly Curtis

Alternate last paragraph:
I hope you will welcome my call soon to arrange a brief meeting when we might meet to discuss your needs and goals and how my background might serve them. I can provide outstanding references at the appropriate time.

KIMBERLY CURTIS

1110½ Hay Street, Fayetteville, NC 28305 • preppub@aol.com • (910) 483-6611

OBJECTIVE

I want to contribute to an organization that can use an accomplished program director and human services professional who excels in working with others while managing scarce resources for maximum efficiency.

EDUCATION

Bachelor's of Science degree in Special Education, University of Nevada, Reno, NV, 1999. Graduated with a 3.5 GPA.

TRAINING

CPR and First Aid
Medication Administration
Non-Violent Crisis Prevention Intervention
Writing Behavioral Objectives
Quality Enhancement/Active Treatment
Nevada State Regulations

EXPERIENCE

HOMELESS SHELTERS DIRECTOR. Community Alternatives Program, Storey County Mental Health Center, Reno, NV (2003-present). Manage daily operations of a network of ten homeless shelters serving thousands of individuals yearly.
- Coordinate services with other agencies that provide adaptive behavior training, personal care, speech therapy, physical therapy, occupational therapy, medical supplies, and durable medical equipment.
- Develop and implement individual habilitation plans which require me to perform extensive cost analyses while also conducting visits to shelters to assure that services are being rendered.

RESIDENTIAL PROGRAM DIRECTOR. The State of Nevada Human Services Program, Las Vegas, NV (2001-03). Managed daily operations of two community residential facilities while also managing two residential program supervisors and thirty employees.
- Wrote Individual Habilitation Plans, Quarterly Reviews, Behavior Assessments, and Individual Programs.
- Handled all financial aspects of the program. Prepared the organization's annual budget and presented it to lawmakers in the state of Nevada.

Other experience: State of Nevada Human Resources Agency, locations statewide.
RESIDENTIAL TRAINER (2000). Responsible to the director of the day care for the daily operation of the facility. Implemented programs. Provided active treatment for the residents.
- Instructed and trained residents in activities of daily living which included personal hygiene, self care, residence maintenance, socialization, and community access.

YOUTH COUNSELOR (1999). Responsible to Human Service Providers Youth Program for the daily operations of counseling youth. Scheduled and organized daily events.
- Wrote reports concerning the weeks events; supervised junior counselors.

CONFERENCES

Assessment and Treatment of Persons with Developmental Handicaps in Sacramento, CA, 2001. Health Survey Process in Sacramento, CA, 2001.
Family Involvement with the Developmental Handicap in Sacramento, CA, 2001.

PERSONAL

Accomplished marathon runner in my spare time. Physically fit. Enjoy all sports.

CAREER CHANGE

Date

Exact Name of Person
Title or Position
Name of Company
Address (number and street)
Address (city, state, and zip)

HOSPICE CASE MANAGER

Dear Exact Name of Person: (or Dear Sir or Madam if answering a blind ad.)

Can you use an articulate and knowledgeable medical professional who excels in contributing to team efforts, instructing and mentoring other professionals as well as educating patients and family members?

I offer a solid background of experience as a nursing professional who has often been called on to instruct, educate, and teach. Currently excelling as a Hospice Case Manager, I manage a case load of up to 21 terminally ill patients, providing supportive care, patient assessment, and education. I joined the staff of Jefferson City Regional Medical Center as a Registered Nurse, and then worked as a Psychiatric Nurse until I was promoted into my current position.

Although I am highly regarded by my present employer and can provide outstanding references at the appropriate time. I am interested in returning to an environment where I would practice clinical nursing responsibilities.

My experience in the nursing field, along with my knowledge of medical facility operations and case management, combine to make me a well-rounded professional. With my enthusiastic approach and reputation as a compassionate individual, I would make a valuable addition to any organization.

I hope you welcome my call soon when I try to arrange a brief meeting to discuss your needs and how I might help you. Thank you in advance for your time.

Sincerely,

Nolan Rainey

Alternate last paragraph:
I hope you will call or write me soon to suggest a time convenient for us to meet and discuss your current and future needs and how I might serve them. Thank you in advance for your time.

NOLAN RAINEY

1110½ Hay Street, Fayetteville, NC 28305 • preppub@aol.com • (910) 483-6611

OBJECTIVE

To offer a combination of experience, education, and personal strengths to an organization that can benefit from my knowledge of the medical field as well as from my communication, teaching, and decision-making skills.

EDUCATION & TRAINING

Completed a three-year program leading to a **Diploma in Nursing,** University of Missouri, Columbia, MO, 1997.

Began a training program in January 2004 with Comprehensive Home Health Care, Jefferson City, MO; earned certification to provide home health care on a case-by-case basis.

EXPERIENCE

Was selected for a departmental transfer while earning a reputation as a professional who can be counted on to apply sound judgment, respond rapidly to problems, and work well under pressure, **Jefferson City Regional Medical Center,** Jefferson City, MO:

2003-present: HOSPICE CASE MANAGER. Manage a case load of as many as 21 terminally ill patients, handling patient assessment and education while coordinating home visits to care for the patient.

- Instruct patients and their family members on matters related to pain management, medications and their side effects, and the disease process.
- Conduct weekly meetings (attended every two week by the physician) with the patient's care team, to discuss care and treatment of the patient.
- Provide supportive care and counseling during home visits to terminally ill patients.

2002-03: PSYCHIATRIC NURSE. Transferred from a ward with 10 patients to a ward with 12 patients.

2001-02: REGISTERED NURSE. Supervised an L.P.N. and a Patient Care Assistant (P.C.A.) while handling nursing assessments, patient care, and case management for an average patient load of from four to eight at any time.

- Provided care support which included IV and LAB therapy as well as medication education for patients. Gained experience in patient administration support such as data entry and records management.
- Implemented a system of checking doctor's orders for accuracy in order to prevent errors; then trained other personnel on how to apply this information.
- Contributed my knowledge and mentoring skills as a preceptor for nursing students.

Other experience:

REGISTERED NURSE. Columbia Hospital, Columbia, MO (1998-01). Cited for my communication skills and ability to deal with patients and their families with compassion and concern, provided patient care including dispensing medications through I.V. therapy and oral injections.

- Was often called on to provide wellness education and predischarge education; was recognized for my ability to explain medical care procedures clearly.
- Rotated charge nurse duties with other qualified members of the nursing team.
- Served as a mentor for student nurses rotating through the hospital's precepting program.

MEDICAL TECHNICIAN. Columbia Providence Hospital, Columbia, MO (1993-97). Worked in a research facility where duties included I.V. therapy, retrieving blood and other samples, giving injections, and providing basic care.

PERSONAL

Am an enthusiastic, energetic, and outgoing individual. Adapt quickly to change.

Date

Exact Name of Person
Title or Position
Name of Company
Address (no., street)
Address (city, state, zip)

Dear Exact Name of Person: (or Dear Sir or Madam if answering a blind ad.)

With the enclosed resume, I would like to make you aware of my interest in exploring employment opportunities with your organization.

As you will see from my resume, I earned my B.B.A. with a 4.0 GPA. Currently employed by the Hospice Agency of Mississippi, I recruit and coordinate the work of 75 volunteers annually who are involved in the important work of helping the dying retain dignity and authority in their final days. I was recruited for this position because of the excellent management skills I demonstrated as Housing Services Coordinator for the Ronald McDonald House.

Because of strong communication skills and sound judgment, I possess an ability to establish warm working relationships with people at all levels. I have greatly enjoyed my work in serving the needs of the dying, and I feel that I have gained an incredible ability to empathize with and truly listen to others. My strong work ethic is supported by my solid academic track record as well as my professional accomplishments, and I can provide outstanding references.

I hope you will call or write me soon to suggest a time convenient for us to meet to discuss your current and future needs. Thank you in advance for your time.

Sincerely yours,

Shelly Fulton

Alternate last paragraph:
I hope you will welcome my call soon to arrange a brief meeting when we might meet to discuss your needs and goals and how my background might serve them. I can provide outstanding references at the appropriate time.

SHELLY FULTON

1110½ Hay Street, Fayetteville, NC 28305   •   preppub@aol.com   •   (910) 483-6611

OBJECTIVE

To apply my customer service skills and business "know-how" to a company needing a self-motivated, computer-proficient professional with strong management abilities and excellent communication skills.

EXPERIENCE

HOSPICE COORDINATOR. The Hospice Agency of Mississippi, Jackson, MS (2002-present). After working part-time as a Hospice Volunteer for two years, was asked to assume an administrative position. Recruit, train, and coordinate up to 75 volunteers yearly who provide comfort to the dying.

- Train hospice volunteers in techniques designed to help the dying spend their last weeks of life in their own homes. Help the dying in their desire to maintain some control of their lives in their final days.

HOUSING SERVICES COORDINATOR. The Ronald McDonald House, Jackson, MS (2000-02). Managed operations of a large home which functioned as a free hotel for people who needed long-term accommodations when visiting their seriously ill loved ones who were in nearby hospital care. Volunteered part-time as a Hospice Worker.

SECRETARY/RECEPTIONIST (Work-Study). University of Mississippi, Hattiesburg, MS (1996-2000). Managed the high-traffic admissions office of this college including administering and confidentially grading tests and responding to large volumes of calls on a multiline phone. Conducted initial telephone interviews to determine which of the commissioned advisors would receive the referral. Greeted all visitors to the college.

Other experience: At the University of Mississippi, demonstrated versatility and dedication to excellence in the following part-time and often-simultaneous positions while financing my education:

Admissions Assistant: Sorted and screened incoming admissions inquiries and forwarded them to the appropriate counselors; managed student files; performed administrative support functions including word processing.

Library Assistant: Helped students locate materials while organizing the card catalog and book shelves.

Tutor: Earned a reputation among undergraduates, graduate students, and professors as the "best tutor" on campus; helped a non-English speaking student on the verge of academic dismissal pass a variety of subjects, including English, with a "B" average.

EDUCATION

Finished at the top of my class with a **Bachelor of Business Administration (B.B.A.) degree,** University of Mississippi, Hattiesburg, MS, 2000; earned a perfect 4.0 GPA.
Graduated **Valedictorian,** Unity Senior High School, Tupelo, MS.
Honors and Awards in high school and college:

- Was nominated to numerous Honor Societies and participated in Student Government in college.
- Was recognized by Who's Who in American Colleges and Universities, and previously in Who's Who in American High Schools.
- Nominated as a Tupelo Scholar. Recipient of Unity Women's Club, Teaching Fellows, and Jackson State University Presidential Scholarships.

PERSONAL

Can motivate others with my tactful communication skills and sound judgment. Welcome challenging work. Offer a strong work ethic supported by a solid academic track record.

Date

Exact Name of Person
Title or Position
Name of Company
Address (no., street)
Address (city, state, zip)

Dear Exact Name of Person: (or Dear Sir or Madam if answering a blind ad.)

I would appreciate an opportunity to talk with you soon about how I could benefit your organization through my knowledge and experience related to income maintenance case management, social work, and social services administration.

As you will see from my resume, I have gained income maintenance knowledge and counseling experience during my positions with the Clay County Department of Social Services. Knowledgeable of all current state and federal procedures and regulations as well as the wide range of programs available for applicable clients, I offer expertise in accessing community and allied health agency resources and coordinating with professionals affiliated with those institutions.

You would find me to be an caring professional dedicated to improving the quality of life of needy individuals and families.

Although I am excelling in my current position, I believe my talents lie in the administrative area, and I am seeking challenging management responsibilities.

I hope you will call or write me soon to suggest a time convenient for us to meet and discuss your current and future needs and how I might serve them. Thank you in advance for your time.

Sincerely,

Samantha Wright

SAMANTHA WRIGHT

1110½ Hay Street, Fayetteville, NC 28305 • preppub@aol.com • (910) 483-6611

OBJECTIVE   To benefit an organization in need of a hardworking, dedicated professional experienced in case management and social work who possesses excellent communication, planning, and organizational skills.

EXPERIENCE   **INCOME MAINTENANCE CASEWORKER.** Clay County Department of Social Services, Moorhead, MN (2003-present). Refined communication and case management skills while handling a wide range of administrative and analytical procedures for over 220 people. Handle cases which require expert knowledge of Assist to Families, Medicaid, and Food Stamp programs.
- Determine Assist to Families eligibility and amount of monthly allocation by reviewing every aspect of every case on an individual basis. Place clients into other social service programs due to changes in family income and other circumstances.
- Knowledgeable of all current state and federal benefit regulations and requirements.
- Process and complete transfer-in reviews; transfer cases to other Minnesota county agencies when necessary. Compile and process monthly reports and update manuals.

DISCHARGE CASEWORKER. Clay County Regional Hospital, Moorhead, MN (2002-03). Polished time-management skills while serving as the Clay County Regional Hospital Discharge Caseworker; handled up to 100 cases simultaneously.
- Deepened my knowledge of the problems faced by the underprivileged.
- Strengthened my ability to establish a rapport with people from diverse cultural and socioeconomic backgrounds.

INVENTORY CONTROL CLERK. Best Buy, Fergus Falls, MN (2001-02). Gained excellent organizational skills utilizing a wide range of inventory controls while maintaining stock.
- Managed receiving and disbursement of supplies while compiling and recording corresponding paperwork and documentation.

OPERATIONS SUPERVISOR. Quick Mart, Fergus Falls, MN (1999-01). Oversaw all store operations, including merchandising, receiving, and ordering as well as handling financial transactions. Trained and supervised a staff of 12.
- Controlled an extensive inventory of products using an automated database. Discovered a knack for conflict resolution answering and resolving customer complaints.

STORE MANAGER. Moorhead General Store, Moorhead, MN (1995-99). Promoted from clerk to manager of this busy factory-owned store. Supervised two employees and managed inventory, accounting records, and bank deposits. Increased daily sales by 43% and increased profit margin by significantly decreasing inventory loss.

SECURITY GUARD. Moorhead Security Services, Inc., Moorhead, MN (1993-95). Applied criminal justice and law enforcement background while acting as a security guard providing safety inspections, preparing detailed security reports, and making hourly inspections.

EDUCATION   Completing an **Associate's degree in Law Enforcement and Criminal Justice** from Concordia College, Moorhead, MN. Completed a number of caseworker training courses.

PERSONAL   Am able to blend professional objectivity and empathy to achieve positive results for needy individuals and families. Enjoy problem-solving and decision-making. Work well as either a team member or a team leader. Consistently receive excellent work evaluations.

Date

Exact Name of Person
Title or Position
Name of Company
Address (no., street)
Address (city, state, zip)

Dear Exact Name of Person: (or Dear Sir or Madam if answering a blind ad.)

With the enclosed resume, I would like to make you aware of my interest in exploring employment opportunities with your organization.

With a B.S. in Sociology along with numerous accreditations, I am currently a Job Training Specialist with the Employment Training Center, where I interview applicants for jobs and determine their eligibility. I am considered an expert on the Employment Training Act, which focuses on socially economically disadvantaged individuals who have disabilities, are dislocated workers, or are homeless.

Prior employment with the Marion County Hospital enabled me to refine my counseling and administrative skills. As the Mental Health Counselor in the Children's Unit, I provided and maintained the therapeutic community for patients by observing behavior, attitudes, and interaction with their peers. I also evaluated patients' behavior and their response to nursing intervention and medications.

You would find me in person to be a congenial individual, and I am known for my ability to establish warm working relationships with others. I have found that "networking" is a key to accomplishing my job in the human services field, and I possess an in-depth understanding of how organizations in the medical, law enforcement, human services, nonprofit, and social services fields interact in the process of serving their clients.

I hope you will call or write me soon to suggest a time convenient for us to meet to discuss your current and future needs. Thank you in advance for your time.

Sincerely yours,

Jacqueline Cain

Alternate last paragraph:
I hope you will welcome my call soon to arrange a brief meeting when we might meet to discuss your needs and goals and how my background might serve them. I can provide outstanding references at the appropriate time.

JACQUELINE CAIN

1110½ Hay Street, Fayetteville, NC 28305   •   preppub@aol.com   •   (910) 483-6611

OBJECTIVE

To contribute my administrative skills to an organization in need of a caring individual with extensive experience in managing job training programs and providing outreach counseling.

EDUCATION

B.S., Sociology, Fairmont State College, Fairmont, WV, 1993.
A.S., Criminal Justice, Citrus College, Glendora, CA, 1990.
Completed numerous training programs and courses related to program management, mental health subjects, outreach counseling, and disabilities.

EXPERIENCE

JOB TRAINING SPECIALIST. Employment Training Center, Fairmont, WV (2004-present). Interview applicants (14-21) for summer jobs in order to determine their eligibility based on the Employment Training Act, which aims to identify socially and economically disadvantaged individuals who have disabilities, are dislocated workers, and are homeless.

COLLEGE INSTRUCTOR. Fairmont State College, Fairmont, WV (2003). Provided educational opportunities for adults while providing innovative literacy and basic skills through various educational programs including ABE, GED, ESL, AHS, and CED.

Refined counseling and administrative skills while excelling in the following positions with Marion County Hospital, Fairmont, WV (1993-03):
OUTREACH COUNSELOR. (2001-03). Provided admission crisis intervention screening and assessment for the adult, adolescent, and child residential treatment center in addition to handling patient referrals.

INSTITUTIONAL FOOD SERVICE SUPERVISOR. (1995-02). Supervised and maintained a high standard of quality for food production and portion control; used standard recipes to approximate quantities of food needed to meet menu requirements; supervised the preparation of all food in sufficient quantities to cover service requirements and the timing of meal preparation to meet deadlines.

MENTAL HEALTH COUNSELOR. (Child Unit) (1993-95). Provided and maintained the therapeutic community for patients by observing conservation, behavior, attitudes, and interaction with their peers; evaluated patients' behavior and response to nursing intervention and medications; took vital signs and recording information in patients' charts.

Highlights of other experience:
- Gained knowledge of insurance underwriting and medical limitation procedures and marketing while servicing established debit territory as an **Insurance Sales Representative**.
- Balanced monthly bills and performed data entry while writing general monthly reports and filed legal documents for MetLife Insurance Company.

VOLUNTEER WORK

Served on a committee focusing on providing ways for parents to survive on their monthly temporary assistance checks provided.
Performed one-on-one client relations in a program designed to assist individuals who had problems adjusting to society after committing a crime.

PERSONAL

Am a patient and friendly professional who works well with anyone. Pick up on new concepts quickly. Am computer-literate and have outstanding administrative skills.

CAREER CHANGE

Date

Exact Name of Person
Title or Position
Name of Company
Address (no., street)
Address (city, state, zip)

Dear Exact Name of Person: (or Dear Sir or Madam if answering a blind ad.)

I would appreciate an opportunity to talk with you soon about how I could contribute to your organization through my enthusiastic and friendly personality.

As you will see from my resume, I am a mature professional who offers a proven ability to work with people of all ages and walks of life. For example, I have worked with legal and social services personnel in a child advocacy program, factory workers and supervisors in a manufacturing environment, medical personnel and patients in a hospital setting, and adolescents in counseling.

With a reputation as individual who excels in putting others at ease and developing rapport, I am accustomed to working under pressure. I have handled numerous emergencies and crises as a Juvenile Corrections Officer and Investigator.

Although I have excelled in the law enforcement community, my outgoing personality and "natural" sales ability would enable me to blossom in a job which requires aggressive marketing and sales. I enjoy traveling and feel that I offer the right combination of maturity, personality, and enthusiasm that your organization seeks.

I hope you will welcome my call soon to arrange a brief meeting at your convenience to discuss your current and future needs and how I might serve them. Thank you in advance for your time.

Sincerely yours,

Brooke Malone

Alternate last paragraph:
I hope you will call or write soon to suggest a time convenient for us to meet and discuss your current and future needs and how I might serve them. Thank you in advance for your time.

BROOKE MALONE

1110½ Hay Street, Fayetteville, NC 28305 • preppub@aol.com • (910) 483-6611

OBJECTIVE
To apply my outstanding communication skills and ability to meet people and quickly develop rapport with them to an organization that can use an enthusiastic and outgoing professional.

EXPERIENCE
JUVENILE CORRECTIONS OFFICER. Maui County, Waikuku, HI (2003-present). Counsel children/adolescents from nine to 16 who are either delinquents or severely undisciplined and placed in the county's juvenile detention center.
- Acquired a great deal of experience in dealing with all types of people from the children and their parents, to professionals including social workers, detectives, and counselors.

INVESTIGATOR & CHILDREN'S ADVOCATE. Family Center, Waikuku, HI (2000-03). Officially commended for my "initiative" and "great commitment," handled a variety of activities related to protecting and helping children who had been abused, neglected, or were alcohol- or drug-dependent.
- Interviewed interested parties to gather information and investigated reported situations to determine actions to be taken.
- Used the results of my investigations while appearing in court to make recommendations on what actions would best protect and help the child.
- Gained experience in dealing with people from all walks of life and of all ages including professionals from the legal, medical, social work, and law enforcement fields.
- Discovered the personal satisfaction of seeing that children and adolescents receive help and guidance. Was cited for my "high energy level" and "willingness to learn."

ASSISTANT PRODUCTION SUPERVISOR. Hawaii Manufacturers, Inc., Waikuku, HI (1995-00). Advanced to a supervisory role based on my performance, flexibility, and dedication while working at this major manufacturer of sportswear.
- Displayed flexibility and an ability to learn new tasks quickly in jobs including dye maker and machine operator.
- Was recognized as a dedicated hard worker who could work well with others and contribute to a pleasant and productive work atmosphere.

Highlights of other experience:
- Became skilled in handling multiple responsibilities including packing completed products, working on an assembly line, and using a dye cutting machine to prepare doll house parts.
- Was known for my ability to build rapport with patients and their families in a hospital pediatrics ward. Assisted in discharge/admittance procedures and helped the nursing staff. Delivered mail and flowers.

EDUCATION
Completed two years towards a B.S. in **Criminal Justice**, University of Hawaii-Maui Community College, Kahului, HI.

TRAINING
Attended numerous seminars and training courses in subjects including:

crisis intervention in dealing with teenagers	first aid
procedures for dealing with youth services	substance abuse awareness
community awareness of occult practices	reality therapy

PERSONAL
Offer well-developed motivational and counseling skills. Find meeting and getting to know new people rewarding. Truly enjoy traveling and new places. Excellent references.

Exact Name of Person
Title or Position
Name of Company
Address (no., street)
Address (city, state, zip)

LABOR CONSULTANT,
Department of Labor

Dear Exact Name of Person: (or Dear Sir or Madam if answering a blind ad.)

With the enclosed resume, I would like to make you aware of my interest in exploring employment opportunities with your organization. I am responding to your advertisement in the *Illinois State Gazette* for an individual who is knowledgeable of Department of Labor standards and who is capable of establishing new work programs in the state of Illinois.

Currently working with the Department of Labor as a Consultant, I play a key role in the planning, design, and establishment of a database of military veterans in Illinois. I also work with state legislative officials on issues pertaining to the database. Although I am excelling in my current position, I work in a part-time consulting role, and I am interested in pursuing full-time employment. I can provide outstanding personal and professional references at the appropriate time.

You will see from my resume that, after graduating from West Point with a B.S. degree in Engineering, I enjoyed a distinguished career as a military officer. Promoted to the rank of Major, I excelled in demanding line management positions worldwide while gaining extensive knowledge of human resources administration. I have earned respect for my creativity and problem-solving skills, and I enjoy the challenge of solving "impossible" problems.

With a reputation as a proactive manager known for personal integrity and high moral standards, I am selectively exploring new challenges in organizations which can use a highly motivated self starter with unlimited personal initiative. I am single and willing to relocate and travel as needed. I understand from your ad that the position requires frequent and prolonged absences.

I hope you will call or write me soon to suggest a time convenient for us to meet to discuss your current and future needs. Thank you in advance for your time.

Sincerely yours,

Bernadine Hanson

BERNADINE HANSON

1110½ Hay Street, Fayetteville, NC 28305   •   preppub@aol.com   •   (910) 483-6611

OBJECTIVE   To benefit an organization through my experience in planning comprehensive and effective programs, training and supervising personnel, and managing a wide range of projects while applying attention to detail, concern for others, and leadership skills.

EDUCATION   **Bachelor of Science,** Engineering, The U.S. Military Academy at West Point, NY, 1990.
Associate of Science, Executive Secretarial Studies, Roosevelt University, Chicago, 1986.

EXPERIENCE   **LABOR CONSULTANT.** Department of Labor, Chicago, IL (2003-present). Work an average of 20 hours weekly while playing a key role in the planning, design, and establishment of a database for 100,000 military veterans in the state of Illinois.
- Make use of existing databases located at federal, state, and local governmental agencies and organizations; prepare and send letters to numerous federal entities while also researching government listings to locate appropriate agencies.
- Apply my knowledge of Excel and Access in creating this organization's database.
- Maintain complete file of work performed.
- Work with state legislative officials on issues pertaining to the database. Designed brochure sent to veterans in the database; coordinated contract with a printer.

Previous U.S. Army experience:
CHIEF OF COMMUNITY ACTIONS & OPERATIONS. Italy (2001-03). At the rank of Major, excelled in a position equivalent to Assistant City Manager for a 12,000-person community. Implemented programs that improved the quality-of-life for American military personnel and their families.

GENERAL MANAGER. Chicago, IL (1995-01). As a Captain, acted as "chief executive officer" of three different organizations. Established training programs, supervised employees in a personnel center, and provided career and performance counseling.

STUDENT, EXECUTIVE DEVELOPMENT PROGRAM. Springfield, IL (1994). Exceeded course standards as one of only nine women in a class of 470 students attending a top-level school which emphasized international issues, training management, and personnel management in large-scale organizations.
- Was cited as an articulate writer and speaker with a positive attitude and superior skills in the areas of research and the collection/compilation of information.

ADMINISTRATIVE SUPERVISOR. The Military Academy at West Point, West Point, NY (1990-93). After graduating from West Point and from subsequent training as a military officer, was selected for highly visible positions as an administrator, advisor, and counselor for students at this prestigious military academy.
- Planned, coordinated, prepared the budget for, and carried out a training programs for 1,150 students; coordinated the assignment and transportation of 2,100 students to 35 locations around the state for summer training.
- Initially served as the senior administrative supervisor in the office of the school's commandant with full responsibility for administrative and records management.

PERSONAL   Familiar with computer software and operating systems including Windows. Known for personal integrity and high moral standards. Held Secret security clearance. Proactive manager who welcomes new challenges. Single; will relocate and travel as needed.

CAREER CHANGE

Date

Exact Name of Person
Title or Position
Name of Company
Address (no., street)
Address (city, state, zip)

LEGISLATIVE AIDE,
House of
Representatives

Dear Exact Name of Person: (or Dear Sir or Madam if answering a blind ad.)

With the enclosed resume, I would like to make you aware of my interest in exploring employment opportunities with your organization.

As you will see from my resume, I hold a B.S. in Business Administration from Johns Hopkins University. In my current position as a Legislative Aide for U.S. House of Representative Anita Shortt, I represent Representative Shortt at political events in counties throughout Maryland, and I have become known as a skilled public speaker with an exceptional ability to "think on my feet." I am comfortable speaking to large groups of several hundred people, and I am also at ease in dealing with high-ranking executives and government officials. I have learned a great deal about the workings of Congress while assisting constituents in the resolution of problems related to social security benefits, Veterans Administration claims, and medical claims.

Prior to working with Representative Shortt, I worked as the Assistant Finance Director for Bob Johnson for United States Senate, and in that capacity I processed up to 400 contribution checks and $100,000 daily. I also maintained cash flow and bookkeeping records and made daily deposits.

Although I have enjoyed the challenge of working for elected officials, I have decided that I wish to pursue a career in the banking field. I am confident that my strong communication and financial skills would be assets in the banking industry, and my extensive customer service experience will be transferable to any organization.

I hope you will call or write me soon to suggest a time convenient for us to meet to discuss your current and future needs. Thank you in advance for your time.

Sincerely yours,

Nick Jackson

Alternate last paragraph:
I hope you will welcome my call soon to arrange a brief meeting when we might meet to discuss your needs and goals and how my background might serve them. I can provide outstanding references at the appropriate time.

NICK JACKSON

1110½ Hay Street, Fayetteville, NC 28305 • preppub@aol.com • (910) 483-6611

OBJECTIVE

I want to contribute to an organization that can use an outgoing individual who offers the ability to work effectively with people from all social and economic levels while solving stubborn problems which require persistence and relentless follow-through.

EDUCATION

Bachelor of Science in Business Administration, Johns Hopkins University, Baltimore, MD, 2000.
Activities:
Elected Chairman, Reception Committee for Business Symposium
Elected President, Business Student Alliance
Elected member of the Student Honor Council
Active player in intramural basketball and football

EXPERIENCE

LEGISLATIVE AIDE. U.S. House of Representative Anita Shortt, Washington, DC (2002-present). For a Congresswoman representing the state of Maryland, assist constituents in the resolution of federal government-related problems including social security benefits, Veterans Administration claims, and medical claims.
- Represent Representative Shortt at political events in counties throughout Maryland.
- Have become a respected strategist, and have been credited with playing a key role in the 2004 reelection of Representative Shortt in a contest which was the closest one ever in the state.
- On my own initiative, developed a new "mobile response system" which has cemented constituent loyalty. Travel extensively throughout the state to hold mobile office hours in dozens of Maryland counties.
- Have become known for my excellent written and oral communication skills while drafting letters for the Representative's signature.

ASSISTANT FINANCE DIRECTOR. Bob Johnson for United States Senate, Baltimore, MD (2000-02). Gained an understanding of campaign financing laws while playing a key role in managing the funds used to finance a U.S. Senate campaign.
- Processed 400 contribution checks and $100,000 daily.
- Maintained cash flow and bookkeeping records and made daily deposits.
- Provided training and guidance to the fundraising team and the accountant.

SALESPERSON. Johns Hopkins University Bookstore, Baltimore, MD (1996-2000). In this part-time job while earning my college degree, refined my customer service and sales skills while working up to 30 hours a week.
- After Johns Hopkins made it mandatory that every student have a personal laptop, provided technical assistance to customers purchasing and using laptop computers.
- Managed the retail bookstore during the evening shift.
- Assisted customers with resume preparation.

ASSISTANT TO THE INTERNAL AUDITOR. ReMax Real Estate, Baltimore, MD (1994-96). In a job which I held for two summers during high school, learned to perform bank reconciliations and became acquainted with QuickBooks Pro accounting software.

Highlights of earlier experience: Refined communication skills as a Salesman for JCPenney; worked part-time during high school.

PERSONAL

Outstanding personal and professional references upon request.

CAREER CHANGE

Date

Exact Name of Person
Title or Position
Name of Company
Address (no., street)
Address (city, state, zip)

MEMBER RELATIONS MANAGER

Dear Exact Name of Person: (or Dear Sir or Madam if answering a blind ad.)

With the enclosed resume, I would like to make you aware of my interest in exploring employment opportunities with your organization.

As you will see from my resume, I am currently the Member Relations Manager for the National Association of Advertising Executives. I have been commended for my ability to develop resourceful new programs and membership tools which cement the loyalty of existing members while attracting new ones. Although I am held in high regard and can provide outstanding references at the appropriate time, I am seeking to move out of the nonprofit world and into the profit-making sector. In my current position, I handle responsibilities similar to those of a Customer Service Manager. In fact, in my previous job I worked as a Customer Service Representative and gained extensive experience in resolving customer problems.

Prior employment in sales enabled me to refine my communication and motivational skills. I am accustomed to the discipline of setting high goals for sales and profitability and working hard to achieve ambitious objectives. I am confident that I could become a valuable asset to your company.

I hope you will call or write me soon to suggest a time convenient for us to meet to discuss your current and future needs. Thank you in advance for your time.

Sincerely yours,

Shannon Johnson

Alternate last paragraph:
I hope you will welcome my call soon to arrange a brief meeting when we might meet to discuss your needs and goals and how my background might serve them. I can provide outstanding references at the appropriate time.

SHANNON JOHNSON

1110½ Hay Street, Fayetteville, NC 28305 • preppub@aol.com • (910) 483-6611

OBJECTIVE

To benefit an organization that can use a creative young professional with well-developed written and oral communication skills as well as a proven ability to handle high-pressure environments while utilizing my flair for enthusiastic and effective public relations.

EDUCATION

Bachelor of Arts degree, the University of Wyoming, Laramie, WY, 2002.
- Majored in Political Science with a concentration in History.
- Completed course work in the following:

Advanced Expository Writing	Business Law	Calculus for Business
Public Speaking Economics	Public Finance	Creative Writing

EXPERIENCE

MEMBER RELATIONS MANAGER. National Association of Advertising Executives, Washington, DC (2003-present). Coordinate communication with member firms who include radio stations, advertising agencies, copy writers, and promotional specialists.
- Aggressively developed new member accounts; now service a large customer base and have surpassed all sales goals set monthly by the association's executive vice president.
- Compiled statistical reports to aid member organizations and published them for the benefit of members.
- Coordinate with station executives and other personnel such as programmers, traffic managers, disc jockeys, and engineers on a daily basis.
- Discovered a "knack" for developing unique and resourceful membership aids, including publications, which cement member loyalty and attract new members.

CUSTOMER SERVICE REPRESENTATIVE. Grand Avenue, Miami, FL (2002-03). Provided customer service while expediting purchase orders and sales transactions involving fabric, wall coverings, furniture, and accessories for this major corporation with 15 showrooms, 17 fabric companies, two mills, and one printing plant nationwide.
- Communicated with the company president, showroom manager, and corporate clients such as Calvin Klein and Talbots.
- For the fabric division, maintained support operations for annual sales of $2 million.
- Facilitated the release of fabric for the Broadway Shows account; sold over $600,000 worth of material.
- Satisfied one disappointed client by replacing $5,000 in flawed imported Indian fabric with fabric from the company's own line. This led to a $300,000 order.

Financed my college education through the following positions:
SALES ASSOCIATE. Go Wyoming, Laramie, WY (2000-02). Refined my knowledge of merchandising and marketing techniques and day-to-day retail operations in this shop selling clothing and college memorabilia.
- Monitored inventory and product flow to ensure proper stock levels.
- Performed accounting duties and checked creditworthiness of customers.

SALES REPRESENTATIVE. The Gap Store, Laramie, WY (2000). For this store selling men and women's clothing and accessories, averaged $2,000 in daily sales.
- Ranked as the "number two" sales representative during a special promotion.

PERSONAL

Am a highly-motivated and well-organized professional who enjoys interacting with a variety of individuals. Relish the opportunity to transform new ideas into working realities. Am a member of the Cheyenne Ad Club and the local Chamber of Commerce.

CAREER CHANGE

Date

Exact Name of Person
Title or Position
Name of Company
Address (no., street)
Address (city, state, zip)

PEACE CORPS VOLUNTEER

is the goal of this mature woman. She has to submit paperwork which explains the various ways in which she believes she could be of value working for the Peace Corps in an underdeveloped community.

Dear Exact Name of Person: (or Dear Sir or Madam if answering a blind ad.)

With the enclosed resume, I would like to make you aware of my interest in exploring employment opportunities with your organization.

In my current position an Instructor at Murray State University, I am a popular instructor of the Stained Glass Course while also teaching in the Adult Continuing Education Department.

I have numerous skills and competencies to offer the Peace Corps, and I am qualified to work in various capacities. As you will see on my enclosed resume, I offer ten years of experience in business management along with a proven ability to set up and manage effective cooperatives. My extensive home economics experience would also make me an asset in a Peace Corps role. I offer numerous areas of practical knowledge, from sewing to cooking to light construction, which I could share with individuals in underdeveloped communities.

I hope you will call or write me soon to suggest a time convenient for us to meet to discuss your current and future needs. Thank you in advance for your time.

Sincerely yours,

Adeline Lowery

Alternate last paragraph:
I hope you will welcome my call soon to arrange a brief meeting when we might meet to discuss your needs and goals and how my background might serve them. I can provide outstanding references at the appropriate time.

ADELINE LOWERY

1110½ Hay Street, Fayetteville, NC 28305   •   preppub@aol.com   •   (910) 483-6611

GOAL	To benefit the Peace Corps through my diversified skills in the fine arts and business.
EXPERIENCE	**INSTRUCTOR.** Murray State University, Murray, KY (2000-present). Am a popular instructor of the Stained Glass Course as well as an instructor in the Adult Continuing Education Department.
SKILL 1	Outstanding Business Management Skills: *Qualified through:* ten years of owning and operating a pet shop.

- Expert in all aspects of boarding, grooming, and preparing pets for shipment domestically and internationally
- Qualified to teach professional pet grooming
- Skilled in all aspects of small business management including marketing, finance, and inventory control
- Proven entrepreneur with experience in every aspect of organizational startup

SKILL 2	Skilled at establishing and managing cooperatives: *Qualified through:* serving as one of the original founders, former President, and now as a member of the Board of Directors of Murray's largest arts and crafts co-op.

- Was involved in forming "from scratch" this not-for-profit cooperative
- Have increased membership from 25 to nearly 50 artists and craftsmen
- Was the guiding hand in assuring that all financial and marketing matters were handled expertly
- Aggressively marketed support for the cooperative in terms of grant money and grant aid; was successful in obtaining funding from the City of Murray and from the Arts Council
- Now serving on the Board of Directors as President Ex-Officio

SKILL 3	Adept at numerous home economics subjects: *Qualified through:* expertise in child rearing, cooking, sewing, dressmaking

- Successfully raised five children
- Offer proven expertise as a dress maker, seamstress, and alteration specialist
- Also offer excellent skills in cooking
- Am able to relate well to others and have been successful in teaching sewing, cooking, and child rearing skills to others.

LANGUAGE	Speak Italian fluently and have a good understanding of French
EDUCATION	Received Certification from Italian Trade Union upon completion of a three-year Apprenticeship in Business Program; Italy Currently enrolled in Spanish II, Principles of Marketing; Murray State University Completed one semester course in computer applications and Windows XP
AFFILIATIONS	Murray Artistic Cooperative Partnership Arts Council of Murray Museum of Murray Murray Museum of Art

CAREER CHANGE

Date

Exact Name of Person
Title or Position
Exact Name of Company
Address (no., street)
Address (city, state, zip)

PREVENTION SERVICES COORDINATOR,

Involvement Prevention Project. This individual is seeking a career change from a nonprofit organization to an academic organization.

Dear Exact Name of Person: (or Dear Sir or Madam if answering a blind ad.)

I am writing to express my interest in exploring employment opportunities with your organization. I am interested in the position of School Counselor which you recently advertised.

As you will see from my resume, I offer an extensive background in the human services field. In my current position as Coordinator of the Involvement Prevention Project, I manage a heavy caseload while providing guidance for socially disadvantaged minority youth. In a prior position with the Boys & Girls Center, I helped teenagers who were dealing with a variety of issues. I offer a proven ability to manage multiple simultaneous cases with maximum efficiency.

Although I have worked with individuals of all ages, I most enjoy working with youth because I have experienced the thrill of success in "turning around" troubled teenagers. I realize that not all youth are troubled, but all young people are wrestling with major issues as they grow up, and I feel I have much to offer a school system that wishes to employ a school counselor who is acquainted with and sensitive to those issues.

I would like to tell you more about myself and my qualifications, and I look forward to meeting with you soon. I hope you will contact me at the telephone number or e-mail address on my resume, and I will respond immediately!

Sincerely,

David Pearson

DAVID PEARSON

1110½ Hay Street, Fayetteville, NC 28305   •   preppub@aol.com   •   (910) 483-6611

OBJECTIVE

To work with a human service agency which seeks an individual with a broad background of program coordination along with proven administrative expertise.

EDUCATION

B.A., Psychology and Sociology, Walburn University of Topeka, Topeka, KS, 1985.
United States Navy Officers Candidate School, Pearl Harbor, HI, 1981.

EXPERIENCE

PREVENTION SERVICES COORDINATOR. Involvement Prevention Project, Kansas City, KS (2003-present). Supervisor: Anthony Harper, (111) 111-1111.
Handle case management counseling and academic guidance for socially disadvantaged minority youth. Facilitate their maturation and effort to become productive fulfilled teenagers, and adults. Coordinate educational, social, cultural and recreational events.

DIRECT CARE SUPERVISOR. McCallum, Inc., Kansas City, KS (2002-03).
Supervisor: Thomas Scott, (222) 222-2222
Handled case management counseling of dually diagnosed adults in therapeutic group home. Assisted the treatment team in facilitating clients' release to a less restrictive setting.

PROGRAM SPECIALIST. Boys & Girls Club Center, Topeka, KS (1999-02).
Supervisor: Angela Grey, (333) 333-3333
Managed cases while providing counseling and academic guidance to club members in an effort to facilitate their maturation and efforts to become productive, fulfilled teenagers and adults. Coordinated educational, social, cultural and recreational events.

SOCIAL SERVICE & RECREATIONAL COORDINATOR. Pinebrook Apartments, Topeka, KS (1995-99). Supervisor: Kristy Wallace, (444) 444-4444
Performed counseling, case management, grant proposal writing, budget balancing, and recruiting and training of volunteers to develop a positive community setting. Total responsibility for planning, coordinating and implementing educational, social, cultural and recreational activities for 533 private housing units.

MENTAL HEALTH CASE MANAGER. Kansas Mental Health Center of Topeka, Topeka, KS (1994-95). Supervisor: Ruth Bowen, (555) 555-5555
Handled case management, counseling, and the writing of assessments for adult dysfunctional clients in the Crisis Stabilization Unit. Assisted the treatment team in discharge planning to facilitate clients' release to a less restrictive setting.

DISTRICT INTAKE COUNSELOR. State of Kansas, Wichita, KS (1990-93).
Supervisor: Karen Poole, (666) 666-6666
Provided counseling, managed cases, and investigated alleged delinquent or dependent youth. Coordinated with law enforcement, State Attorney, and the Child Protection Team.

SOCIAL WORKER. Lawrence Youth Development Center, Lawrence, KS (1988-90).
Supervisor: Julia Willis, (777) 777-7777
Provided counseling and case management. Wrote assessments, performance contracts, transfer summaries, monthly progress reports, and release letters for delinquent youth to facilitate their timely release to a less restrictive setting.

REFERENCES

Outstanding references available upon request.

Date

Exact Name of Person
Title or Position
Name of Company
Address
City, State, Zip

PROGRAM ASSISTANT, WOMEN'S CENTER

Dear Exact Name of Person: (or Dear Sir or Madam if answering a blind ad.)

With the enclosed resume, I would like to make you aware of my interest in exploring employment opportunities with your organization.

After receiving my B.S. in Sociology, I applied my knowledge as a Case Worker in the domestic violence area for the Fairbanks Memorial Hospital. In that capacity, I conducted client intake and exit evaluations, provided information/referral resources, and conducted "one-on-one" counseling sessions. I became known for my tact and good manners while answering and responding to the Crisis Hot Line.

Currently excelling as Program Assistant for the Interior Alaska Women's Center, I handle multiple functions for this busy nonprofit organization. While representing the program in the community, I recruit and supervise program participants, facilitate small group Survival Skills training for women and men, and supervise teen community service workers. I have been credited with organizing and supervising some of the organization's most successful fundraisers.

I hope you will call or write me soon to suggest a time convenient for us to meet to discuss your current and future needs. Thank you in advance for your time.

Sincerely yours,

Lisa Barker

Alternate last paragraph:
I hope you will welcome my call soon to arrange a brief meeting when we might meet to discuss your needs and goals and how my background might serve them. I can provide outstanding references at the appropriate time.

LISA BARKER

1110½ Hay Street, Fayetteville, NC 28305 • preppub@aol.com • (910) 483-6611

OBJECTIVE   To benefit an organization that can use a dedicated and hardworking human services professional who offers outstanding administrative and communication skills.

EDUCATION   **B.S., Social Work,** Alaska Pacific University, Anchorage, AK, 2001.
Earned a certificate in *Theology*, University of Alaska Fairbanks, AK, 1995.

A.A., Social Work, with a minor in **Psychology**, University of Alaska Fairbanks, Fairbanks, AK, 1994.

EXPERIENCE   **PROGRAM ASSISTANT.** Interior Alaska Women's Center, Fairbanks, AK (2004-present). Handle multiple functions for this busy nonprofit organization:
Administration: Conduct intake assessments and case management.
Public Relations: Represent program in community affairs and provide resource information and referrals.
Bookkeeping/Accounting: Prepare financial reports.
Training/Supervision: Recruit and supervise program participants, facilitate small group Survival Skills training for women and men, and supervise teen community service workers.
Fundraising: Organize and supervise fundraisers. Have organized some of the organization's most successful fundraisers.

TELECOMMUNICATOR. Fairbanks Penny Saver, Fairbanks, AK (2002-03). Sold and developed special ad projects, created ad layouts, certified space reservation tickets, and provided information to prospective clients.

CASEWORKER (Domestic Violence). Fairbanks Memorial Hospital, Fairbanks, AK (2001-02). Conducted client intake and exit evaluations; provided information/referral resources.
- Conducted "one-on-one" counseling sessions.
- Managed casework files and records.
- Answered and responded to the Crisis Hot Line.

MARKETING REPRESENTATIVE. Alaska Family Services, Fairbanks, AK (2001-03). For the public sector, conducted door-to-door canvassing in the process of making medical coverage presentations and enrolling Medicaid recipients into Wellness Plan.

RECORDS OFFICER. Fairbanks North Star Borough, Fairbanks, AK (2000-01). Conducted intake and orientation of applicants for Summer Youth Employment Training Program and served as an Assistant Teacher.

Highlights of other experience:
Assisted students with classwork and activities as a **Teacher Aide**.
Provided tutorial services, monitored behavior, and conducted placement and follow-up with foster homes as a **Staff Care Worker**.

PERSONAL   Am a computer-literate professional with experience in Word. Type 50 wpm. Am a quick learner as well as flexible and adaptable. Excellent references.

Exact Name of Person
Exact Title
Exact Name of Company
Address
City, State, Zip

**PROGRAM DIRECTOR,
ARTS COUNCIL**

Dear Exact Name of Person (or Dear Sir or Madam if answering a blind ad):

　　With the enclosed resume, I would like to make you aware of my background as an arts management professional with exceptional communication, organizational, and motivational skills. I offer the proven ability to recruit, train, and manage volunteers; direct grant writing and fundraising activities; and increase public awareness and involvement in the arts. My husband and I have recently relocated to your area, and I am seeking an employer that can make use of my nonprofit experience.

　　In my most recent position, I served as Program Director for the seventh largest arts council in Wyoming, which has an annual operating budget of nearly $800,000. With the Orchard Valley Arts Council, I developed and implemented a number of new programs, including a comprehensive dance program that generated more than $10,000 annually in class fees as well as a drama troupe for teenagers which was funded by an annual grant that I secured. In addition to events planning and coordination, I excelled in marketing and public relations, designing brochures, writing press releases, and creating program books that raised community awareness of the Arts Council's programs.

　　Earlier, as Executive Director for the Sweetwater Arts Council, I oversaw all operational aspects of the organization, from developing and managing an annual budget of $100,000 to acting as liaison between the arts council and local schools, arts organizations, and the local government. I developed new training procedures for incoming members of the Board of Directors, designing and producing all printed training materials, handbooks, and information packets. I also created and implemented the first-ever Your First Arts Festival for mentally challenged children and adults in Sweetwater County.

　　As you will see, I earned my Bachelor of Science in Theatre Arts and have supplemented my degree program with additional courses in Arts Management from Western Wyoming Community College. I am currently completing the Certificate in Nonprofit Management program at Laramie County Community College.

　　If you can use a dedicated Arts Management professional who offers skills in volunteer management, fundraising, and program development, I hope you will contact me soon.

Sincerely,

Charlene Bosco

CHARLENE BOSCO

1110½ Hay Street, Fayetteville, NC 28305 • preppub@aol.com • (910) 483-6611

OBJECTIVE
To benefit an organization that can use a dynamic, experienced Program Director with exceptional communication and organizational skills who offers the proven ability to recruit, train, and manage volunteers; direct grant writing and fundraising activities; and increase community awareness and involvement in the arts.

EDUCATION
Bachelor of Science in Theatre Arts, University of Wyoming, Laramie, WY, 1999.
• Graduated with a 3.6 GPA; minored in Dance and Music.
Supplemented my degree program with additional courses in Arts Management, Western Wyoming Community College, Rock Springs, WY, 2003.
Completed the Laramie County Community College Certificate in Nonprofit Management program, Laramie County Community College, Cheyenne, WY, 2004.

AFFILIATIONS
Member, Wyoming Theatre Conference, 2003-present.
Sweetwater Arts committee, Wyoming Senior Games, 2001-present.

EXPERIENCE
PROGRAM DIRECTOR. Orchard Valley Arts Council, Cheyenne, WY (2004-present). Assisted the Executive Director of Wyoming's seventh largest arts council, which has an annual budget of nearly $800,000; duties included program development; recruiting, training, and supervision of volunteers; and fundraising.
• Oversaw the planning, development, and implementation of new and existing arts programs; created innovative and effective marketing plans and publicity materials.
• Recruited and supervised the activities of up to 20 volunteers, training them to assist in the administrative operations of the organization while also teaching them details of stage production so they could provide technical assistance at OVAC events.
• Developed a comprehensive dance program which was attended by more than 100 students in its first year, generating more than $10,000 in annual revenue for the Council.
• Established a drama troupe for teenagers, securing a $10,000 yearly grant for the company and collaborating with community youth on program development; the troupe received more than 30 invitations to perform for local organizations.
• Coordinated the Youth Theatre Showcase, scheduling over 50 groups to perform before 100 representatives of arts councils and related agencies; designed and produced press releases, brochures, and programs for the event.
• Assisted the Executive Director with grant writing, reports, and administrative duties.

EXECUTIVE DIRECTOR. Sweetwater Arts Council, Rock Springs, WY (2001-03). Oversaw all operational aspects of this county-wide organization; provided supervisory and administrative support in addition to acting as liaison between the Arts Council and local schools, arts organizations, and local government.
• Collaborated with the members of the Board of Directors to formulate policies; prepared and administered the yearly arts agenda.
• Developed and managed an annual operational budget of $100,000.
• Prepared applications and gave recommendations for a local sub-granting program.
• Planned, organized, coordinated, and promoted two major festivals; served as coordinator for the Sweetwater County Youth Games Program, Sweetwater Arts Division.

MUSIC TEACHER. Laramie County Schools, Cheyenne, WY (1999-01). Taught six classes daily in music while directing and producing plays for public performance.

PERSONAL
Excellent personal and professional references are available upon request.

CAREER CHANGE

Date

Exact Name of Person
Title or Position
Name of Company
Address (no., street)
Address (city, state, zip)

PROGRAM MANAGER, FAMILY SERVICES, is seeking to transfer her skills from the human services field to the profit-making arena. She desires to utilize the Accounting degree she earned previously but has not used extensively.

Dear Exact Name of Person: (or Dear Sir or Madam if answering a blind ad.)

I would appreciate an opportunity to talk with you soon about how I could contribute to your organization through my strong customer service orientation and proven ability to manage time and heavy caseloads with thoroughness and professionalism.

In my current position with the state's child support system, I deal with a wide range of people including children whose welfare is often in jeopardy, court officials and legal professionals, parents, teachers, and law enforcement personnel. Because of my strong analytical and negotiating skills, I have been selected as the senior representative for managing interstate cases, and I frequently train other program managers in the procedures I use to bring cases to satisfactory conclusions.

You will notice that I earned a degree in Accounting prior to my experience in the law enforcement community and the social services field. Although I have enjoyed the challenges involved in helping others in those human services jobs, I have made the decision to transfer my versatile skills to the profit-making arena. I am certain that I could be a valuable contributor to any business that is in need of a mature, adaptable individual who can get along with others.

I hope you will welcome my call soon to arrange a brief meeting at your convenience to discuss your current and future needs and how I might serve them. Thank you in advance for your time.

Sincerely yours,

Monica Paul

Alternate last paragraph:
I hope you will call or write me soon to suggest a time convenient for us to meet and discuss your current and future needs and how I might serve them. Thank you in advance for your time.

MONICA PAUL

1110½ Hay Street, Fayetteville, NC 28305　•　preppub@aol.com　•　(910) 483-6611

OBJECTIVE　　To offer my strong interpersonal skills and experience in developing effective programs to an organization that can benefit from my proven ability to identify solutions and implement them in a spirit of harmony and good will.

EXPERIENCE　　**PROGRAM MANAGER.** Wisconsin State Family Services, Milwaukee, WI (2004-present). Became very adept at dealing with people of all socioeconomic levels in highly stressful situations while overseeing child support programs related to establishing paternity, locating absent parents, and enforcing court orders.
- Apply my organizational and time management skills while creating ideas for new ways to handle heavy caseloads and ensure that each client receives thorough attention.
- Coordinate regularly with court representatives to schedule and arrange for court appearances.
- Have refined my negotiating skills and constantly apply them while dealing with attorneys during the process of settling court cases.
- Selected as senior representative for managing interstate cases, trained others in proper procedures and the smartest ways to bring cases to satisfactory conclusions.

SCHOOL LIAISON OFFICER and **INSTRUCTOR.** Milwaukee Sheriff's Department, Milwaukee, WI (1998-03). Designed and implemented the county's first school liaison program and acted as the resource consultant for administrative and guidance offices to use when dealing with drugs and other problems involving students.
- Earned special certification as a law enforcement instructor and used this knowledge to teach law enforcement principles to high school students.
- Applied teaching skills to present stress management, juvenile law, search and seizure, and other topics in the county's internal training programs.
- Polished my ability to get along with people of all ages and walks of life while working with the entire range of school-age children and young adults, faculty and staff members at the county schools, and law enforcement professionals.

COUNSELOR/JUVENILE OFFICER. Milwaukee Sheriff's Department, Milwaukee, WI (1995-98). Refined my investigative and interviewing techniques working with the court system to help children in trouble or in crisis situations.
- Received special recognition for my contributions in improving programs supporting the welfare of children.
- Displayed a high level of empathy and concern for children whose lives had been damaged by rape, incest, abuse, or neglect. Specialized in working with runaways and with other difficult types of cases.

EDUCATION　　**Bachelor's degree in Accounting**, Marquette University, Milwaukee, WI, 1995. Completed specialized law enforcement training programs leading to certification in Basic Law Enforcement.

COMPUTERS　　Offer experience with computers using both Microsoft Word and Excel

PERSONAL　　Am a problem solver with a talent for finding ways to streamline and improve procedures. Enjoy helping others and can deal with the most difficult and trying circumstance. Have extensively volunteered my time in service to the Salvation Army. Excellent references.

Date

Exact Name of Person
Title or Position
Name of Company
Address
City, State, Zip

PROJECT DIRECTOR, DISASTER RELIEF PROGRAM

Dear Exact Name of Person: (or Dear Sir or Madam if answering a blind ad.)

With the enclosed resume, I would like to make you aware of my interest in exploring employment opportunities with your organization.

As you will see from my resume, I enjoy helping others and finding ways to improve the quality of their lives. I am adept at planning large-scale humanitarian relief projects and skilled at organizing the details so that projects are successful and productive.

Currently as Project Director for the Disaster Relief Program, I lead and direct the efforts of a management team which plans and coordinates emergency and long-term response following natural disasters. Part of my job is to plan and supervise the construction of housing and program sites supporting 12,500 volunteers, and I oversee activities which provide food and housing for hundreds of volunteers and staff members. I am a co-developer of successful operational plans in which large groups of volunteers have been used to provide large-scale emergency relief efforts worldwide.

In previous employment, I was a Program Coordinator for a "Migrant Education" program involving more than 170 children in 18 migrant labor camps. In that capacity, I addressed the basic issues of ensuring that children received basic educational service while addressing the spiritual needs of children and families.

I hope you will call or write me soon to suggest a time convenient for us to meet to discuss your current and future needs. Thank you in advance for your time.

Sincerely yours,

Ryan Johnston

Alternate last paragraph:
I hope you will welcome my call soon to arrange a brief meeting when we might meet to discuss your needs and goals and how my background might serve them. I can provide outstanding references at the appropriate time.

RYAN JOHNSTON

1110½ Hay Street, Fayetteville, NC 28305   •   preppub@aol.com   •   (910) 483-6611

OBJECTIVE

To offer my broad base of experience in project management, problem solving, marketing, and administration to an organization that can use my compassion and true concern for others as well as my specialized education and experience in disaster relief and aid projects.

EXPERIENCE

PROJECT DIRECTOR. Disaster Relief Program, Washington, DC (2002-present). Lead and direct the efforts of a management team which plans and coordinates emergency and long-term response following natural disasters.

- Plan and supervise the construction of housing and program sites in support of more than 12,500 volunteers providing relief efforts in countries all over the world.
- Oversee activities which provide food and housing for an average of 350 volunteers and staff members on a daily basis.
- Plan for and manage construction activities including scheduling, logistics support, and purchasing for 280 to 300 construction projects annually.
- Direct multimillion-dollar budgets.
- Played a key role in the development and founding of Northfield Schools, an alternative program for delinquent adolescents.
- Was a co-developer of successful operational plans in which large groups of volunteers were used to provide large-scale emergency relief efforts.

PROGRAM COORDINATOR. Migrant Workers Advocacy Agency, Malletts Bay, VT (1999-01). Helped establish a "Migrant Education" program at Malletts Bay, VT: this was a program involving more than 170 children in 18 migrant labor camps on Malletts Bay. Addressed the basic issues of ensuring that children received basic educational services and, in a nondenominational fashion, also addressed the spiritual issues of children.

PRESIDENT & GENERAL MANAGER. Vermont Builders Supply, Burlington, VT (1999). Established and managed a successful general contracting business which built homes, remodeled upscale homes, and performed light commercial work.

Highlights of earlier experience: Built a unique business which transported large yachts cross country after accomplishing continued growth as a partner in a general residential and light commercial construction company.

- Became the youngest assistant manager and manager for two different hospitality companies. Gained experience in all aspects of the industry from custodial duties, to bartending, to kitchen cook, to catering, to accounting, to reservations.

EDUCATION

Received certification as a trainer following advanced training by the Department of Psychiatry's post-disaster mental health course, University of Vermont, Burlington, VT, 2003.
Completed two years of college course work in Business and Liberal Arts, Champlain College, Burlington, VT.

AFFILIATIONS

Served on the board of directors of organizations which included the following:
State of Vermont Migrant Task Force, 1998-2004
Coalition Board of Directors, 2002-2003

PERSONAL

Enjoy knowing I am helping others and finding ways to improve the quality of their life. Offer a reputation as a compassionate, caring person. Am adept at large-scale planning and organizing the details so that projects are successful and productive.

Exact Name of Person
Title or Position
Name of Company
Address (number and street)
Address (city, state, and zip)

PUBLIC INFORMATION ASSISTANT, ACTIVITIES OFFICE

Dear Exact Name of Person: (or Sir or Madam if answering a blind ad.)

I would appreciate an opportunity to talk with you soon about how I could contribute to your organization through my outstanding communication skills and ability to "get things done."

Since earning my B.A. in Business Management from Utah Valley State College, I have worked as a Public Information Assistant for the college. In addition to excelling in my full-time job, I am active in my community. For example, I was active in the re-election campaign of a prominent county commissioner and, on my own initiative, I spearheaded a successful campaign to stop semi-trucks from carrying hazardous waste through the city. I fearlessly approached local and state-level elected figures, distributed petitions, attended environmental seminars, and held rallies to make people aware of the potential for disaster. I am very proud that my leadership led to a grant for $300,000 from the Department of Labor!

A highly self-motivated individual who can handle pressure and deadlines, I often worked in simultaneous jobs while earning my college degree. I offer strong abilities in areas which range from financial management to creative marketing.

I hope you will welcome my call soon to arrange a brief meeting to discuss your current and future needs and how I might serve them. Thank you in advance for your time.

Sincerely,

Jessica Sullivan

Alternate last paragraph:
I hope you will call or write me soon to suggest a time convenient for us to meet and discuss your current and future needs and how I might serve them. Thank you in advance for your time.

JESSICA SULLIVAN

1110½ Hay Street, Fayetteville, NC 28305 • preppub@aol.com • (910) 483-6611

OBJECTIVE To offer communication, sales, training, and marketing skills as well as knowledge of finance and inventory control to an organization that can use a detail-oriented professional with the ability to handle pressure, deadlines, and challenges.

EDUCATION **B.S., Business Management,** Utah Valley State College, Orem, UT, 2003.
- Completed my degree in three years and maintained a 3.0 GPA while working.

COMMUNITY INVOLVEMENT Have been active in community affairs including being personally invited by Salt Lake County Commissioner Johnson to serve on his campaign committee.
- Played an important part in efforts which resulted in the commissioner's being elected despite several polls predicting he would lose.
- Spearheaded a successful campaign to stop semi-trucks from carrying hazardous waste through the city: approached local and state-level elected figures, distributed petitions, attended environmental seminars, and held rallies to make people aware of the potential for disaster; my leadership led to a grant for $300,000 from the Department of Labor!

EXPERIENCE **PUBLIC INFORMATION ASSISTANT.** Utah Valley State College Activities Office, Orem, UT (2003-present). Provide support services for faculty, staff, students, and campus visitors while ordering merchandise and controlling inventory for the student supply store; supervised and scheduled student employees.
- Became familiar with a wide range of services available on campus such as where to obtain class schedules and how to locate facilities.
- Provide management leadership which has led this service facility to operate at its maximum level of efficiency.
- Am respected by students as someone in authority who is always cheerful and ready to help with problems; am a source of advice on where to find reasonable priced housing, food, and transportation.
- Represent the university to potential new students and personally recruited six young adults for UVSC.

Financed my education and refined my time management and organizational abilities while holding these often-simultaneous jobs, participating in community affairs, and attending college:
NIGHT MANAGER. Walgreens, Orem, UT (2001-03). Refined my computer operations skills and provided supervision for 12 employees while handling additional functional areas such as scheduling, collections, and inventory control.
- Learned to take care of the financial activities while preparing daily sales reports and making night deposits.

SALES REPRESENTATIVE & BOOKKEEPER. Utah Glassworks, Co., Orem, UT (1998-01). Learned how various glasswork is made and how to operate glass making tools while providing administrative support by ordering materials, preparing bids, preparing receipts for customers, and making determinations on the profitability of potential jobs.

PERSONAL Attended several workshops and seminars sponsored by local colleges and which emphasized listening, leadership, teaching, and problem-solving skills. Am a creative thinker with a talent for dealing with people fairly and honestly. Excellent references.

Exact Name of Person
Title or Position
Name of Company
Address (no., street)
Address (city, state, zip)

REGIONAL DIRECTOR, AMERICAN LUNG ASSOCIATION

Dear Exact Name of Person: (or Dear Sir or Madam if answering a blind ad.)

I am applying for the Director of Public Relations position with your company which was advertised in the *Columbia News*. With a creative marketing background along with experience in promoting and coordinating events, I am confident that I am the professional you are seeking.

In my current position as Southeast Regional Director for the American Lung Association, I handle multiple responsibilities which include conducting signature events, organizing and managing fundraising events, and conducting professional health seminars throughout Missouri.

Because of my outgoing personality and ability to network effectively with individuals and organizations, I have been successful in a variety of activities which required enthusiasm, intelligence, and relentless follow-through. For example, as a volunteer with the American Lung Association, I raised $20,000 for a Missouri State Golf Tournament, and I organized a Walk-A-Thon fundraiser for the American Diabetes Association. Through my volunteer activities, I have become relatively "high profile" and well liked in the medical community, and I offer a strong network of contacts and relationships which I could put to work for your benefit.

If you can use my considerable talents and skills, I hope you will contact me to suggest a time when we might meet to discuss your needs. I can provide outstanding references at the appropriate time.

Sincerely,

Victoria Brown

VICTORIA BROWN

1110½ Hay Street, Fayetteville, NC 28305   •   preppub@aol.com   •   (910) 483-6611

OBJECTIVE   To obtain a challenging position with an organization seeking a vibrant and enthusiastic young professional with a flair for marketing and promotion.

EXPERIENCE   **REGIONAL DIRECTOR**. American Lung Association (ALA), Columbia, MO (2004-present). Am excelling in handling broad responsibilities for program management, public awareness promotion, and child/adult advocacy for the state of Missouri. Work as a lung cancer liaison for major hospital and home health care agencies.
- On the county level, develop new chapters for the ALA, organize patient education programs, and recruit medical professionals for chapter councils.
- On the state level, organize signature events. Have earned the American Lung Association Professional Staff Certification.

CONSULTANT, OPERATIONS & PROMOTIONS COORDINATOR. Edmonds Services, Columbia, MO (2001-04). Coordinated and managed the production department including employee training and scheduling while expertly performing computerized inventory control and analysis.
- Improved client relations, developed effective new marketing strategies, conducted research for new products, and administered testing of advertising/promotional concepts.

ACCOUNT REPRESENTATIVE. Avon, Columbia, MO (2000-01). Managed the sales of the products in addition to conducting clinics and maintaining client information. Maintained detailed records for accurate monthly reports and controlled inventory. Personally reviewed by Avon's Los Angeles Headquarters Manager which resulted in the parent company's expansion in this area.
- Increased sales by over 100% in six months.

VOLUNTEER & FUNDRAISING ACTIVITIES   *American Lung Association:*
- $20,000 Missouri State Golf Tournament
- $5,000 Grindstone Fun Run
- $2,500 Walgreens
- Conducted two Children With Lung Disease Day Camps
- Increased professional and patient membership

Find-A-Friend One-On-One Program:
- Executive Board Member since 2004
- Mentor Find-A-Friend
- Find-A-Friend Fundraiser $14,000

American Diabetes Association:
- Developed and organized a "Walk-A-Thon" fundraiser
- Pro-bono coordination of volunteers

Other activities:
- Kicked off annual membership drive for Columbia Chamber of Commerce; was the Chamber of Commerce Award Recipient 1999.
- WKKR-TV11 You Care Award - 1999.
- Served on the Grindstone Festival Committee for 1999.
- Served on the Missouri Barbecue Festival Committee for 2000.

EDUCATION   **B.S., Mass Communication**, Columbia College, Columbia, MO, 2000.
- Dean's List, Fall Semester, 2000.
- Senior Representative for the American Communication Conference, 1999.

Date

Exact Name of Person
Exact Title
Exact Name of Company
Address
City, State, Zip

RESIDENT COUNSELOR, CHILDREN'S HOME

Dear Exact Name of Person: (or Dear Sir or Madam if answering a blind ad):

With the enclosed resume, I would like to make you aware of my desire to explore employment opportunities with your organization. I have recently completed my B.S.W. degree in Social Work and offer strong communication and counseling skills.

As you will see from my resume, I have excelled in counseling positions in a camp environment, in a home for displaced children, and at the Boys and Girls Club of America. While working as a Resident Counselor at the Tulsa Children's Home, I became known for my creativity and program development skills. On my own initiative, I organized a store at the home so that youth aged 9-18 could learn money-handling and budgeting skills. I was commended for my efforts which resulted in building self-esteem and a feeling of self-worth.

In a job as a Case Manager at the Boys and Girls Club of America, I worked as an intern in the spring of 2004. In that capacity, I organized an after-school program at Midwest High School designed to build self-esteem in children. Known as "Bright Outreach," the program I developed began with 10 children and grew to serve 40 children. After my internship, the program received formal funding so that it could continue. For my leadership and initiative, I received a certificate of appreciation.

As a teenager, I discovered my orientation toward the social work field while working as a Camp Counselor at Birch Lake Summer Camp with children aged 6-13. In 2003, I also volunteered as Office Manager and Receptionist at The Tulsa House, where I published a book of poems written by the disabled clients of that nonprofit organization.

If you can use a caring and enthusiastic young professional with a true desire to make a difference in the lives of others, I hope you will contact me to suggest a time when we might meet to discuss your needs. I can provide excellent references.

Sincerely,

Janice Meyer

JANICE MEYER

1110½ Hay Street, Fayetteville, NC 28305　　•　　preppub@aol.com　　•　　(910) 483-6611

OBJECTIVE	I want to contribute to an organization that can use an outgoing young professional who offers considerable sales skills and proven management potential along with a desire to serve the public and work with others in achieving top-quality results.
EDUCATION	Earned **Bachelor of Social Work (B.S.W.) degree,** University of Tulsa, Tulsa, OK, 2004. Completed professional training which included Teaching Parent Model.
COMPUTERS	Proficient with Windows operating systems and Microsoft Word software.
EXPERIENCE	**RESIDENT COUNSELOR.** Tulsa Children's Home, Tulsa, OK (2004-present). At this orphanage which is "home" for 600 children, provide training related to life skills for youth aged 9-18 while also implementing parent training; developed programs for each child which resulted in building self-esteem and a feeling of self-worth.

> • **Program Development:** On my own initiative, developed a store at the Tulsa Children's Home so that children could earn money and learn skills in handling money and budgeting for their expenses; designed and managed the store's policies and procedures.

COUNSELOR. Boys and Girls Club of America, Oklahoma City, OK (2004). As an Intern with the Oklahoma County, interviewed and placed prospective mentors and worked as the trusted "right arm" to the program manager.

> • **Program Development:** Organized an after-school program designed to build self-esteem in children and worked closely with children making failing grades; the "Bright Outreach" program at Midwest High School was widely praised and considered a success and I was praised for my creativity and professional style. Began with 10 students and grew the program to 40 students. The program received funding after its pilot year and is being continued.
>
> • **Award:** Received a prestigious Certificate of Appreciation for my work in Blackwood Middle School.

HISTORIAN. Midwest High School, Tulsa, OK (2003). Developed a scrapbook which provided the school's first permanent record of its after-school program; planned photographic events and arranged photo opportunities with children, tutors, and staff.

OFFICE MANAGER & RECEPTIONIST. The Tulsa House, Tulsa, OK (2003). While working as a volunteer, applied my creativity in developing a book of poems by the disabled clients of this nonprofit organization serving the less fortunate.

> • **Social worker responsibilities:** Routinely handled many duties of a social worker; processed intakes, made referrals to other agencies, supplied clients with clothing and hygiene kits, and followed up.

CAMP COUNSELOR. Birch Lake Summer Camp, Birch Lake, OK (2000-02). Found many opportunities to express my creativity and resourcefulness while scheduling events, planning educational programs, and working with children aged 6-13.

> • **Programming:** Planned a talent show for the children and nurtured their creativity.

SALES REPRESENTATIVE. Old Navy, Tulsa, Oklahoma City, OK (1996-00). Began working at the age of 16 and worked for four years part-time.

PERSONAL	Caring and nurturing professional who yearns to make a difference in the social work field.

CAREER CHANGE

Date

Exact Name of Person
Title or Position
Name of Company
Address (no., street)
Address (city, state, zip)

SENIOR DISTRICT EXECUTIVE, YMCA

Dear Exact Name of Person: (Or Dear Sir or Madam if answering a blind ad.)

I am writing to express my strong interest in a position as a Sales Representative with your company. With the enclosed resume, I would like to make you aware of my strong leadership ability and management skills. Although I am excelling in my current job and can provide excellent personal and professional references at the appropriate time, I am attracted to your company's outstanding reputation, and I feel my strengths and abilities could be well suited to your needs.

As you will see from my resume, I am currently involved in program management with the YMCA. While interacting routinely with corporate executives, political leaders, and entrepreneurs, I have earned a reputation as a powerful motivator and organizer. For each of the past three years, I have been the recipient of the prestigious American Chief Winner Award because of my initiative and bottom-line results in exceeding financial goals and human resources recruiting objectives.

I have been honored by election to the "1000 Most Promising Young Men of America," an organization designed to identify and encourage the nation's most promising young leaders. I have also been honored by election to the steward board of my church—and I am the youngest person ever elected in the history of my church. I have a gift for earning people's confidence and enlisting their support.

Although I have been involved in nonprofit management positions since my college graduation in 2002, I have decided to transfer my management skills and strong bottom-line orientation into the profit-making sector. I offer a reputation for unlimited personal initiative, creativity, and leadership.

If you can use a proven young professional who excels in working with people at all organizational levels, I hope you will write or call me to suggest a time when we might meet to discuss your needs and how I might help you. Thank you in advance for your time.

Yours sincerely,

Joshua Guthrie

JOSHUA GUTHRIE

1110½ Hay Street, Fayetteville, NC 28305 • preppub@aol.com • (910) 483-6611

OBJECTIVE
I want to contribute to an organization that can use a strong young leader who offers a track record of outstanding performance in organizing people to work as part of a team toward common goals and who also offers proven skills in budgeting and project management.

EDUCATION
College: Earned **B.S. degree in Political Science,** Cornell University, Ithaca, NY, 2002.
- Chose numerous courses which examined human resources policies and labor laws.
- Active in the Who's Who campus organization.

AFFILIATIONS
Member, Chamber of Commerce
Member, Young Achievers Association, Cornell University
Elected to "1000 Most Promising Young Men of America": this organization recognizes the most outstanding young leaders in the nation.

EXPERIENCE
SENIOR DISTRICT EXECUTIVE. YMCA, Syracuse, NY (2004-present). Am solely responsible for programming, budgeting, and operations management of activities in this county; administer a budget while providing leadership to four major programs: Finance, Public Relations, Outdoor Program, and Membership Enrollment.
- Routinely interact with the county's corporate leaders and entrepreneurs while inspiring them to work toward YMCA goals.
- Am continuously involved in strategic planning; develop concepts and strategies for the future and develop detailed plans to achieve those goals; am considered a "master" in organizing and leading others and in enlisting their support for quality programs.
- Developed detailed operational plans for action to be taken at the highest organizational level, the middle level, and the lowest level.
- Have become skilled in establishing performance standards and measurable goals for individuals and organizations, and have refined my ability to measure performance.

Honors & Awards:
- For each of the past three years, have been a recipient of the prestigious American Chief Winner Award because of my leadership in achieving 10% growth annually in membership development and in exceeding annual fundraising goals.

BUDGET DIRECTOR & PROGRAM SUPPORT SPECIALIST. Syracuse Group Home, Syracuse, NY (2002-04). In my first job after college graduation, controlled operating budgets for five different group homes while motivating and guiding the staff.
- Led other professionals in the strategic planning process.
- On my own initiative, developed an Access database which permitted easy reference to the vast network of group homes throughout New York.

Other experience:
YOUTH SPORTS COUNSELOR. Boys and Girls Club of America, Syracuse, NY (2000-02). Worked part-time while completing my college degree; coordinated youth sports activity programs while acting as a counselor for middle and elementary school children.
- Responsible for the Male Achievers Program for Young Males 10-18.

PERSONAL
Outstanding personal and professional references upon request. Strong work ethic.

Date

Exact Name of Person
Title or Position
Name of Company
Address (no., street)
Address (city, state, zip)

Dear Exact Name of Person: (or Dear Sir or Madam if answering a blind ad.)

With the enclosed resume, I would like to make you aware of my interest in becoming a member of your fine staff.

As you will see from my resume, I have excelled as an educator since earning my B.S. degree in History from the University of New Hampshire. I was aggressively recruited by the college to play basketball, and as a captain I led the college to its first semifinals. For three years in high school, I was named Player of the Year in New Hampshire.

Since graduation, I have excelled as an educator and coach and have earned the respect of peers, students, and parents for my creativity as well as my strong communication and problem-solving skills. Although I am held in the highest regard within the teaching community, I have come to the realization that a long career in teaching is not for me. I have, however, thoroughly enjoyed the challenge of teaching social studies, government, and history to preteens, and I have been successful in 7th grade, 8th grade, as well as behavior-and-emotional-disorder classrooms. I have become particularly respected for my highly inventive nature and for my ability to apply my creativity in practical ways to help students; for example, I created and implemented end-of-grade practice tests which prepared students for an exam which can count up to 20% of their final grade. I offer a proven ability to walk into an established situation and, on my own initiative, develop and implement effective new approaches without alienating veterans in the field.

I am confident that I could become an enthusiastic and committed member of your staff, and I offer hands-on knowledge related to the educational system. I have exceptionally strong written and oral communication skills, and colleagues have told me that I possess an unusually strong ability to motivate and influence others. In my previous job, I coached a middle school basketball team to second place finish in the county. I would enjoy utilizing my knowledge and motivational skills in helping you accomplish your goals.

If you can use a dedicated, congenial, and enthusiastic hard worker known for the ability to produce the highest quality results under the pressure of long hours and tight deadlines, I hope you will contact me to suggest a time when we might meet to discuss your needs and goals. With an outstanding personal and professional reputation, I can provide superior references.

Sincerely,

Jason Revels

JASON REVELS

1110½ Hay Street, Fayetteville, NC 28305   •   preppub@aol.com   •   (910) 483-6611

OBJECTIVE   To benefit an organization that can use an articulate communicator, strong problem-solver, and talented organizer with extensive knowledge of government and the legislative process along with a desire to apply that knowledge for the benefit of an elected official.

EDUCATION   **Bachelor of Science (B.S.) degree in History,** University of New Hampshire, Durham, NH, 1998.
- Inducted into Beta Gamba Chi; recognized in the top 10% in the Social Science Department of the Association of Northeastern Colleges.
- As a captain, led the college to the first semifinal game in its history.
- Named **All-Region NCAA,** a respected college basketball honor.

Graduated from Portsmouth High School, Portsmouth, NH, 1994.
- Named **Player of the Year** in New Hampshire, 1994.
- Named to New Hampshire All-Star High School Basketball Team.

AFFILIATIONS   Member, Northern Historical Society; National Educators Association (NEA).

EXPERIENCE   **SOCIAL STUDIES TEACHER & COUNSELOR.** Strafford County Schools, Portsmouth High School, Portsmouth, NH (2003-present). As a 9th grade teacher, teach social studies to 110 students and prepare them for the end-of-grade writing, reading, and math tests.
- On my own initiative, teach remediation classes in the morning and afternoon in order to ensure that every student has an opportunity to achieve mastery learning.
- Played an organizational and leadership role in the Drama Teamsters.
- Counsel students/parents about matters related to student achievement and well-being.
- Coach the basketball team, and groomed two players named to the All Star team.

COMMUNICATIONS SKILLS TEACHER & COACH. Strafford County Schools, Strafford Middle School, Portsmouth, NH (2000-02). As an 8th grade teacher, taught English and reading skills to 142 students while also administering end-of-grade tests and exams.
- On a daily basis, counseled 28 children and helped them set high personal goals.
- Became respected by other teachers for my ability to develop creative materials which helped prepare students for high school.
- Coached the basketball team to the second place finish in the county.
- On my own initiative, created and administered end-of-grade practice tests which helped children ready themselves for a test which counts up to 20% of their total yearly grade.

BEHAVIOR & EMOTIONAL DISORDER TEACHER. Strafford County Schools, Northwood School, Portsmouth, NH (1998-00). As an 8th grade teacher, taught social studies skills to children who could not attend public schools; became a valuable part of the intervention process for children with extreme discipline problems, and helped many of them return to mainstream classrooms.

SUPERVISOR, SUMMER PLAYGROUND. Hillsborough County Parks and Recreation, Manchester, NH (1996-98). Invented and planned daily activities for children aged 5-14; supervised a staff of three professionals overseeing up to 50 children.
- Refined my organizational skills while resourcefully administering summer activities.

PERSONAL   Highly motivated individual who desires to apply my knowledge of government, social studies, and the educational process. Strong computer skills. Excellent references.

Exact Name of Person
Title or Position
Name of Company
Address (no., street)
Address (city, state, zip)

**SOCIAL WORKER,
DEPARTMENT OF
CHILDREN'S SERVICES**

Dear Exact Name of Person: (or Dear Sir or Madam if answering a blind ad.)

I would appreciate an opportunity to talk with you soon about how I could contribute to your organization through my experience in social work as well as my sincere desire to help others and contribute to a service organization.

In my current position with the Burleigh County Department of Children's Services, I specialize in providing children's services as I screen for abuse, neglect, and dependency. Although I enjoy the challenges involved in clinical social work, I am eager to assume a management position through which I can mentor junior employees and play a role in improving the efficiency of the human services system.

I hope you will call me soon to arrange a brief meeting at your convenience to discuss your current and future needs and how I might serve them. I can provide outstanding personal and professional references at the appropriate time. Thank you in advance for your time.

Sincerely,

Danielle Burks

DANIELLE BURKS

1110½ Hay Street, Fayetteville, NC 28305 • preppub@aol.com • (910) 483-6611

OBJECTIVE   To benefit an organization that can use a dedicated and hardworking professional skilled in social work who offers excellent management and administrative skills.

EDUCATION   Currently working towards **Master of Social Work** degree, University of Marywood, Bismarck, ND.
Bachelor of Arts degree, Political Science, Oregon State University, Corvallis, OR, 1998.
Associate of Applied Science degree, Criminal Justice, Minot State University, Minot, ND, 1996.

EXPERIENCE   **SOCIAL WORKER III.** Burleigh County Department of Children's Services, Bismarck, ND (2004-present). As Intake Worker for Children's Services, screen abuse, neglect, and dependency reports according to statutory definitions, and accept appropriate candidates for investigations.
- Make referrals to law enforcement agencies as necessary. Determine eligibility for crisis programs offered by the agency. Carry a beeper to respond to reports in off-duty hours.

SOCIAL WORKER II. Burleigh County Department of Children's Services, Bismarck, ND (2002-04). As Child Care Coordinator, determined eligibility of clients requesting state aid which would permit low-income families to work and attend school.
- Completed monthly reimbursement turnaround documentation authorizing payments to child care providers. Educated the staff of other agencies as well as the community concerning strict child care regulations and the child care program.
- Actively sought and recruited providers.
- Monitored registered and nonregistered homes as well as day care centers to ensure they were complying with state regulations; reported those not in compliance and any complaints to the county care section for investigation.
- Carried a beeper during off-duty hours for Protective Services.

SOCIAL WORKER I. Burleigh County Department of Children's Services, Bismarck, ND (2001-02). Provided job and education-related counseling, and oversaw clients in the program.
- Promoted attendance in educational programs and provided services to support their participation.
- Aided clients in reaching the goal of becoming self-sufficient from government assistance.
- Saw other clients for general intake purposes in support of other services offered through the agency.

INCOME MAINTENANCE CASEWORKER I. Bismarck Family Center, Bismarck, ND (1999-01). Redetermined client's eligibility for assistance support; managed clients' files and performed monthly and yearly reviews. Made revisions as necessary.
- Recommended clients for benefits and terminated clients who were found to be ineligible. Uncovered fraudulent clients; referred suspected fraud to the appropriate authorities and recouped overpayments.

AFFILIATION   Member, Association of Social Workers

PERSONAL   Am a detail-oriented professional sincerely dedicated to helping others. Have a knack for dealing with people and can get along with anyone regardless of background. Remain calm and productive in pressure situations. Excellent references on request.

Exact Name of Person
Exact Title
Exact Name of Company
Address
City, State, Zip

SOCIAL WORKER,
FAMILY SERVICES

Dear Exact Name of Person: (or Dear Sir or Madam, if answering a blind ad):

With the enclosed resume, I would like to introduce you to my background as a Social Worker and Investigator with specialized experience in assisting children who are victims of sexual abuse, physical abuse, and neglect.

As you will see from my resume, I served my country for ten years in the Air Force in the accounting field, and it was that experience in counseling soldiers about personal and financial problems which made realize that I wanted to make a career in Social Work. After leaving the Air Force I became a full-time student and earned my Bachelor of Science in Social Work (B.S.W.). While earning my degree, I volunteered for two years at a women's shelter and made a difference in the lives of many victims of violence.

After excelling in an internship with the Yellowstone County Family Services, I was offered a full-time position as a Social Worker. Subsequently I advanced to the position of Investigator for Child Protective Services, and I directed services to the child and family in an attempt to protect the child from further neglect and abuse.

In my most recent position as a Social Worker III, Child Placement Unit, I have handled a caseload of 27 cases while specializing in sexual abuse cases where children have been removed from the home or are in foster care. I am skilled at numerous legal processes, including terminating parental rights, and I have become very knowledgeable about the variety of programs and services available to provide intervention and problem solving for abusive parents and their children.

Through my enthusiasm, motivational abilities, empathy, and compassion for others, I can make valuable contributions to an organization such as yours. I hope you will welcome my call soon when I try to arrange a brief meeting to discuss your goals and how my background might serve your needs. I can provide outstanding references at the appropriate time.

Sincerely,

Shirley Cantwell

Alternate last paragraph:
I hope you will write or call me soon to suggest a time when we might meet to discuss your needs and goals and how my background might serve them. I can provide outstanding references at the appropriate time.

SHIRLEY CANTWELL

1110½ Hay Street, Fayetteville, NC 28305   •   preppub@aol.com   •   (910) 483-6611

OBJECTIVE   To offer my reputation as a compassionate, dedicated, and enthusiastic professional to an organization that can use my education and experience related to social work and human services as well as my willingness to "go the extra mile" for my clients.

EDUCATION   **Bachelor of Science** in **Social Work (B.S.W.),** Montana State University, Billings, MT, 2001. Previously completed social work courses at University of Montana, Missoula, MT. Completed numerous training programs including the following:

MAPP Certification	Core I Training
Crossing Threshold	Risk Assessment Training
Child Sexual Abuse Training	Child Placement Training
Stress Management	Civil Rights Training
Child Development	Families at Risk
Hazardous Communications	Fire Extinguisher Training

Life Books for Children Experiencing the Trauma of Separation and Loss
Legal Aspects of Child Protective Services; Medical Aspects of Child Protective Services

EXPERIENCE   **SOCIAL WORKER III, CHILD PLACEMENT UNIT.** Yellowstone County Family Services, Billings, MT (2004-present). Handle a caseload of 27 cases while specializing in sexual abuse cases in which the children had been removed from the home or were in foster care.

- Gained experience in writing petitions and summons, and am experienced in handling non-secure hearings. After trial dates are set, testify in criminal court. Am experienced in handling judicial proceedings involved in terminating parental rights.
- Thrive on the challenge of bringing stability, good parenting, and a sense of permanence into the lives of children whose biological parents are incapable of being responsible parents.
- Am skilled at assessing parenting capabilities of potential adoptive or foster parents.
- Conduct individual and group interviews to make assessments of families and child.
- Handle resource development, community liaison, and case management.

INVESTIGATOR, SOCIAL WORKER III, CHILD PROTECTIVE SERVICES. Yellowstone County Family Services, Billings, MT (2003-04). Investigated allegations of child abuse and neglect by interviewing, observing, and interpreting verbal and nonverbal behavior of the child, suspected perpetrators, family, and collateral witnesses.

- Developed and implemented effective treatment plans, when necessary, removed the child from the abusive environment to protect the child from neglect or abuse. Completed and filed juvenile court petitions, summons, and court reports; testified in abuse cases.

Other experience:
SOCIAL WORKER. Silverbow County Family Services, Butte, MT (2001-02). Investigated allegations of child abuse and neglect, performing emergency assessments and evaluations to determine the risk level of the child; made recommendations for action and referrals to local services.
SOCIAL WORK INTERN. Yellowstone County Children's Services, Billings, MT (2000-01). Excelled in an internship in which I responded to petitions to adopt by stepparents, and completed agency home studies for both adoption and foster care.

PERSONAL   Excel in interviews and in confrontations about sensitive subjects, such as sexual abuse. Am persistent—will not give up until I have obtained the very best assistance for my client.

Date

Exact Name of Person
Title or Position
Name of Company
Address
City, State, Zip

Dear Exact Name of Person: (or Dear Sir or Madam if answering a blind ad.)

With the enclosed resume, I would like to make you aware of my interest in exploring employment opportunities with your organization.

As you will see from my resume, I have enjoyed a track record of promotion based on my strong management and organizational skills. Currently as a Social Worker and Counselor, I play a key role in efficiently managing a private, nonprofit residential group home facilities for low-functioning mentally challenged adults. I ensure the health and safety of clients, which involves investigating possible abuse and neglect cases, upholding standards, and protecting client rights. I am in charge of recommending and approving requests for client therapeutic leave.

Prior employment with the Knox Health Care as a Habilitation Specialist enabled me to act as advocate protecting clients' legal rights and supervising client progress. I also assisted clients in acquiring daily living, vocational, and cognitive skills through individual and group classes.

As a respected member of my profession, I am a member of the Interagency Council, Human Rights Committee, and Interdisciplinary Team, and I serve as chairperson for the Interdisciplinary Team and as liaison with the school system.

I hope you will call or write me soon to suggest a time convenient for us to meet to discuss your current and future needs. Thank you in advance for your time.

Sincerely yours,

Drake Reese

Alternate last paragraph:
I hope you will welcome my call soon to arrange a brief meeting when we might meet to discuss your needs and goals and how my background might serve them. I can provide outstanding references at the appropriate time.

DRAKE REESE

1110½ Hay Street, Fayetteville, NC 28305   •   preppub@aol.com   •   (910) 483-6611

OBJECTIVE

To benefit an organization in need of a resourceful administrator who is knowledgeable of group home management and the treatment of mentally challenged adults.

EXPERIENCE

Have established a track record of exceptional performance and promotion while refining my management and organizational skills during this company's restructuring from Tennessee Family Care to Tennessee Regional Hospital.

SOCIAL WORKER & COUNSELOR. Tennessee Regional Hospital, Knoxville, TN (2003-present). During a time of organizational transition, have played a key role in the efficient management of a private, nonprofit residential group home facilities for low-functioning mentally challenged adults.

- Ensure health and safety of clients, including investigating possible abuse and neglect cases, upholding standards, and protecting client rights.
- Record client progress, update case files, and supervise program changes to facilitate greater progress. Act as family and guardian point-of-contact.
- Recommend and approve requests for client therapeutic leave.
- Active on numerous professional boards and committees. Member of Interagency Council, Human Rights Committee, and Interdisciplinary Team. Chairperson for interdisciplinary team. Liaison with school system.

HABILITATION SPECIALIST. Knox Health Center, Knoxville, TN (2002-03). Acted as an advocate protecting clients' legal rights in addition to supervising client progress.

- Assisted clients in acquiring daily living, vocational, and cognitive skills through individual and group classes.
- Coordinated client work/training programs and technical assistance appointments.
- Member of interdisciplinary team. Trained staff on program implementation.

ASSISTANT FACILITY ADMINISTRATOR. Tennessee Family Care, Knox County, Knoxville, TN (2001-02). Rapidly promoted to handle a wide range of personnel and administrative functions including hiring, training, evaluating, and supervising staff personnel.

- Assisted in setup of the Knoxville unit including opening three new group homes.
- Coordinated health and safety issues including sanitary inspections and licensure qualifications.
- Supervised management of eight group homes including hiring, training, and evaluating personnel while handling disciplinary and other personnel issues.
- Conducted management team meetings. Supervised home managers.

AREA HOME MANAGER. Tennessee Family Care, Anderson County, Oak Ridge, TN (1999-00). Gained valuable managerial skills administering a wide range of personnel procedures including the hiring, training, and evaluating of group home personnel.

- Supervised direct care staff for 15-bed facility.

HABILITATION AIDE & RESIDENT TECHNICIAN. Tennessee Family Care, Anderson County, Oak Ridge, TN (1998-99). Assisted in providing 24-hour primary and direct care for clients. Taught clients educational skills as well as hygiene skills such as grooming.

EDUCATION

Bachelor of Arts, Political Science, University of Tennessee, Knoxville, TN, 1991.

Date

Exact Name of Person
Title or Position
Address (no., street)
Address (city, state, zip)

**SPECIAL
EDUCATION
TUTOR.**
With prior experience
as a Program
Coordinator for a
child abuse
prevention program,
this individual is
seeking her first
"real" professional
position.

Dear Exact Name of Person: (or Dear Sir or Madam if answering a blind ad.)

I would appreciate an opportunity to talk with you soon about how I could contribute to your organization through my experience in working with abused and exceptional children as well as my concerned and caring leadership style.

A recent graduate of the University of Oklahoma with a B.A. degree in Psychology, I completed courses related to child development, personality, social psychology, the family and society, and exceptional children including autistic, learning disabled, and mentally challenged youth.

My actual experience with "special" children includes tutoring a child with reading disabilities and low self-esteem and working with another child who is autistic. Working with these children allowed me to help them through positive reinforcement and my strong desire to reach them. This experience enabled me to appreciate the advantages I grew up with and strengthened my determination to help others with special needs.

While a student at University of Oklahoma, I participated through the Campus Central Office service organization as Program Coordinator and Advocate for the Child Abuse Prevention Program. I cared for children whose parents were receiving counseling, helped set up a program in Tulsa, conducted regular business and training meetings, and participated in presenting educational programs to local and campus groups.

I hope you will welcome my call soon to arrange a brief meeting at your convenience to discuss your current and future needs and how I might serve them. Thank you in advance for your time.

Sincerely yours,

Carolyn Whitter

CAROLYN WHITTER

1110½ Hay Street, Fayetteville, NC 28305 • preppub@aol.com • (910) 483-6611

OBJECTIVE   To offer my "newly minted" degree in psychology and my experience in relating to children and adolescents to an organization that can use a mature and dependable young professional.

EDUCATION   **B.A., Psychology,** University of Oklahoma, Norman, OK, 2004.
- Learned to manage time and coordinate a busy schedule while working a minimum of 20 hours a week to help pay for college expenses; participated in numerous volunteer activities.
- Completed specialized course work related to family life and society, child development, and exceptional children including autistic, learning disabled, and mentally challenged.

EXPERIENCE   **SPECIAL EDUCATION TUTOR.** Internship, University of Oklahoma (2004). Worked with two students in a Franklin Elementary School program for "exceptional children."
- Provided positive reinforcement and feedback for a child with reading disabilities and low self-esteem. Worked closely with a crisis intervention counselor and supervised schoolwork for an autistic child.
- Learned the importance of providing positive reinforcement at every opportunity when working with children with disabilities.

PROGRAM COORDINATOR & ADVOCATE. Campus Central Office, Child Abuse Prevention Program, University of Oklahoma (2000-04). While earning my degree at the University of Oklahoma, provided care for abused children while their parents attended counseling. Conducted biweekly meetings to provide information and training for volunteers.
- Gained a broad base of "hands-on" experience with abused children and became familiar with the types of situations they endured.
- Played a major role in setting up the program in Tulsa. Was highly effective in passing my knowledge and observations on to less experienced workers.

MEMBERSHIP CHAIRMAN. Campus Central Office, University of Oklahoma (2002-03). Refined my organizational skills through attention to the details of coordinating activities with 32 other committees. Handled the collection of, and accounting for, membership dues from 750 students.
- On my own initiative, set up an automated system to simplify accounting.

RETAIL SALES ASSOCIATE. Old Navy, Norman, OK (1999-02). Excelled in providing outstanding customer service while handling daily functions including customer sales, inventory control, stocking, and closing out the register.
- Consistently received "superior" performance evaluations in every area.

Highlights of other experience:
Learned to be patient and tactful in dealing with customers as a waitress; applied my communication skills in a campaign to solicit funds from university alumni.

COMPUTERS   Familiar with Microsoft software including Word and Excel.

PERSONAL   Am an enthusiastic and outgoing person. Have a desire to work with disadvantaged children and adolescents. Offer superior communication skills. Excellent references.

Exact Name of Person
Title or Position
Name of Company
Address (no., street)
Address (city, state, zip)

**STAFF ASSISTANT,
UNITED WAY**

Dear Exact Name of Person: (or Dear Sir or Madam if answering a blind ad.)

With the enclosed resume, I would like to express my interest in exploring employment opportunities with your organization.

A recent graduate of Western Michigan University with a Bachelor of Applied Science degree in Human Services, I offer a reputation as a versatile hard worker with strong computer skills.

In a sense, I feel that I have had the equivalent of an "internship" in a nonprofit organization through the part-time job I have held with the United Way. While operating a computer with specialized software including Word and Excel, I play a key role in supporting the needs of the membership department. Although I am excelling in my current position, I feel that I am ready to step up to a new level of responsibility and your trade association seems a perfect fit with my considerable skills.

I can provide excellent references at the appropriate time, and I hope you will contact me to suggest a time when we might meet to discuss your current and future needs and how I might serve them. Thank you in advance for your time.

Sincerely,

Edith Rivers

EDITH RIVERS

1110½ Hay Street, Fayetteville, NC 28305 • preppub@aol.com • (910) 483-6611

OBJECTIVE To obtain an internship in a nonprofit organization that can use a hardworking young professional with proven administrative skills and executive abilities.

EDUCATION Earned a **Bachelor of Applied Science in Human Services**, Western Michigan University, Kalamazoo, MI, 2004.
- Appointed to the President's List, 2002-04.
- Member of Kappa Alpha Chi Honor Society.
- Excelled in numerous elective courses related to psychology including Grief Counseling.

Studied Applied Management at Jackson Community College, Jackson, MI, 2001.
Completed course work in Life Science, Gainesville College, Gainesville, GA, 1994-95.

EXPERIENCE **STAFF ASSISTANT**. United Way, Kalamazoo, MI (2004-present). In this part-time job while completing my Associate's degree, perform a variety of administrative and clerical duties and helped manage the membership department.
- Maintain membership records and dues.
- Generate invoices on renewal accounts and invoices for all departments as needed; produce printouts of overdue members to help support account executives.
- Handle the setup and execution of administrative duties necessary for all networking and social events of the department.
- Manage executive calendars and keep track of meetings and appointments.
- Help improve efficiency by making recommendations on the most effective means of accomplishing the mission of the Membership Department.
- On my own initiative, created a database which has improved the efficiency of mass mailings.
- On numerous occasions, have been asked to serve as the point of contact for visiting VIPs and high-profile members.

LAB ASSISTANT & RECEPTIONIST. Dr. Richard Cummings, Kalamazoo, MI (2003). Autoclaved instruments, received shipments, and prepared operators in addition to answering telephone, greeting/assisting patients, confirming insurance policies and appointments, and closing books.

LEARNING CENTER OPERATOR. U.S. Army Community Center, Ft. Stewart, GA (2001-02). Kept up-to-date inventory of all U.S. Army technical manuals; issued equipment and scheduled usage of classrooms for the community center.

WORK CENTER SUPERVISOR. U.S. Navy, Kings Bay, GA (1996-01). Scheduled preventative maintenance on work center equipment while providing counseling to employees regarding personal matters including financial issues and credit card debt; wrote supporting evaluations for junior personnel.
- Prepared and presented lectures on work center procedures and safety.
- Implemented a maintenance program for the newly formed work center; ordered and received all supplies for the center.

COMPUTERS Offer computer knowledge including Word, Excel, and Access. Can type 50 w.p.m.

PERSONAL Experienced in working with and assisting the public. Outstanding references on request.

Exact Name of Person
Exact Title
Exact Name of Company
Address
City, State, Zip

STATE PROGRAM MANAGER, DEPARTMENT OF FAMILY SERVICES

Dear Exact Name of Person: (or Dear Sir or Madam if answering a blind ad.)

With the enclosed resume, I would like to make you aware of the background in program management and staff development which I could put to work for your organization.

While excelling in the track record of advancement which you will see summarized on my resume, I have applied my strong organizational skills in implementing new programs, organizing conferences and seminars, training and counseling professional-level employees, and transforming ideas into operational realities. On numerous occasions, I have developed effective formats for grant, reports, documents, and quality assurance protocol which have been described as "models."

In my current position, I have served as a Program Manager for the state of Maryland while spearheading the development of new housing options and employment opportunities for physically and mentally challenged adults. With a reputation as a vibrant and persuasive communicator, I routinely interface with legislators, state and federal officials, as well as with local program managers. It has often been my responsibility to take a new law and make sure it is efficiently and resourcefully implemented at the local level while assuring compliance with federal and state guidelines. I am continuously involved in teaching and training others—not only the professionals whom I directly supervise but also professionals regionally and locally who turn to me for advice and assistance in problem solving.

I feel confident that my resourceful leadership, expertise in staff training and staff development, and pragmatic approach to operations management and service operations delivery could be valuable to your organization. If you feel that you could use my considerable experience in initiating new programs, making existing programs work better, and establishing effective working relationships, I hope you will contact me to suggest a time when we might meet to discuss your needs and how I might serve them. I can provide outstanding personal and professional references at the appropriate time.

Yours sincerely,

Norah Stephens

NORAH STEPHENS

1110½ Hay Street, Fayetteville, NC 28305 • preppub@aol.com • (910) 483-6611

OBJECTIVE

To benefit an organization that can use a results-oriented program manager and skillful coordinator of services who offers a reputation for creative leadership, a proven ability to initiate and develop new programs, along with experience in administering existing services.

EXPERIENCE

STATE PROGRAM MANAGER. Maryland Department of Family Services, Baltimore, MD (2004-present). Supervise two professionals–a Residential Specialist and a Vocational Specialist–while establishing and administering statewide policies related to the provision of services and programs for the 3% of Baltimore residents afflicted with developmental disabilities.

- Have spearheaded the exciting development of new housing options for the physically handicapped (PH); whereas physically and mentally challenged individuals traditionally have had to live in group homes, I have provided leadership in pioneering a new program through which those individuals and families have purchased their own homes.
- Negotiated with a nonprofit credit union and the Maryland Housing Agency to develop a new mortgage product using the "Home Sweet Home" program as a model; supervised the development of literature explaining the product.
- Am considered an expert on the Maryland Portal Law which governs how handicapped individuals gain access to services provided by the state; travel extensively to local communities to work with mental health professionals and mental health centers to provide training and problem-solving assistance related to this law and other matters.
- Have worked tirelessly to assure maximum vocational opportunities for mentally and physically challenged individuals; played a key role on an advisory committee which explored ways to help high school graduates with developmental disabilities transition into jobs and training programs.
- Provided leadership during a statewide summit that increased employment options for disabled adults.

STATE TEAM LEADER. Maryland Division of Human Services, Baltimore, MD (2003-04). Supervised three professionals while traveling throughout the state to monitor statewide compliance with a Medicaid Program known as the Community Options Program which provides the developmentally disabled with housing options other than group homes.

- Coordinated statewide training for case managers and service providers.
- Was essentially in the role of Quality Assurance Manager as I developed review documents and quality control protocol to assure local compliance with state law.

REGIONAL PROGRAM COORDINATOR. O'Berry Center, Baltimore, MD (2001-03). Played a key role in increasing the efficiency of services provided to the developmentally disabled while acting as a Consultant in Maryland. Worked with state and federal regulators while functioning as the region's technical expert on the Community Options Program.

REGIONAL PROGRAM COORDINATOR. Anne Arundel County Area System, Annapolis, MD (1996-01). Supervised four professionals while also functioning as a Case Manager with a case load of 18 persons with developmental disabilities; administered 18 separate budgets.

Other experience: **PROGRAM COORDINATOR.** STAR, Inc., Baltimore, MD (1994-95). While earning my master's degree, oversaw operations of three group homes.

EDUCATION

Master of Arts in Education, University of Maryland, Baltimore, MD, 1996.
Bachelor of Science in Special Education, University of Baltimore, MD, 1992.

Date

Exact Name of Person
Title or Position
Name of Company
Address (no., street)
Address (city, state, zip)

STATION MANAGER,
American Red Cross

Dear Exact Name of Person: (or Dear Sir or Madam if answering a blind ad.)

With the enclosed resume, I would like to make you aware of my interest in exploring employment opportunities with your organization.

As you will see from my resume, I hold a B.S. in Marketing from the University of New Mexico. In my current position as Station Manager for the American Red Cross, I oversee the provision of emergency help and financial assistance while delivering needed programs and services for the needy. In addition to managing the station, I oversee and support the blood center. I was promoted to my current position based on my outstanding performance in my previous position as Assistant Station Manager. In that position, I gained experience in emergency planning and disaster response while providing help to thousands of individuals rendered homeless by hurricanes and tornadoes.

You would find me in person to be a congenial fellow who prides myself on my ability to get along with all types of people. Although my major in college was marketing, I am respected for my solid financial skills, and I am proud of the financial leadership I have provided to the American Red Cross in Farmington. When I took over the station, its staff and programs were in disarray, and I provided the leadership needed to rebuild inefficient programs and retraining an unmotivated staff. I believe there is no finer Red Cross station in the U.S. than the one we now have in Farmington.

I hope you will call or write me soon to suggest a time convenient for us to meet to discuss your current and future needs. I can provide outstanding personal and professional references at the appropriate time. Thank you in advance for your time.

Sincerely yours,

Yolanda Harris

YOLANDA HARRIS

1110½ Hay Street, Fayetteville, NC 28305   •   preppub@aol.com   •   (910) 483-6611

OBJECTIVE   I want to benefit an organization that can use a resourceful manager who excels in managing people, programs, projects, and finances while performing astute strategic planning that continuously assures that the organization is focused on its future goals and needs.

EDUCATION   Earned **Bachelor of Science in Marketing,** University of New Mexico, Gallup, NM, 2000.
- Excelled academically with a 3.8 GPA even though I worked 30 hours a week in order to finance my college education.
- Volunteered my time to community projects such as AIDS Awareness; traveled to numerous high schools to talk to young people about the advantages of abstinence from sex and about the dangers of sexually transmitted diseases (STD).

EXPERIENCE   **STATION MANAGER.** American Red Cross, Farmington, NM (2003-present). Was specially selected for this sought-after promotion to manage the American Red Cross station in Farmington. Provide emergency communications, financial assistance, help manage the station, deliver needed programs and services for the military, oversee and support the blood center, and recruit blood donors.
- **Financial control:** Provide vital input into budgets for numerous programming activities; continuously develop new outreach programs. Establish goals for fundraising as well as for reducing expenses.
- **Employee training and supervision**: Oversee the recruiting, training, and management of more than 200 volunteers annually in addition to the paid staff of 10 individuals.

ASSISTANT STATION MANAGER. American Red Cross, Gallup, NM (2000-2002). Provided emergency communications for needy individuals and their families during a period of time when major hurricanes and tornadoes wreaked havoc on the state and created numerous homeless individuals.
- **Emergency planning and disaster response**: Directed the activities of more than 250 volunteers and paid staff who responded to the needs of individuals displaced from their homes by natural disasters. Organized homeless shelters and blood drives.

SALES ASSOCIATE. Target, Gallup, NM (1998-99). Worked part-time while pursuing my college degree, and became a valued sales associate in this Target "superstore." Assisted customers with purchases and wrote gift certificates.
- Was strongly encouraged to become a part of the company's management training program after college graduation.

DENTAL ASSISTANT & RECEPTIONIST. Edward Z. Haye, DDS, Gallup, NM (1996-98). In a part-time job while in high school and college, scheduled appointments for clients, operated computer, typed, filed, assisted dentist with patients, and made bank deposits.

REFERENCES   Outstanding references available upon request. My father was a medical doctor and I grew up in a home where helping others was considered a daily necessity.

Date

Exact Name of Person
Title or Position
Name of Company
Address (no., street)
Address (city, state, zip)

STATION MANAGER. Dear Exact Name of Person: (or Dear Sir or Madam if answering a blind ad.)

This American Red
Cross Station Manager
is seeking an
opportunity with a
de-mining organization
which provides
humanitarian
assistance.

With the enclosed resume, I would like to make you aware of my interest in exploring employment opportunities with your organization. I am responding to your recent advertisement for a Humanitarian Assistance Manager for your de-mining operations.

As you will see from my resume, I have completed numerous American Red Cross (ARC) sponsored training courses in the process of being promoted to my current position as Station Manager. In my current position, I provide guidance and leadership for American Red Cross support programs while planning and organizing educational programs. I also administer an international communications network and provide confidential counseling. Known as an articulate public speaker, I make presentations to groups of as many as 500 people.

While working with the American Red Cross, I have worked closely with the U.S. Army and U.S. Air Force, and I have traveled with U.S. military forces to countries including Saudi Arabia, Afghanistan, and Iraq. On one occasion, I was handpicked as a Disaster Services Family Service Technician in Oklahoma City, where I was placed in charge of providing financial support and assistance to victims of the bombing and their families. Most recently I spent eight months in Iraq (my second trip there) providing disaster assistance, setting up homeless shelters, and responding to the vast human needs.

My background seems well suited to your needs for a sensitive and caring individual to become a part of your humanitarian efforts in global de-mining activities. I hope you will meet with me in person to further discuss the position you have in mind. I can provide outstanding references at the appropriate time. Thank you in advance for your time.

Sincerely yours,

Lauren Miller

LAUREN MILLER

1110½ Hay Street, Fayetteville, NC 28305 • preppub@aol.com • (910) 483-6611

OBJECTIVE

To offer expertise in case management, emergency response, and office administration to an organization in need of a creative, mature professional able to manage multiple tasks, motivate volunteers, and make sound decisions.

EXPERIENCE

STATION MANAGER. The American Red Cross (ARC), Ft. Bragg, NC (1995-present). Provide guidance and leadership for ARC support programs at the largest U.S. military base in the world. Have traveled with military organizations while providing Red Cross assistance to individuals in Saudi Arabia, Afghanistan, and Iraq. Regularly plan and organize educational programs, administer an international communications network, provide counseling, and make presentations to groups of as many as 500 people while involved in:

Verifying details of family emergencies
Providing for loans or grants during emergencies
Counseling personnel and making referrals to other agencies
Recruiting, training, and supervising adult and youth volunteers
Contacting various groups to solicit funds to meet local needs
Preparing press releases; planning advertising campaigns and promotions
Accompanying military units on humanitarian projects
Collecting loan payments when prior repayment plans failed
Preparing and maintaining records and statistics to meet existing guidelines
Using software which automates recordkeeping and casework reporting
Arranging transportation and lodging for clients
Analyzing client's budgets to determine eligibility for assistance
Arranging for and coordinating training in areas including health and safety, HIV/AIDS education, disaster awareness, and volunteer responsibilities

- Represented the Ft. Bragg and Pope AFB station during the war in the Middle East and during the War on Terrorism. Lived and worked in Afghanistan and Iraq.
- Earned a reputation as a skilled public speaker; frequently spoke to family support groups, clubs, and committees on subjects including domestic violence.
- On special assignment, served as a Disaster Services Family Service Technician in Oklahoma City providing assistance to families of bombing victims.
- Coordinated with agencies such as military aid societies, social services, and hospice organizations to provide comprehensive services for military families.

Highlights of earlier American Red Cross experience:
RECREATION SUPERVISOR. Planned and administered therapeutic recreational activities for two 150-bed hospitals, including coordinating outside agency/group visits; developed sensitivity to patient rights and worked with hospital administrative personnel.

EDUCATION & TRAINING

Nine graduate hours in Personnel Administration & Community Relations.
B.A., Elementary Education, University of North Carolina at Greensboro, NC, 1994.
Attended numerous Red Cross-sponsored training courses on topics including:

introduction to disaster services	paid and volunteer staff relations
emergency assistance to families	damage assessment
administration during small disasters	mass care; first aid and CPR
case management: the art of helping, financial assistance, and referrals	

PERSONAL

Extensive training in Microsoft Word. Use office equipment such as fax machines, multiline phones, typewriters, and computers. Excellent references on request.

Date

Exact Name of Person
Exact Title
Exact Name of Company
Address
City, State, Zip

Dear Exact Name of Person (or Dear Sir or Madam if answering a blind ad):

With the enclosed resume, I would like to make you aware of my interest in exploring employment opportunities with your organization. I am responding to your recent advertisement for an Executive Director.

As you will see from my resume, I have worked for the Shawnee County Health Department since 1985, and I have excelled in a track record of promotion to my current position as Supervisor of the Women's and Children's Health Program. While working within the county's health department, I have become accustomed to interacting with multiple clinics and multiple programs. In my current position, I hire, train, and manage up to 25 individuals while planning and administering multiple budgets totaling more than $2.5 million. I have earned a reputation as a caring individual who is skilled at building consensus and inspiring others to work toward common goals.

An outgoing and energetic individual, I take great pride in the multiple accomplishments of the county's health department, and I have played a key role in many important programs. I co-developed the Shawnee County Healthy Living Program which provided preventive health screening services to the county's 2,000 employees. I have also played a key role in the Pregnant Living Program which has reduced the incidence of teen pregnancies. In addition to organizing numerous projects related to breast cancer awareness and other areas, I developed the Childhood Poison Prevention Program and the Heart Control Program.

While serving the health care needs of the county's indigent population, my main "hobby" has been gaining advanced knowledge through earning additional academic credentials. In addition to earning my L.P.N. and R.N. credentials, I received a Bachelor of Science in Nursing and a Master's in Public Health degree. I am proficient with numerous software programs which I have utilized in my job in order to prepare budgets, track expenditures, and control the funding of multiple programs.

I can provide outstanding personal and professional references at the appropriate time, but I would ask that you not contact the Shawnee County Health Department until after we have a chance to discuss your needs. Since I am in a key management role, I wish my interest in your organization to remain confidential at this time. Thank you in advance for your consideration and professional courtesies.

Yours sincerely,

Lavina Cleveland

LAVINA CLEVELAND

1110½ Hay Street, Fayetteville, NC 28305   •   preppub@aol.com   •   (910) 483-6611

OBJECTIVE   To benefit an organization that can use a strong leader and resourceful problem solver who offers proven experience in motivating employees and inspiring teamwork, managing finances and preparing budgets, as well as in developing and implementing new programs.

COMPUTERS   Proficient with software including Excel, Access, Word, and PowerPoint.

EDUCATION   **Master's in Public Health,** Emporia State University, Emporia, KS, 2004. GPA 3.8.
Bachelor of Science in Nursing (B.S.N.), Friends University, Wichita, KS, GPA, 1999.
Associate's Degree in Nursing (A.D.N.), Wichita State University, Wichita, KS, 1989.
Licensed Practical Nurse (L.P.N.), Washburn University of Topeka, Topeka, KS; 1985.

EXPERIENCE   *Shawnee County Health Department, Topeka, KS. Have excelled in the following track record of promotion within the public health field while continuing my education in my spare time. Have worked in a public health environment with multiple clinics serving populations across the life span, from birth to old age.*
2000-present. SUPERVISOR. Was promoted in 2000 to supervise the Women's and Children's Health Program, and have earned a reputation as a caring leader who is skilled at building consensus and inspiring others to work toward common goals.
- **Employee supervision:** Hire, train, and supervise up to 25 individuals who include RNs, LPNs, community health assistants, nurse practitioners, and secretaries. Devise and implement regular inservice training for staff.
- **Budget preparation and management:** Plan and administer multiple budgets totaling more than $2.5 million for activities pertaining to child health, family planning, breast cancer awareness, rape crisis, lead programs, and outreach activities. Create spreadsheets in Excel in order to monitor expenditures and assure that disbursements are within state guidelines.
- **Executive decision making:** Am part of monthly management team meetings, weekly supervisory meetings, and annual Board of Director meetings.
- **Program development:** Played a role in developing and implementing the **Healthy Living Program** which provided 2,000 county employees with preventive health screening and health education. Played a major role in managing the **Pregnant Living Program** funded by the state to decrease unwed pregnancies.

1991-00. CLINIC CHARGE NURSE. Supervised up to three RNs, aides, and communicable disease specialists while working in the Family Health Clinic.
- **Project management:** Organized projects with the Shawnee Regional Hospital to promote health concepts such as breast cancer awareness. Developed the **Childhood Poison Prevention Program** and the **Heart Control Program.**

1989-91. STAFF NURSE. Worked as a School Health Nurse at Birchcreek Junior High and Sunshine Elementary; made home visits and performed physical assessments; rotated as a clinical nurse among all health department clinics including Child Health, Family Planning, TB Chest, Immunization, Maternity, Neurology, Neuromuscular, Orthopedic, and Dental.

1985-89. LPN. Assisted MDs and worked as a Liaison Nurse to Shawnee Regional Hospital, transitioning patients to the from the public health environment; taught classes.

AFFILIATIONS   **President,** KS Public Health Nurse's Administrators; **Member,** Healthy Choice for Humanity; KS Public Health Association, Shawnee County School Health Committee.

Date

Exact Name of Person
Title or Position
Name of Company
Address (no., street)
Address (city, state, zip)

Dear Exact Name of Person: (or Dear Sir or Madam if answering a blind ad.)

I would appreciate an opportunity to talk with you soon about how I could contribute to your organization through my experience and administrative skills related to the social services and mental health field.

As you will see from my resume, I have been involved since childhood in helping others as a role model and mentor. While earning my B.S. degree in Marketing and my A.A. in Business Administration, I worked with troubled youth and convinced many young people that hard work and a positive attitude combined with staying in school can overcome a bad start in life.

For the past two years after graduating from college, I have worked in classroom and camp environments with children who have varying disabilities including autism, cerebral palsy, and Downs Syndrome. As a teacher in a classroom of behaviorally disturbed children in Iowa, I learned how to develop and implement effective lesson plans for disruptive students. As a teacher with the Cedar Falls Area Schools, I taught reading to autistic and mentally handicapped children and, on my own initiative, I learned sign language in order to help a child with Downs Syndrome learn to better communicate in his world. Most recently I was recruited by a classroom teacher for autistic students as one of seven staff members responsible for starting up a new summer program for autistic youth aged 4-20.

If we meet in person, you will see that I am an outgoing young professional with excellent communication skills and a very positive attitude. I truly believe that hard work and a positive attitude can help people overcome even the most disadvantaged childhood, and I take pride in the fact that I have helped many youth get off the wrong track and set high goals for themselves.

I offer excellent computer skills including proficiency with Windows, and I have a knack for rapidly learning new software and hardware. I am certain I could easily master whatever system you have.

I hope you will write or call me soon to suggest a time when we might meet to discuss your goals and needs and how I might serve them. I feel certain that I could become a valuable and productive member of your team.

Sincerely yours,

Amanda Barnes

AMANDA BARNES

1110½ Hay Street, Fayetteville, NC 28305 • preppub@aol.com • (910) 483-6611

OBJECTIVE

To benefit an organization that can use a dynamic and articulate young professional who sincerely enjoys helping others while utilizing strong organizational skills, computer knowledge, and a thoroughly positive attitude.

EXPERIENCE

TRAINING COORDINATOR & CLIENT ENABLER. Iowa Autism Society, Waterloo, IA (2003-present). Contribute to team efforts in a habilitation program which allows clients who are autistic or have communication handicaps to develop communication, social, and leisure skills which will allow them to live independently.

- Work closely with family members, other trainers, case managers, and the Director of Recreational and Community Service.
- Assist clients in the development of skills such as ordering their own food in restaurants or playing games with another person.
- Complete written reports of skills, activities, progress, and concerns at each session along with monthly progress reports.
- Participate in community outings with clients in order to increase their independence in areas such as using public transportation, managing money, and handling household responsibilities such as doing laundry and setting the table.
- Assist in efforts to educate the general public about autism.

ASSISTANT TO THE DIRECTOR & TEACHER. Lil' Angels Camp, Waterloo, IA (2000-02). Was specially recruited by a classroom teacher for autistic students as one of seven staff members to assist in starting up and implementing a new summer camp for autistic children funded by Black Hawk County Health, grants, and donations.

- Planned and implemented activities for youth aged 4-20.
- As the youngest member of the teaching/administrative team, won the respect of my peers for my creativity, reliability, and willingness to always "go the extra mile."
- Helped children learn behavior skills while involving them in activities that promoted their academic, physical, and social development.
- Strongly expressed and implemented my belief that autistic children, like all children, need to learn and use good manners.

SUBSTITUTE TEACHER. Polk County Area Schools, Des Moines, IA (2000). For youth aged kindergarten-grade 12, provided instruction based on daily lesson plans; learned to prepare and implement effective lesson plans for classrooms of children with behavioral problems.

- Instilled in children the concept that hard work and a good attitude are the keys to success in life, and that they can overcome disadvantages in their background through initiative and a positive attitude.

Other experience: While in college, worked as a mentor/counselor three days a week with troubled youth; taught them that one can overcome a poor beginning in life and that staying in school is essential to happiness and success.

- Believe I helped many youth discover hope and set new goals in life.
- Have a strong "helping instinct" expressed through volunteer roles in programs including Feed the Homeless, Adopt a Family, Sports Youth Program, and as Secretary and Teacher in a Sunday School program.

EDUCATION

Bachelor of Science degree in **Marketing**, University of Iowa, Cedar Falls, IA, 2000.
Associate of Arts degree in **Business Administration**, Drake University, IA, 1998.

CAREER CHANGE

Date

Exact Name of Person
Title or Position
Name of Company
Address (no., street)
Address (city, state, zip)

TRAINING MANAGER

Dear Exact Name of Person: (or Dear Sir or Madam if answering a blind ad.)

With the enclosed resume, I would like to make you aware of my interest in the position of Executive Director.

As you will see from my resume, I have excelled in managerial roles in both profit-making and nonprofit organizations. After college, I spent several years as an entrepreneur in a corporate environment, where I was extensively involved in financial planning and budgeting as well as project management and personnel supervision.

It has always been important to me to make contributions to my community and to our less fortunate citizens in particular, so I made a career transition in the 1990s into the nonprofit world. As a nonprofit executive, I utilized my leadership and vision to create and manage highly effective programs aimed at helping youth, treating substance abusers, and promoting environmental awareness. I created multiple new programs, including the Friendship Program and the Immersion Program, and I advanced to Program Manager for Experiential Education. While becoming a recognized authority on adventure and environmental education programs, I gained vast experience in starting up new programs "from scratch" and in developing the networks and alliances which are critical to the success of new initiatives.

I believe the key to my success has been my ability to develop effective working relationships with others while inspiring people to work toward common goals. A creative individual who is accustomed to "thinking outside the box" while solving problems and identifying new opportunities, I am comfortable in stepping into situations where it is up to me to provide team leadership and evaluate program effectiveness.

Because of my reputation as a highly effective team builder, I was recruited in 2004 by a business corporation to assume a newly created position as its Training Manager. While I have enjoyed the challenge of evaluating the company's programs and improving its personnel hiring, training, and management systems, I miss the unique challenges–and the unique problems–of a nonprofit environment.

I am confident that I could make valuable contributions for your company, and I would be honored to meet with you to discuss the important work you do in our community. I hope you will give me an opportunity to meet with you to discuss your needs, and I will furnish outstanding professional references at the appropriate time.

Sincerely,

Eric Sutton

ERIC SUTTON

1110½ Hay Street, Fayetteville, NC 28305 • preppub@aol.com • (910) 483-6611

OBJECTIVE

To benefit an organization that can use an inspiring and creative leader who offers extensive experience in managing budgets, people, projects, and programs while motivating others to achieve ambitious goals.

EDUCATION

Bachelor of Science degree in Communications Media, Georgia State University, Atlanta, GA, 1985. Completed a minor in **Environmental Outdoor Education.**

Continuing education: Excelled in continuing education courses which included:

Conflict Management/Conflict Resolution	Violence Interruption Process
Team Building	Adventure Therapy
Love and Logic	Reality Therapy
Team Community Leadership Training	Budget Planning
Personnel Supervision	Operations Management

Certifications: Certified by Mercer University as a Trainer for School Based Peer Mediation and Conflict Resolution and Team Community Leadership; Certified in Psychological Assessing by the Mercer University. Certified to administer medications.

EXPERIENCE

TRAINING MANAGER. Highland Companies, Macon, GA (2004-present). Because of my reputation as an effective team builder and trainer, was recruited for this position by the corporate CEO. Have improved the personnel hiring, training, and management systems.

PROGRAM MANAGER. Merrimack, Inc., Atlanta, GA (1995-2003). Created multiple new programs—including the Friendship Program and the Immersion Program—and was promoted to Program Manager for Experiential Education. Became the respected "internal expert" on adventure and environmental education programs. Managed budgets and supervised employees/volunteers on various projects.

- *The Immersion Program:* Developed a regional network of adventure guide professionals, nonprofit organizations, and businesses which provided technical gear and back country sites which we incorporated into a new treatment model for drug/alcohol abuse and psychological disorders.
- *The Friendship Program:* Developed a network of community resources and established strong relationships with the Fulton County Public Schools, Salvation Army, retirement facilities, the park service, Emory University, and other organizations.

COMMUNITY DEVELOPMENT SPECIALIST. Georgia Outreach Organizations, Macon, GA (1993-95). Developed a network of businesses and nonprofit organizations to support multiple programs while creating programs that enriched life experience opportunities for disenfranchised youth.

- *The River Run Team*: Served as Outreach Coordinator for a new program which offered children an opportunity to explore scientific and social issues related to ecology while interacting with some of Georgia's river channels. Newspaper articles credited this program with instilling a "community conscience" in school-age children.
- *Georgia Youth Program:* Acted as Youth Program Coordinator for a program funded by the Wal-Mart Foundation designed to teach communities how to help their youth.

Highlights of other experience: Sports Referee; Wilderness Field Trip Leader; Swimming Instructor and Camping Trip Leader; Boy Scout Summer Camp Program Director; YMCA Summer Camp Director; Outreach for Alcohol-Free Schools. Entrepreneur.

PERSONAL

Outgoing individual with exceptional interpersonal skills. Known for my ability to gain the trust of others and establish warm working relationships with others.

TWO-PAGE RESUME

ANDREW MITCHELL

1110½ Hay Street, Fayetteville, NC 28305   •   preppub@aol.com   •   (910) 483-6611

OBJECTIVE   To contribute to an organization that can use a talented administrator with exceptional planning, organizational, and management skills.

EDUCATION   **B.A. in Sociology and Social Welfare,** Delaware State University, Dover, DE, 1991.

UNIT DIRECTOR,
YMCA

EXPERIENCE   **UNIT DIRECTOR.** YMCA, Dover, DE (2004-present). Plan, organize, direct, promote, and supervise a public housing community's YMCA. Coordinate all programs within the unit. Evaluate programs and submit periodic reports to the Executive Director. Assist in the recruitment, selection, supervision, direction, and evaluation of staff. Promote and stimulate participation and membership through school visitations and recruitment. Maintain the facility including equipment and supply requisition. Maintain working relationship with schools, parents, volunteers, the board of directors, and other agencies.

ASSISTANT CENTER DIRECTOR. Dover Park and Recreation Area, Dover, DE (2003-04). Planned, promoted, and coordinated special events, classes, and sports and summer day camps. Ensured building and grounds were clean, safe, and attractive. Worked with schools, churches, and area businesses in an effort to provide recreational activities for youths 6 and older. Provided assistance for city-wide recreational functions and aided other center staff in implementing their programs. Recruited instructors for classes, guest speakers to conduct workshops, and volunteers to coach in our sports program.

YOUTH PROGRAM ASSISTANT. Kent Acres Home, Dover, DE (2003). Supervised seven emotionally and mentally challenged children with behavior disorders. Assisted supervisor in the operation of a homelike setting for the clients, teaching clients how to care for their building, prepare meals, attend to personal hygiene, and gain interpersonal and academic skills. Maintained visual observation of clients and prepared reports on behaviors and treatment plans. Maintained positive working relationship with school officials, health and medical professionals, and community agencies.

SERVICE DIRECTOR. Milford Youth League, Milford, DE (1998-02). Planned, organized, implemented, and evaluated a comprehensive Youth Club Program. Oversaw operations of a youth recreational facility. Supervised paid and volunteer staff. Ensured that facility and equipment were maintained. Recruited members and volunteers, and collaborated with other social service agencies through public relations. Conducted numerous presentations on Youth Clubs' mission, purpose, and program to area civic clubs, school officials, and church groups. Assisted Area Director in developing program budgets. Directed leadership clubs in fundraising projects to supplement expenses for conferences, special field trips, and program supplies. Secured funds to send ten delegates across the state for a State Exchange Program.

HEALTH & PHYSICAL EDUCATION DIRECTOR. Milford Youth League, Milford, DE (1996-98). Conducted league competitions and individual sports for boys ages 6-18. Recruited volunteers to officiate, coach, drive vans, and supervise members in sports, field trips, and overnight parties. Secured guest speakers and physicians to conduct health and nutrition workshops, and provide dental and physical examinations for youth. Assisted Service Director as needed and managed the building in the absence of the Service Director.

YOUTH GROUP SUPERVISOR. Youth Center, Milford, DE (1996). Provided supervision and security for male juveniles ages 10-18. Processed boys for intake and out-take procedures. Maintained daily log detailing what occurred during each shift. Transported and supervised recreation, education, sleeping, meals, worship, and visiting activities for the boys.

SPORTS ASSISTANT. Dover Youth Club, Dover, DE (1993-96). Supervised basketball, soccer, and cheerleading programs for youths. Monitored practices and games in baseball, softball, basketball, football, soccer, ice hockey, and cheerleading. Prepared service agreements and job descriptions for volunteers desiring to become a part of the organization. Provided instruction to designate personnel the use of scoring and timing devices. Prepared and distributed to the public and news media, public announcements, flyers, and posters. Maintained participation accounts of youth/coach ratio in each program and submitted accurate figures to supervisor.

RECREATION LEADER. Dover Youth Club, Dover, DE (1990-93). Coordinated recreational activities for the Dover Outreach Program. Supervised children ages 6-19 in holiday festivities, games, free play, and dance. Maintained attendance register for all participants and their guests by classes and activities in accordance with procedures; posted data on weekly worksheet. Supervisor of Special Projects. Met with operating officials at various post schools and neighborhoods in an effort to plan and implement recreational activities to suit their needs.

INTERESTS   Enjoy artwork, automobile mechanics, reading, tennis, basketball, and swimming.

Date

Exact Name of Person
Exact Title
Exact Name of Company
Address
City, State, Zip

VICTIM ADVOCATE,
FAMILY CENTER

Dear Exact Name of Person: (or Dear Sir or Madam if answering a blind ad):

With the enclosed resume, I would like to introduce you to my background as an articulate communicator and experienced social worker whose outstanding organizational and case management skills have been proven in challenging environments where I worked with various consumer populations.

As you will see from my resume, I have earned a Bachelor of Science in Sociology with a minor in Social Work which I have supplemented with additional courses in case management, staff development, and law enforcement response to sexual assault.

My case management experience has been extensive and versatile, and I have worked with social services consumers ranging from victims of domestic violence and sexual assault, to the homeless and the chronically/severely mentally ill, to substance abusers and inmates in maximum security correctional facilities. Throughout my career in counseling and social work, I have managed heavy caseloads while developing effective relationships with community officials and other service providers.

Most recently, I single-handedly developed and ran a satellite office for an organization which provides counseling, victim advocacy, and referral services to victims of domestic violence and sexual assault. While overseeing all counseling, operational, and administrative functions of the office, I performed liaison with officials from the law enforcement and judicial communities as well as local service providers and outside agencies providing assistance to victims prosecuting their abusers.

In earlier positions, I assisted homeless and substance abuse consumers with vocational counseling and housing issues, and I worked with individuals suffering from chronic and severe mental illness to provide them with increased independence.

If you can use a highly skilled human services professional, I hope you will write or call me soon to suggest a time when we might meet to discuss your needs and goals and how my background might serve them. I can provide outstanding references at the appropriate time.

Sincerely,

Isabelle Evans

ISABELLE EVANS

1110½ Hay Street, Fayetteville, NC 28305   •   preppub@aol.com   •   (910) 483-6611

OBJECTIVE   To benefit an organization that can use a dedicated human services professional with exceptional communication and organizational skills who offers a strong background in case management of a wide range of mental health consumers.

EDUCATION   **Bachelor of Science** degree in **Sociology**, with a minor in **Social Work**, University of Bridgeport, West Haven, CT, 1997.
Completed additional course work in social services which included the Trinity College Case Management training, University Center for Psychiatric Rehabilitation; a 40-hour Staff Development Training course, Connecticut Coalition Against Domestic Violence; and Law Enforcement Response to Sexual Assault training, Connecticut Coalition Against Rape.

EXPERIENCE   **VICTIM ADVOCATE.** Hartford Family Center, Hartford, CT (2004-present). Provide individual supportive counseling, assessment, case management, and advocacy to victims of domestic violence and sexual assault while managing an office of this organization.
* Oversee all operational, administrative, and counseling functions of a satellite office serving a two-county area.
* Perform assessments and refer consumers to appropriate agency or community-sponsored programs.
* Manage as many as 20 open cases at any time, providing court advocacy, information, and support to victims participating in the judicial process.
* Serve as a key member of the Multi-Disciplinary Community Committee; network with law enforcement, the judicial system, service providers, and community leaders to raise awareness and increase convictions in domestic violence cases.
* Develop and distribute a variety of informational handouts and materials to domestic violence and sexual assault victims; distribute materials to service providers.

INTENSIVE CASE MANAGER. Hartford Health Center, Hartford, CT (1998-03). Serviced a heavy case load of chronically/severely mentally ill consumers as well as substance abusers and the homeless, providing continual assessment of consumer needs and crisis intervention.
* Trained new case managers/team members and medical students completing practicums.
* Provided case management to 30 consumers, working to increase their level of independent functioning and use of community resources while reducing hospitalization. Assisted homeless and mentally ill consumers in obtaining a stable living environment through vocational training and assistance with employment, housing, and health care.

CASE MANAGER & GRANT MANAGEMENT TEAM MEMBER. YMCA, Hartford, CT (1996-98). Provided assessment, counseling, vocational education, job placement assistance, and child care to 20 families at the housing development facility.
* Assisted consumers with development of problem-solving skills; provided crisis intervention and referrals to other service providers within the community.

MENTAL HEALTH CASE MANAGER. West Haven, CT (1995-96). Served a caseload of 30-35 chronically/severely mentally ill adults, working with consumers, developing treatment plans to reduce their hospitalization and increase their use of community resources; performed assessments of consumers mental state and needs, revising treatment plans.

PERSONAL   Excellent personal and professional references are available upon request.

Exact Name of Person
Title or Position
Name of Company
Address (no., street)
Address (city, state, zip)

**YOUTH ACTIVITIES
DIRECTOR,
YOUTH CENTER**

Dear Exact Name of Person: (or Dear Sir or Madam if answering a blind ad.)

I would appreciate an opportunity to talk with you soon about how I could contribute to your organization through my versatile background in the areas of planning, directing, and providing administrative support for recreation and community services programs.

As you will see from my enclosed resume, I offer a wide range of skills which include budget formulation and planning, program development and implementation, personnel management, public speaking, and contracting. In my most recent position as a Youth Activities Director and Recreation Program Director, I supervised 65 employees while supporting three teen centers, eight youth centers, and four youth sports programs which served from 100 to 175 people a day.

Through my versatile experience, skills, and knowledge, I am confident I could make an impact on the quality of your organization's programs. The recipient of several "on-the-spot" awards for contributions and professionalism, I have consistently found ways to improve the quality of sports, leisure, and recreational programs.

I have a reputation for being able to deal with people at all levels from community and civic leaders, to parents, to children and youth, to supervisors, to my peers. I get along well with others and can be counted on to get the job done.

I hope you will welcome my call soon to arrange a brief meeting at your convenience to discuss your current and future needs and how I might serve them. Thank you in advance for your time.

Sincerely yours,

Sharon Jenkins

Alternate last paragraph:
I hope you will call or write me soon to suggest a time convenient for us to meet and discuss your current and future needs and how I might serve them. Thank you in advance for your time.

SHARON JENKINS

1110½ Hay Street, Fayetteville, NC 28305   •   preppub@aol.com   •   (910) 483-6611

OBJECTIVE   To offer my experience in planning, directing, and administration of recreation and community services programs to an organization that can benefit from my knowledge in formulating and justifying budgets, supervising employees, and organizing youth and adult activities.

EXPERIENCE   **YOUTH ACTIVITIES DIRECTOR**. Community Youth Center, Sacramento, CA (2001-present). Wear a variety of hats as acting director, program manager, and recreation specialist for three teen centers and eight youth centers which offer comprehensive youth sports programs and special events.

- Supervise 65 employees in facilities which provided activities for 100 to 175 people daily.
- Implemented instructional classes which resulted in a 50% increase in revenue.
- Planned and implemented a summer day camp which was cited as the best in California.
- Developed a strong volunteer force which enabled the program to enjoy a 25% decrease in operational costs. Developed employment contracts to hire camp counselors and provide summer jobs for area youth.
- Gained further exposure to interpreting and implementing government regulations.
- Handle publicity to ensure awareness of the availability of programs/resources.
- Plan and supervise programs ranging from instructional classes, to gymnastics and tumbling, to karate, to piano, to baton twirling, to modern dance, to cultural events.
- Implement an after-school peer "homework helper" program and regular counseling.
- Plan trips for football games, museums, amusement parks, and ski resorts as well as day camps, horseback riding, swimming, bowling, and a variety of other activities.
- Apply organizational and written skills preparing standard operating procedures, policy letters, employee performance reports, and other reports.
- Analyze and administer two operating funds totaling more than $1.1 million annually.

RECREATION PROGRAM DIRECTOR. Community Youth Center, Sacramento, CA (1999-00). Handled a multitude of daily activities including supervising five employees, planning and conducting special events, providing new residents with information and assistance, coordinating with various local agencies and offices, and ordering supplies and equipment.

- Dealt with local vendors: had the authority to approve purchases up to $10,000.
- Coordinated accommodations, car rentals, and other details for tours/recreation activities.
- Represented the recreation center with presentations and slide shows for groups.

RECREATION ASSISTANT. Family Recreation Center, San Jose, CA (1995-98). Assisted in planning and carrying out programs for youth from ages six through 19; these programs included social, educational, recreational, cultural, and competitive activities.

- Prepared a minimum of five well-attended and successful programs a month.
- Implemented an outreach recreational program for families in outlying areas.
- Supervised and evaluated employees, summer hires, and volunteers.
- Earned several cash awards for my contributions and professionalism.

EDUCATION   Completing **A.A.S. in Social Services,** American River College, Sacramento, CA; degree anticipated in 2005.
Completed approximately 300 hours of training for youth and community services managers.

PERSONAL   Was praised for my organizational and "people" skills as coordinator of a highly successful program. Consistently earned laudatory remarks for summer camp programs and was singled out among coordinators throughout California for exceptional programs.

Exact Name of Person
Title or Position
Name of Company
Address (no., street)
Address (city, state, zip)

YOUTH PROGRAM ASSISTANT, MENTAL HEALTH CENTER

Dear Exact Name of Person: (or Dear Sir or Madam if answering a blind ad.)

I would appreciate an opportunity to talk with you soon about how I could contribute to your organization through my enthusiastic manner, adaptability, and ability to work with people of all ages and developmental levels. Although I am a productive and valued professional in my present situation, I have family and friends in your area, and I am in the process of permanently relocating to your community.

As you will see from my resume, I am a versatile professional with a broad base of experience in mental health and social services. My experience includes involvement with substance abuse education and counseling, residential management, therapeutic recreation program supervision and planning, and administrative operations.

Currently pursuing a bachelor's degree in Sociology after completing three years of study in Psychology, I have shown myself to be a compassionate and caring professional who can handle crisis and high-risk situations. I have worked with clients ranging from the elderly, to violent and emotionally disturbed youth, to rape and abuse victims of all ages, to substance abusers of all ages. I have consistently earned the respect, trust, and confidentiality of my clients and their family members as well as the mental health, medical, and legal professionals with whom I am in frequent contact.

I am confident that I possess a thorough knowledge of the concepts, practices, and techniques of the field of mental illness and developmental disabilities.

If you are looking for a dedicated and reliable professional with a reputation for being well rounded, approachable, and self-reliant, I hope you will call or write me soon to suggest a time convenient for us to meet to discuss your current and future needs and how I might serve them. Thank you in advance for your time.

Sincerely,

Katie Moses

KATIE MOSES

1110½ Hay Street, Fayetteville, NC 28305   •   preppub@aol.com   •   (910) 483-6611

OBJECTIVE

To combine my education and experience in the field of mental health/social service operations to benefit an organization in need of a bright, enthusiastic, innovative professional who excels in dealing with people, defusing difficult situations, and solving problems.

EXPERIENCE

YOUTH PROGRAM ASSISTANT. Jefferson County Mental Health Center, Pine Bluff, AR (2002-present). Provide psycho-educational services to JCMHC, juvenile sex offenders, and emotionally disturbed adolescents in a high-risk adolescent facility: ensure that clients who require out-of-home care due to their psychiatric needs receive focused attention to assist them in the development of social skills, independent living skills, and behavioral management.

- Plan and implement group activities and monitor participation; provide and administer medication. Interact daily with in-house therapists, social workers, probation officers, and other mental health professionals.
- Handle administrative duties which include weekly summaries, treatment plans, record keeping for individual and group adolescent facility client funds, high-risk intervention notes, and incident and accident reports; contribute basic medical terminology/computer skills and abilities.
- Attend regular staff meetings, treatment team meetings, and conferences.
- Design, develop, and organize new and ongoing activity programs and have become well-versed in the principles and techniques of therapeutic recreation methods.
- Conduct in-home visits to clients and their family members as well as providing both group and individual counseling in the residential facility.
- Teach behavior modification techniques and gained experience in crisis intervention, high-risk intervention, and crisis management in an environment working with adolescent males.

DAY PARENT & CERTIFIED NURSING ASSISTANT. Pine Bluff, AR (2000-02). In a self-employed position as a private contractor, provided outpatient services to mentally ill and developmentally disabled clients.

SUBSTANCE ABUSE COUNSELOR. Family Care Services, Little Rock, AR (1998-00). Provided individual, group, and family counseling as well as education for substance abuse treatment services including referrals, screenings, and assessments.

- At a "Willie M" residential facility, supervised male and female adolescent youth with emotional and violent behavior problems.

CHILD ABUSE COUNSELOR & PROGRAM COORDINATOR. Jefferson County Family Clinic, Pine Bluff, AR (1994-97). Conducted research, planned, and carried out a child abuse educational program which included workshops and seminars as well as counseling.

EDUCATION

B.S. in Sociology in progress, University of Arkansas, Little Rock, AR.
Previously studied Psychology, University of Arkansas, Little Rock, AR, 1994-97.

AFFILIATIONS

Attended numerous mental health and social service seminars and workshops.
Certified in these areas:

High-Risk Intervention	Protection Intervention Course	Medicaid billing
American Sign Language	CPR	First Aid

Hold membership in the Rape Crisis Center, the Businesswomen's Association of America, and Big Sisters and Big Brothers of Arkansas.

Date

Exact Name of Person
Exact Title
Exact Name of Company
Address
City, State, Zip

YOUTH PROGRAMS ADMINISTRATOR

Dear Exact Name of Person (or Dear Sir or Madam if answering a blind ad):

With the enclosed resume, I would like to express my interest in exploring employment opportunities with your organization. I am seeking an employer who can use a highly intelligent and reliable young professional with an outstanding track record. My husband and I will soon be relocating to Oklahoma, and I am seeking an employer that can use a dedicated hard worker with strong problem-solving skills.

In my most recent position, I programmed and managed a variety of youth services at a military base in Florida. After excelling in creating written flyers and newsletters as well as training and managing youth counselors, I was promoted to handle senior management responsibilities because of my strong communication and problem-solving skills.

In prior positions with the Pensacola Police Department in Florida as well as with the Logistic Support Division in Florida, I excelled as a Communicators Operator and Dispatcher. I have become skilled at handling emergency situations with common sense and insight. At the Pensacola Police Department, I monitored the activities of more than 30 officers per shift as I performed liaison with 911 and various elements of the Pensacola Police Department.

If you can use a dedicated professional who offers the proven ability to produce quality results in any type of work environment, I hope you will contact me soon to suggest a time we might meet to discuss how I could contribute to your organization. I can provide excellent professional and personal references at the appropriate time. Thank you for your time and consideration.

Sincerely,

Sarah Jordan

SARAH JORDAN

1110½ Hay Street, Fayetteville, NC 28305   •   preppub@aol.com   •   (910) 483-6611

OBJECTIVE

To benefit an organization that can use an experienced young professional with strong problem-solving and communication skills along with an enthusiastic customer service attitude.

EDUCATION & TRAINING

Completed two years toward Bachelor's degree with a concentration of course work in Human Resources and Sociology, University of West Florida; am finishing my degree in my spare time.

Completed training including Child Care Modules, Child Abuse Training certifying me to become an Administrator of Medications, Food Handlers training, Moving Ahead Military Child Care Training, and training pertaining to ADHD and anger diffusion.

EXPERIENCE

YOUTH PROGRAMS ADMINISTRATOR. City of Ft. Lauderdale, FL (2000-present). For youth programs at this prominent city in Florida, have been the lead counselor for up to 1,500 school-age children K-12; supervise up to 12 other caregivers. Program activities in areas including academics, art, science, and physical education; manage several new programs. Coordinator of Project Learn, and Programmer for the Boys and Girls Clubs.
- Coordinate activities that enhance learning and growth; play a key role in organizing and implementing community activities such as carnivals, Halloween and Santa Claus events, military appreciation activities, talent shows, Easter egg hunts, and others.
- Conduct parents' meetings and handle accounts receivable; praised for keen negotiating skills.
- Became very knowledgeable of children's anger disorders and worked closely with children diagnosed with ADHD, ODD, autism, bipolar disorders, and physical challenges.

DISPATCHER. Logistic Support Division, Elgin AFB, FL (1996-2000). Was recruited as a Dispatcher for the Logistic Support Division, and was rapidly promoted to Manager of the Protocol Division, which involved organizing and managing arrangements for VIPs visiting Florida.
- Dispatched vehicle operators to military flightline and various other places on and off the base. Provided customer service by phone and in person.
- Issued military licenses; handled and relayed secure information. Was responsible for maintenance of two-way radios. Input data, created spreadsheets, and developed presentations using Word, Excel, and PowerPoint.
- Responsible for employees' work schedule, lunch breaks, and annual leave.

POLICE DEPARTMENT DISPATCHER & COMMUNICATIONS OPERATOR. Pensacola Police Department, Pensacola, FL (1994-96). Established an excellent reputation within the Pensacola community and participated in many emergency situations.
- Processed emergency and non-emergency information to officers.
- Was promoted to train new dispatchers; monitored the activities of more than 30 officers per shift while also monitoring and operating seven police channels using Computer Aided Dispatch system. Acted as the liaison between 911 and the Sheriff's Department.

Other experience: Became a part of the work force in Florida by becoming a temporary worker with Escambia Temporary Service in Pensacola.

COMPUTERS

Proficient in using computers with MS Word, Excel, PowerPoint, and other software.

PERSONAL

Outstanding references on request. Thrive on solving problems through people.

You may already realize that applying for a federal government position requires some patience and persistence in order to complete rather tedious forms and get them in on time. Depending on what type of federal job you are seeking, you may need to prepare an application such as the SF 171 or OF 612, or you may need to use a Federal Resume, sometimes called a "Resumix," to apply for a federal job. But that may not be the only paperwork you need.

Many Position Vacancy Announcements or job bulletins for a specific job also tell you that, in order to be considered for the job you want, you must also demonstrate certain knowledge, skills, or abilities. In other words, you need to also submit written narrative statements which microscopically focus on your particular knowledge, skill, or ability in a certain area. The next few pages are filled with examples of excellent KSAs. If you wish to see many other examples of KSAs, you may look for another book published by PREP: "Real KSAs--Knowledge, Skills & Abilities--for Government Jobs."

Although you will be able to use the Federal Resume you prepare in order to apply for all sorts of jobs in the federal government, the KSAs you write are particular to a specific job and you may be able to use the KSAs you write only one time. If you get into the Civil Service system, however, you will discover that many KSAs tend to appear on lots of different job announcement bulletins. For example, "Ability to communicate orally and in writing" is a frequently requested KSA. This means that you would be able to use and re-use this KSA for any job bulletin which requests you to give evidence of your ability in this area.

What does "Screen Out" mean? If you see that a KSA is requested and the words "Screen out" are mentioned beside the KSA, this means that this KSA is of vital importance in "getting you in the door." If the individuals who review your application feel that your screen-out KSA does not establish your strengths in this area, you will not be considered as a candidate for the job. You need to make sure that any screen-out KSA is especially well-written and comprehensive.

How long can a KSA be? A job vacancy announcement bulletin may specify a length for the KSAs it requests. Sometimes KSAs can be 1-2 pages long each, but sometimes you are asked to submit several KSAs within a maximum of two pages. Remember that the purpose of a KSA is to microscopically examine your level of competence in a specific area, so you need to be extremely detailed and comprehensive. Give examples and details wherever possible. For example, your written communication skills might appear more credible if you provide the details of the kinds of reports and paperwork you prepared.

KSAs are extremely important in "getting you in the door" for a federal government job. If you are working under a tight deadline in preparing your paperwork for a federal government position, don't spend all your time preparing the Federal Resume if you also have KSAs to do. Create "blockbuster" KSAs as well!

FEDERAL RESUME OR RESUMIX

CRAIG SEAN DUNCAN

SSN: 000-00-0000

1110 Hay Street
Fayetteville, NC 28305
Home: (910) 483-6611
Work: (910) 483-2439
E-mail address: preppub@aol.com
Vacancy Announcement Number: 123XYZ

Here you see the Federal Resume of a military professional who is applying for jobs at the GS-09 and above level.

SUMMARY of SKILLS

Offer well-developed knowledge of **administrative operations** and **automated data processing** as well as strong **motivational, leadership, and counseling** skills.

EXPERIENCE

ADMINISTRATIVE ASSISTANT. U.S. Navy, McIver Medical Center, Norfolk, VA (March 1999-present).
Supervisor: Commander F. Sweeney, (910) 483-6611
Pay grade: RP1
Hours worked per week: 40
Duties: Provide clerical and logistics support for chaplains at a major medical center; assist in programs which provide for the free exercise of religion; administer to the spiritual, moral, and ethical needs of patients, their families, and staff members.
Accomplishments:
· Described as a highly resourceful professional, was cited for my contributions during a ten-day training exercise designed to prepare medical students for field duty; provided support for the religious program and in other functional areas.
· Was awarded the Navy and Marine Corps Achievement Medal and selected for special training in providing instruction, technical writing, and blueprint reading.

ADMINISTRATIVE ASSISTANT TO THE CHAPLAIN. U.S. Navy, USS Kennedy, Miami, FL (December 1996-March 1999).
Supervisor: Captain Francis Sweeney
Pay grade: RP1
Hours worked per week: 40
Duties: Counseled personnel and handled the processing of regular performance reports, counseling statements, and other administrative actions.
Accomplishments:
· Was awarded a Navy Achievement medal for my efforts in creating and managing a project which resulted in a resource learning center with five computer stands: obtained $25,000 in funding and established Internet access for users while at sea.
· Was entrusted with numerous functional duties ranging from trainer to ADP system security specialist, to career counselor, to financial counselor.
· Coordinated details and arranged transportation which allowed personnel to attend a special Christmas Eve mass.

ADMINISTRATIVE ASSISTANT TO THE CHAPLAIN. U.S. Navy, USS Gateway, San Diego, CA (September 1995-December 1996).

Supervisor: LTC Frank Sweeney

Pay grade: RP2

Hours worked per week: 40

Duties: Was cited for numerous contributions to the effectiveness of the ship's religious programs and support for personnel requiring counseling and support services during crisis and emergency situations.

Accomplishments:

- Was described in official performance evaluations as "intelligent, impressively articulate, and refreshingly conscientious."
- On my own initiative, developed a cross-training program.
- Developed and wrote the standard operating procedures (SOP) for using the ship's library and implemented a functional reorganization.
- Utilized my computer skills to create a database of all books and video tapes as well as a tracking system for library materials.

SENIOR ADMINISTRATIVE ASSISTANT. U.S. Navy, Chief of Personnel, Department of the Navy, Washington, DC 28305 (August 1993-September 1995).

Supervisor: LTC F. Sweeney, Sr.

Pay grade: RP4

Hours worked per week: 40

Duties: Learned administrative skills in the fast-paced, high-stress environment of the office of the Chief of Personnel.

Accomplishments:

- Was awarded a Navy Achievement Medal for my contributions which included coordinating the reorganization of office work space for increased productivity.
- Handled multiple responsibilities in ADP security, training, and career counseling.

EDUCATION

B.S. in History, Honolulu Community College, Oahu, HI, 1993.

TRAINING

Attended Navy and Marine Corps schools which included basic infantry and administration as well as the "Class A" and "Class F" career courses.

Completed nonresident training courses which included the following subjects:

religious program operations	inventory control
program management	customer service
human behavior	administrative assistance

CLEARANCE

Was entrusted with a Secret security clearance.

COMPUTERS

Am experienced with FORTRAN, C++, Microsoft Word, Excel, and WordPerfect.

FEDERAL RESUME OR RESUMIX

MEGAN STEWART
1110 1/2 Hay Street, Fayetteville, NC 28305
Home: (000) 000-0000; work: (000) 000-0000
E-mail: preppub@aol.com
SSN: 000-00-0000

Position, Title, Series, Grade: GS-00-00
Announcement Number: 0000-00-0000

<table>
<tr>
<td>ENVIRONMENTAL LAW ATTORNEY
utilizes this "resumix" to apply for a federal government job</td>
<td>EDUCATION</td>
<td>Juris Doctor degree, Georgetown University School of Law, Washington, DC, 1992.
Bachelor of Arts degree in International Relations, Ocean County College, Toms River, NJ, 1989.</td>
</tr>
</table>

TRAINING

Have completed military training programs for legal professionals which have included the following:
Environmental Law Course – environmental law and updates, 1998
Ethics Course – laws and policy governing ethics, 1997
Fiscal Law Course – laws governing federal expenditures, 1996
Criminal Law Course – rules of evidence and case law, 1996

LAW LICENSE

Licensed to practice law in New Jersey since 1992.

COMPUTERS

Offer skills in automated legal research utilizing Lexis.

EXPERIENCE

Advanced to Captain while serving in the U.S. Army:
ENVIRONMENTAL LAW ATTORNEY. HHC, 187th Legal Services Division, Ft. Dix, NJ 11525 (2004-present). Annual salary: CPT. Supervisor: LTC James Clamore, (111) 111-1111. As a specialist in environmental law, am the advisor on federal and state environmental laws, construction, and land use issues which impact this military post with a million dollar annual budget.

- Am involved in negotiations with the Environmental Protection Agency on multiple violations of the Safe Water Drinking Act.
- Represent Ft. Dix in current negotiations of a conditional settlement in a case before the state's Department of Environment and Natural Resources (NJDENR): am working within the guidelines of military limitations on not paying environmental fines or using appropriated funds for environmental projects without congressional approval.
- Am working on a project related to four acres of contaminated land owned by the U.S. Army which are to be disposed of.
- Established a satellite office and integrated my activities into the operations of my client – the Public Works Business Center (PWBC) – in order to gain the strongest understanding of the technology and science of the infrastructure, pollution control and prevention programs, and natural resource management activities.
- Taught National Environmental Policy Act (NEPA) procedures to the PWBC's resident specialist in order to encourage him to use their checklist and take advantage of the expertise of other specialists such as the Air Emissions Program Manager and Endangered Species Wildlife Biologist.
- Initiated a program for tracking compliance involving resource

conservation and placing special emphasis on laws concerning hazardous waste: created sample documents required by law and posted them on a website for the benefit of units which needed to track their compliance with the laws.

- Work closely with the O'Keefe National Wildlife Reserve to increase land for training while also recovering and protecting the habitat of five endangered species.
- Advise a number of committees which include: Environmental Quality Control, Qualified Recycling Program, Integrated Natural Resources Management Plan Steering, and Installation Environment and Facilities Maintenance Working Group.

ADMINISTRATIVE LAW ATTORNEY. ARCOM, 3-139th Regiment, Fort Carson, CO 87955 (2001-04). Annual salary: CPT (O3). Supervisor: LTC Lindsey Jenkins, (222) 222-2222. Officially evaluated as "a leader others look to for guidance," provided legal advice on administrative and regulatory issues to all organizations, units, and staff sections.

- Earned respect for my ability to provide timely, accurate guidance on even the most difficult legal questions while preparing legal opinions and advising managers and investigating officers on legal issues for this community of 32,000.
- Wrote preventive law articles for the post newspaper.
- Singled out as a leader among captains, was cited for setting the pace for the administrative division during a period of severe personnel shortages.

LEGAL CENTER MANAGER and **CHIEF OF LEGAL ASSISTANCE AND CLAIMS.** Department of Defense, 5495 Lee Avenue, Washington, DC 11028-5545 (1996-01). Salary: CPT (O3). Supervisor: MAJ Mark C. Vance, (333) 333-3333. Officially evaluated as "truly spectacular" in a demanding field grade position, was cited for my maturity, good judgment and superb leadership of a legal center which served a community of military, family members, civilians, and retirees.

- Supervised three judge advocates while advising executives, supervising a tax assistance office, and administering a preventive law program.
- Provided advice and services on family law, consumer law, estate planning, military administrative law, personal finances, and civil law issues.
- Was credited as the key player in the center's recognition with a Chief of Staff Award.
- Provided oversight for the most successful tax assistance office in the region which serviced clients and generated refunds for its clients during the fiscal year.

Other experience:
TRIAL COUNSEL. The District Municipal Court of Toms River, 7957 Allendale Drive, Toms River, NJ 11655 (1996-99). Salary: 30,000. Supervisor: Neil Pershing, (444) 444-4444. Cited as "particularly persuasive in oral arguments and presenting the government's case in sentencing," represented the U.S. in difficult and complex courts-martial cases such as cases of sexual assault, child sexual abuse, and drug distribution.

- Sought out for my guidance on tough issues, was also effective in developing and teaching classes on sexual harassment, Law of War, substance abuse, and military justice.

ATTORNEY. Pettiford, Shockley & Associates, 206 Saxony Avenue, Toms River, NJ 11645 (1992-96). Salary: 28,000. Supervisor: Robert Tyler, (555) 555-5555. Quickly became known for my ability to handle stress and change in a busy center which provided legal counseling, representation, and guidance.

- Handled activities which ranged from preparing court documents and correspondence to educating clients on how to use nonlegal alternatives.
- Wrote articles for the base newspaper; taught classes to soldiers; executed wills and powers of attorney while helping personnel prepare for overseas assignments.

PERSONAL   Am known for sound judgment, keen insight and analytical skills, and vision.

FEDERAL RESUME OR RESUMIX

JOSEPH STONE
SSN: 000-00-0000

1110 Hay Street
Portland, OR 28305
Home: (910) 483-6611
Work: NA
Vacancy Announcement Number: 123XYZ

Country of Citizenship: USA
Veterans' Preference:
Reinstatement Eligibility:
Highest Federal Civilian Grade Held:

This is a Federal Resume of a military officer (Captain) seeking a second career in the Civil Service. He has a medical background.

SUMMARY
Offer well-developed **planning and organizational abilities, strong leadership skills,** and a reputation for possessing **excellent written and verbal communication skills.**

EXPERIENCE
MEDICAL SUPPORT MANAGER. U.S. Army, B Company, 407th Forward Support Battalion, Ft. Lewis, WA 45745 (August 1996-present).
    Supervisor: CPT Francis Sweeney
    Pay grade: O-2 (1LT)
    Hours worked per week: 40
    Duties: As Executive Officer at the rank of Captain, assisted the General Manager (Commander) with planning and carrying out training and all phases of support for company activities to include controlling more than $6 million worth of equipment. Was entrusted with additional duties which included overseeing motor pool and supply operations, physical security, weapons room, environmental regulations compliance, and family support activities. Managed the NBC (nuclear, biological, and chemical) defense and training plans.
    Accomplishments:
- Officially evaluated as "the best lieutenant in the company," was cited for my drive, incredible knowledge, and attention to detail which allowed me to produce outstanding results in every area of responsibility.
- Automated the supply room and completed a 100% inventory of all supplies and equipment while transforming a dysfunctional section into one recognized as a model of efficiency.
- Prepared weekly reports sent to higher-level material review personnel and achieved a 96% average during regular evaluations.
- Maintained strict standards for my personnel which resulted in "commendable" ratings during several critical external evaluations.
- Was described in formal evaluations as consistently performing above my rank and level of experience and as a mature professional who was relentless in pursuing excellence.
- Was credited with accomplishing in only six months what others had been unable to do in two years through my ability to find solutions and push myself and my subordinates to succeed.

FIRST-LINE SUPERVISOR. C Co., 7/62 Inf BN, Ft. Eustis, VA (Sep/94-Aug/96).
Supervisor: CPT F. Sweeney
Pay grade: O-2 (1LT)
Hours worked per week: 40
Duties: Supervised and provided leadership for a 39-person medical platoon which provided health services support to an 875-person unit. Planned, organized, and coordinated patient evacuation, trauma management, and supply support as well as controlling the operation and maintenance of $2 million worth of property and equipment. Supervised individual and group training. Handled multiple responsibilities for a variety of programs including weight control, drug and alcohol abuse and prevention, and safety.

Accomplishments:

Evaluated as a proactive and energetic leader who set the pace for excellence, was cited for my technical and tactical skills during a rotation at the National Training Center— lowered by 10% the number of people who would have died of their wounds and was named as being directly responsible for 500 simulated casualties being evacuated, evaluated, and processed.

EDUCATION

Completed one semester of graduate studies in International Relations, Webster University, Ft. Knox, KY, spring 1998.

B.S., Chemistry, Culowhee University, Culowhee, NJ, 1994.

- Recognized as ROTC Distinguished Military Graduate based on my academic standing and leadership skills.
- Named in Outstanding College Students of America based on my GPA.
- Elected Executive Officer of the National Society of Pershing Rifles, a military fraternity, for the 1993-94 school year.
- Named to Phi Beta Sigma freshman honorary society and Delta Beta Epsilon chemistry honorary society for my 4.0 GPA in chemistry, 1992.
- Received a full four-year ROTC scholarship and three two-year scholarships based on my academic and leadership potential.
- Placed on the Dean's List every semester and graduated with a 4.0 GPA in my major and 3.97 overall (*summa cum laude*).

Graduated from Our Lady of the Sacred Heart Montessori School, NJ, 1990.

- Placed first among 53 seniors in a small parochial high school.

TRAINING

Excelled in extensive military training which has included the following programs:
- Command and Staff Service School (6 weeks), 1999
- SERE (Survival, Evasion, Resistance, and Escape) High-risk School (19 days), 1998
- Individual Terrorism Awareness Course (INTAC) (five days), 1998
- Infantry Officers Advanced Course (seven months), 1997
- AMEDD OBC (four months), 1994
- Air Assault School (three weeks), 1992
- Airborne School (two weeks), 1991

LANGUAGES

Speak and read the Arabic language well and write on a basic level—completed a six-month Basic Military Language Course.

CLEARANCE

Was entrusted with a Top Secret security clearance.

FEDERAL RESUME OR RESUMIX

TAMEIKA L. JACKSON
SSN: 000-00-0000

1110 1/2 Hay Street
Boston, MA 28305
Home Phone: (910) 483-6611
Work Phone: (910) 483-2439

Country of Citizenship: USA
Veterans' Preference:
Reinstatement Eligibility:
Highest Federal Civilian Grade Held:

**Federal Resume
Office Management
Experience**

SUMMARY OF SKILLS

Over ten years of experience in office management and personnel management, customer service and public relations, as well as computer operations and office equipment operation. Extensive knowledge of specialized terminology needed to type correspondence, reports, and memoranda along with knowledge of grammar, spelling, capitalization, and punctuation. Ability to type 40 words per minute.

EXPERIENCE

OFFICE MANAGER. June 2003-present. 40 hours per week. Prep Personnel, 1110 Hay Street, Boston, MA 28305. Ms. Frances Sweeney, (910) 483-6611. Manage office operations, customer service, and the organization of accounting information for the company accountant. Type correspondence, memoranda, and reports in final form. Utilize my excellent knowledge of functions, procedures, and policies of the office.

The Position Vacancy Announcement specified a three-page limit for this Federal Resume.

- Have become known for my gracious manner when answering the phone.
- Utilize my communication skills while speaking with potential customers as well as existing clients by phone and in person to answer their technical questions about the company's cleaning services.
- Manage both commercial and residential accounts.
- Schedule appointments for company services and determine correct prices.
- Handle a wide range of bookkeeping functions; investigate and analyze previous invoices in order to attach them to current work orders.
- Have been commended for my ability to deal graciously with the public and have been credited with increasing company revenue through my public relations and customer service skills.

PERSONNEL ADMINISTRATIVE SPECIALIST. April 1991-June 2003. 40 hours a week. HHC, 93rd TRANSCOM, Ft. Kobbe, Panama APO AE 28305. SFC F. Sweeney, (telephone unknown). Expertly performed a wide range of office duties, and was selected as Noncommissioned Officer In Charge (NCOIC) when my unit was deployed to Somalia.

- Was specially selected as Rear Detachment S-1 NCOIC as a Specialist (E-4) even though this position is normally held by an SFC (E-7).
- Utilized a computer with Microsoft Office for word processing.
- Handled personnel administration activities which included processing hundreds of soldiers in and out of our 400-person organization.
- Performed clerical support functions related to the preparation of personnel reports as well as documents pertaining to personnel assignments.
- Prepared finance documents related to personnel payroll.

PERSONNEL ADMINISTRATION SPECIALIST & UNIT CLERK. February 1987-April 1991. 40 hours a week. HHC, COSCOM, Frankfurt, Germany, APO AE 28305. 1SG Franc Sweeney, (telephone unknown). Utilized my skills in office procedures while excelling in a job as a Unit Clerk (1987-90) and then as a Personnel Administration Specialist (1990-91) within the same organization.

- Received a special award for my leadership as Unit Clerk in reducing a large backlog of personnel documents (SIDPERS) to zero—our unit was the first one to achieve that goal within 2d Army. The citation for the Army Achievement Medal which I received praised my efforts in "reducing 347 critical data blanks on the SIDPERS System to zero, allowing Headquarters Company to become the first of 16 units to reach this target." **Was commended for dedication and self-sacrificing devotion to duty.**
- As Personnel Administration Specialist, provided administrative support to Headquarters and Headquarters Company; posted changes to personnel files for 298 personnel, maintained personnel records including medical and dental records for hundreds of employees; and assisted personnel in coordinating appointments for annual physicals, immunizations, dental exams, photographs, and other matters.
- Became known for my excellent written and oral communication skills.
- On a formal evaluation of my performance during this period, **was commended for my "ability to adapt to changing requirements" and recommended for "rapid promotion to increased supervisory responsibility."**

Her experience is in office management and administrative support. She will be applying for jobs at the GS-05 level.

ADMINISTRATIVE SPECIALIST & PERSONNEL SPECIALIST. March 1983-January 1987. 40 hours a week. 5th Engineering Battalion, Ft. Drum, NY 28305. MSG Francis Sweeney (telephone unknown). Excelled in a job as a Clerk Typist and advanced to handle more complex office administration duties because of my cheerful attitude and ability to handle large volumes of work which had to be performed accurately and quickly.

- Prepared and maintained personnel reports for upper management review.
- Prepared military and nonmilitary correspondence in draft and final form.

You will notice that a Federal Resume is different from the "civilian" resume. You don't provide your employers' names and phone numbers, or your salary history, on a "civilian" resume!

EDUCATION & TRAINING
Certificate, USAR Unit Administration Basic Course, 1998.
Certificate, Administrative Specialist Course, U.S. Army, 1997.
Certificate, Primary Leadership Course, U.S. Army, 1997.
Certificate of Training, Battalion Training Management Course, U.S. Army, 1997.
Certificate of Training, Maintenance Management Course, 1994.
Certificate of Completion, Clerk-Typist Course, U.S. Army, 1984.
Graduate of Steadfast High School, Oakland, CA, June, 1982.

CLEARANCE
While in military service, held a Secret clearance.

OFFICE SKILLS
Proficient with all office equipment: computers, typewriters, copiers, fax machines.

MEDALS AND AWARDS
While in military service, received numerous awards and medals including the Army Service Ribbon, Army Reserve Components Overseas Training Ribbon, Army Achievement Medal, NCO Professional Development Ribbon, Army Good Conduct Medal, Army Commendation Medal, National Defense Service Medal, Rifle M16 Sharpshooter Badge.

EXAMPLE OF A KSA

ROSS A. CHELSEA

SSN: 000-00-0000

CRIMINAL INVESTIGATOR, GS-00-13 ANNOUNCEMENT #XYZ123

Knowledge of law enforcement concepts, principles, and practices.

CRIMINAL ATTORNEY uses this two-page KSA as part of his application for a federal government job. KSA stands for "Knowledge, Skills, and Abilities."

In my current position as a Criminal Attorney for the Las Cruces Police Department, Protective Services Division, GS-11 (2002-present), my knowledge of law enforcement concepts, principles, and practices is exhibited while planning, organizing, and conducting criminal and non-criminal investigations, and performing mobile and stationary surveillance to observe the activities of individuals involved in the investigation. When sufficient evidence is obtained to justify such action, I prepare requests for and obtain search warrants. Process crime scenes to obtain such physical evidence as latent fingerprints, hair and skin samples, fibers, etc. Operate concealed cameras, audio and videocassette recorders, directional microphones, and other technical investigative aids. Conduct and document interviews with victims, witnesses, and suspects, using learned interrogative techniques to obtain corroborative statements to support the physical evidence.

Most recently, I was assigned to an internal investigation with the Washington Headquarters Services. The position involved investigating fraudulent or inappropriate use of government property by federal employees. Under the auspices of the Washington Headquarters Services, I conducted a week-long surveillance of the suspect, during which time I observed him misusing his government vehicle on numerous occasions, to include allowing non-government personnel the use of the vehicle. In addition, there was some evidence involving contracting fraud, specifically fraudulent payments to government officials by another government employee. This aspect of the investigation is still ongoing.

In April of 2002, a case involving theft of government property involving a number of Hispanic artifacts was turned over to the National Security Agency for investigation. The thefts had occurred in 1998, at which time the International Affairs Division reported the matter to the Las Cruces Police Department. The LCPD took no action, as the case involved Federal government property, and thus was under the jurisdiction of the LCPD. Because the value of the stolen property was only $10,500, the case was assigned a low priority by the LCPD. As a result, almost no action had been taken until the case was turned over to the National Security Agency and assigned to me. The investigation called for a detailed internal audit of the museum's accounting and inventory records. After careful examination of the NSA's invoices, bills of lading, shipping manifests, and payment records, I was able to positively identify the 10 pieces that had been stolen and confirm the dates that they were received. Despite the four-year time lag between the commission of the crime and the start of the investigation, my efforts resulted in recovery of all the stolen artifacts and the identification and apprehension of a suspect, who was charged with felony theft of government property.

I also conducted an internal investigation in a 2000 case involving suspicious payments to a long-term government contractor that was deferred to the NSA by the LCPD Investigator, who had no investigator on-site. I was assigned to the case, which involved a comprehensive and detailed audit of accounting files for the office of the

Representative Department. I reviewed all LCPD contracts, invoices, work orders, payment requests, and authorizations, reconciling all figures to ensure that actual payment amounts matched the figures agreed to in the contract, and that all work which had been paid for was actually performed. As a result of this investigation, it was determined that there were no irregularities in LCPD payments to the contractor. No charges were brought in the matter.

In 1995, I was assigned to an investigation for the Washington Headquarters Services office related to possible fraudulent acquisition of surplus government property. The investigation centered on recent transfers of government surplus communications equipment and vehicles, including dump trucks, heavy construction equipment, boats, light trucks, etc. by the Department of Transportation. After conducting a thorough audit of all accounting paperwork for both agencies, I was able to prepare a complete list of items received from government surplus in order to determine whether or not these items had been obtained under false pretenses. These items were supposedly requisitioned for use by the requesting agencies, but on investigation, I determined that the property was being sold, given to, or used improperly for the benefit of private individuals or companies. As a result of my audit, one investigation was closed and the property in question was seized by the government. Due to the extent of the property fraudulently obtained, other related investigations are still ongoing.

Earlier as Lead Detective/ Police Officer (1990-93), I supervised four or more Investigative Police Officers per assigned shift, overseeing their performance in the full range of law enforcement duties, including but not limited to conducting initial and follow-up investigations, processing crime scenes to obtain physical evidence, and processing search and arrest warrants. Served as a uniformed police officer and leader/trainer in the Protective Services Division, ensuring the safety and protecting the civil rights of individuals while they were on controlled property that was owned or under the control of one of its tenant agencies. Maintained order, preserved the peace, and protected all controlled property. Conducted initial and follow-up investigations of reported thefts, burglaries, assaults, and threats, as well as instances of vandalism and narcotics violations. Interviewed victims, witnesses, and suspects during the investigative process.

Education and Training Related to the KSA:
Juris Doctor (J.D.) degree from New Mexico State University, Las Cruces, NM, 1993. Bachelor of Science in Criminal Justice, with concentrations in Sociology and Correctional Administration, minor in International Studies, New Mexico State University, Las Cruces, NM, 1990.

Completed numerous additional training and development courses at the New Mexico Police Academy in Albuquerque, NM, which included:
- Advanced Physical Security Training Course, 80 hours, 2001
- Data Recovery and Analysis Training Course, 40 hours, 2001
- Financial Investigations Practical Skills Training Course, 40 hours, 2000
- Criminal Intelligence Analyst Training Course, 80 hours, 1999
- Personnel Security Adjudication Training Course, 40 hours, 1999
- Basic Criminal Investigation Course, 320 hours, 1998
- Basic Police Course, 320 hours, 1998

Completed supervisory training courses sponsored by the Las Cruces Police Department, Las Cruces, NM, including:
- Supervising: A Guide for All Levels, 8 hours, 2000
- Constructive Discipline for Supervisors, 6 hours, 2000
- Basic Supervision Course, 6 hours, 2000

EXAMPLE OF A KSA

ROSS A. CHELSEA
SSN: 000-00-0000
CRIMINAL INVESTIGATOR, GS-13 ANNOUNCEMENT #XYZ123

Knowledge of the Principles of Conducting Investigations.

ATTORNEY
will use these KSAs
in order to apply for
a federal
government
position.

In my current position as a Special Attorney for the Criminal Investigation Section of the Las Cruces Police Department, Protective Services Division, GS-11 (2002-present), I plan, organize, and conduct criminal and non-criminal investigations, performing mobile and stationary surveillance to observe the activities of individuals involved in the investigation. When sufficient evidence is obtained to justify such action, prepare requests for and obtain search warrants. Process crime scenes to obtain such physical evidence as latent fingerprints, hair and skin samples, fibers, etc. Operate concealed cameras, audio and videocassette recorders, directional microphones, and other technical investigative aids. Conduct and document interviews with victims, witnesses, and suspects, using learned interrogative techniques to obtain corroborative statements to support the physical evidence.

Most recently, I was assigned to an internal investigation involving fraudulent or inappropriate used of government property by a federal employee. Under the auspices of the Washington Headquarters Services office, I conducted a week-long surveillance of the suspect, during which time I observed him misusing his government vehicle on numerous occasions, to include allowing non-government personnel to use the vehicle. In addition, there was some evidence involving contracting fraud, specifically fraudulent payments to government officials by another government employee. This aspect of the investigation is still ongoing.

In April of 2002, a case involving theft of government property, specifically a number of Hispanic artifacts was turned over to the National Security Agency for investigation. The thefts had occurred in 1998, at which time the International Affairs Division reported to the Las Cruces Police Department. The Las Cruces police took no action, as the case involved Federal government property, and thus was under the jurisdiction of the LCPD. Because the value of the stolen property was only $10,500, the case was assigned a low priority by the LCPD. As a result, almost no action had been taken until the case was turned over to the National Security Agency and assigned to me. The investigation called for a detailed internal audit of the museum's accounting and inventory records. After careful examination of the NSA's invoices, bills of lading, shipping manifests, and payment records, I was able to positively identify the 10 pieces that had been stolen and confirm the dates that they were received. Despite the four-year time lag between the commission of the crime and the start of the investigation, my efforts resulted in recovery of all the stolen artifacts and the identification and apprehension of a suspect, who was charged with felony theft of government property.

I conducted an internal investigation in a 2000 case involving suspicious payments to a long-term government contractor that was referred to the NSA by the LCPD Investigator, who had no investigator on-site. I was assigned to the case, which involved performing a comprehensive and detailed audit of accounting files for the office of the NSA Customer Representative Department. I reviewed contracts, work orders, payment requests, and authorizations, reconciling all figures to ensure that actual payment amounts matched the figures agreed to in the contract, and that all work which had been paid for was actually performed. As a result of this three-week investigation, it was determined that there were no irregularities in the payments to this contractor, and no charges were brought in the matter.

In 1995, I was assigned to an investigation for the Washington Headquarters Services office related to possible fraudulent acquisition of surplus government property. The investigation centered on recent transfers of government surplus communications equipment and vehicles, including dump trucks, heavy construction equipment, boats and light trucks by the Department of Transportation. After conducting a thorough audit of all accounting paperwork for both agencies, I was able to prepare a complete list of items received from government surplus in order to determine whether or not these items had been obtained under false pretenses. These items were supposedly requisitioned for use by the requesting agencies, but on investigation. I determined that the property was being sold, given to, or used improperly for the benefit of private individuals or companies. As a result of my audit, one investigation was closed and the property in question was seized by the government. Due to the extent of the property fraudulently obtained, other related investigations are still ongoing.

ATTORNEY
will use these KSAs in order to apply for a federal government position.

Earlier as Lead Detective/Police Officer (1990-93), I supervised four or more Investigative Police Officers per assigned shift, overseeing their performance of the full range of law enforcement duties, including but not limited to conducting initial and follow-up investigations, processing crime scenes to obtain physical evidence, and processing search and arrest warrants. Served as a uniformed Police Officer and leader/trainer in the Federal Protective Services Division, ensuring the safety and protecting the civil rights of individuals while they were on Federal property that was owned or under the control of one of its tenant agencies. Maintained order, preserved the peace, and protected all Federally owned or controlled property. Conducted initial and follow-up investigations of reported thefts, burglaries, assaults, and threats, as well as instances of vandalism and narcotics violations. Interviewed victims, witnesses, and suspects during the investigative process.

Education and Training Related to the KSA:
Juris Doctor (J.D.) degree from New Mexico State University, Las Cruces, NM, 1993. Bachelor of Science in Criminal Justice, with concentrations in Sociology and Correctional Administration, minor in International Studies, New Mexico State University, Las Cruces, NM, 1990.

Completed numerous additional training and development courses at the New Mexico Police Academy in Albuquerque, NM, which included:
- Advanced Physical Security Training Course, 80 hours, 2001
- Data Recovery and Analysis Training Course, 40 hours, 2001
- Financial Investigations Practical Skills Training Course, 40 hours, 2000
- Criminal Intelligence Analyst Training Course, 80 hours, 1999
- Personnel Security Adjudication Training Course, 40 hours, 1999
- Basic Criminal Investigation Course, 320 hours, 1998
- Basic Police Course, 320 hours, 1998

MORE EXAMPLES OF KSAs

MELANIE T. EUBANKS

SSN: 000-00-0000

LEGAL ASSISTANT, GS-09 ANNOUNCEMENT #XYZ123

KSA #1: Skill in interpersonal relations.

LEGAL ASSISTANT
will use these KSAs in order to apply for a federal government position.

In my most recent position as Legal Assistant within the Department of Defense, I demonstrated my skill in interpersonal relations on a daily basis while interacting on a personal and professional level with attorneys of diverse specialties. I dealt with a heavy volume of office traffic, tactfully and diplomatically fielding questions and complaints from civilian and military attorneys, subcontractors, military personnel, and office visitors both in person and over the telephone and radio. I performed liaison between attorneys and engineers, relaying important information or taking messages if I could not resolve a problem or answer an inquiry. Frequently received calls from attorneys who were angry or upset due to problems or other delays; handled these calls expertly, using tact and diplomacy to defuse the situation, then presenting the attorneys' concerns to the appropriate person in order to efficiently resolve the conflict. Answered multi-line phones in a courteous and professional manner, routing incoming calls to the appropriate person, taking telephone messages, and providing callers with information over the phone.

In earlier positions as Secretary to the Chiefs of the Plans and Operations Division and of the Logistics Communication Division, I interacted daily with a large number of people, both on the phone and in person. I recorded telephone messages and answered multi-line phones, effectively communicating with callers in order to ascertain the purpose of their call. Responded to caller inquiries, furnishing information and resolving their problems when possible and directing calls to the supervisor or appropriate personnel when I was unable to assist them. Maintained lines of communication and developed strong working relationships with higher, lateral, and subordinate counterparts at military headquarters in order to facilitate the exchange of information concerning each division's affairs.

Education and Training Related to This KSA:

In addition to the Certificates I received from Central Florida Community College and the Bethune-Cookman College, the following courses have been helpful in refining my skills in this area:
- Correspondence English Usage, Kessler AFB, Mississippi
- Legal Terminology, Kessler AFB, Mississippi
- Legal Composition, Andrews AFB, Maryland
- Building a Professional Image, Andrews AFB, Maryland

MELANIE T. EUBANKS

SSN: 000-00-0000

LEGAL ASSISTANT, GS-09 ANNOUNCEMENT #XYZ123

KSA #2: Ability to communicate in writing.

In my most recent position as a Legal Assistant for the Department of Defense, I composed and prepared all correspondence for the office. Demonstrated my understanding of legal terminology as I carefully proofread and edited this material, making necessary changes to ensure precision of language, correct grammatical usage, and compliance with the appropriate format under the rules and regulations of correspondence. Also prepared all personnel actions for the office, to include personnel action requests, travel orders, transportation and training requests, and performance appraisals and incentive awards. Used style manuals, technical and non-technical dictionaries, and other references to ensure correctness of grammar and usage as well as precision of language. This position involved writing, editing, proofreading, and final printing of a large volume of letters, memos, reports, and other correspondence, as I posted transactions for over 35 attorneys and more than 150 program managers. Was known for my sound judgment, exceptional communication and organizational abilities, and attention to detail.

In earlier positions as the Secretary and Stenographer to the Chiefs of the Plans and Operations Division and Logistics Communication, I composed all office correspondence, including letters, memos, reports, and personnel actions. Using style manuals, technical and non-technical dictionaries, and other reference materials, ensured correctness of grammar and usage, precision of language, and adherence to proper formats according to the rules and regulations of correspondence. I composed and prepared initial drafts of all correspondence, proofread and edited the initial draft, made necessary changes and prepared the final documents. As I worked closely with a senior rater, this position involved preparing a heavy volume of personnel recommendations for awards, and civilian employee appraisals. Performed stenography duties, recording minutes of weekly staff meeting and other information which I then compiled, edited, and modified for use in memos, reports, letters, and other correspondence. Prepared, edited, and finalized a wide range of classified and non-classified documents, including staff papers, directives, and other military and non-military reports.

In an earlier position as Legal Assistant to the Commander of the 23rd Intelligence Division, I prepared, edited and finalized all correspondence, to include OERs, APRs, military awards and decorations, letters, reports, and memos. I proofread and edited all materials submitted for publication in a newsletter, ensuring correctness of grammar and usage, precision of language, and adherence to length requirements, and styles.

Education and Training Related to This KSA:

In addition to the Certificates I received from Central Florida Community College and the Bethune-Cookman College, the following courses have been helpful in refining my skills in this area:

- Correspondence English Usage, Kessler AFB, Mississippi
- Legal Terminology, Kessler AFB, Mississippi
- Legal Composition, Andrews AFB, Maryland
- Building a Professional Image, Andrews AFB, Maryland

LEGAL ASSISTANT will use these KSAs in order to apply for a federal government position.

ABOUT THE EDITOR

Anne McKinney holds an MBA from the Harvard Business School and a BA in English from the University of North Carolina at Chapel Hill. A noted public speaker, writer, and teacher, she is the senior editor for PREP's business and career imprint, which bears her name. Early titles in the Anne McKinney Career Series (now called the Real-Resumes Series) published by PREP include: *Resumes and Cover Letters That Have Worked, Resumes and Cover Letters That Have Worked for Military Professionals, Government Job Applications and Federal Resumes, Cover Letters That Blow Doors Open,* and *Letters for Special Situations.* Her career titles and how-to resume-and-cover-letter books are based on the expertise she has acquired in 25 years of working with job hunters. Her valuable career insights have appeared in publications of the "Wall Street Journal" and other prominent newspapers and magazines.

PREP Publishing Order Form

You may purchase our titles from your favorite bookseller! Or send a check, money order or your credit card number for the total amount*, plus $4.00 postage and handling, to PREP, 1110 1/2 Hay Street, Fayetteville, NC 28305. You may also order our titles on our website at www.prep-pub.com and feel free to e-mail us at preppub@aol.com or call 910-483-6611 with your questions or concerns.

Name: _____

Address: _____

E-mail address: _____

Payment Type: ☐ Check/Money Order ☐ Visa ☐ MasterCard

Credit Card Number: _____ Expiration Date: _____

Put a check beside the items you are ordering:

☐ $16.95—REAL-RESUMES FOR RESTAURANT, FOOD SERVICE & HOTEL JOBS. Anne McKinney, Editor

☐ $16.95—REAL-RESUMES FOR MEDIA, NEWSPAPER, BROADCASTING & PUBLIC AFFAIRS JOBS. Anne McKinney, Editor

☐ $16.95—REAL-RESUMES FOR RETAILING, MODELING, FASHION & BEAUTY JOBS. Anne McKinney, Editor

☐ $16.95—REAL-RESUMES FOR HUMAN RESOURCES & PERSONNEL JOBS. Anne McKinney, Editor

☐ $16.95—REAL-RESUMES FOR MANUFACTURING JOBS. Anne McKinney, Editor

☐ $16.95—REAL-RESUMES FOR AVIATION & TRAVEL JOBS. Anne McKinney, Editor

☐ $16.95—REAL-RESUMES FOR POLICE, LAW ENFORCEMENT & SECURITY JOBS. Anne McKinney, Editor

☐ $16.95—REAL-RESUMES FOR SOCIAL WORK & COUNSELING JOBS. Anne McKinney, Editor

☐ $16.95—REAL-RESUMES FOR CONSTRUCTION JOBS. Anne McKinney, Editor

☐ $16.95—REAL-RESUMES FOR FINANCIAL JOBS. Anne McKinney, Editor

☐ $16.95—REAL-RESUMES FOR COMPUTER JOBS. Anne McKinney, Editor

☐ $16.95—REAL-RESUMES FOR MEDICAL JOBS. Anne McKinney, Editor

☐ $16.95—REAL-RESUMES FOR TEACHERS. Anne McKinney, Editor

☐ $16.95—REAL-RESUMES FOR CAREER CHANGERS. Anne McKinney, Editor

☐ $16.95—REAL-RESUMES FOR STUDENTS. Anne McKinney, Editor

☐ $16.95—REAL-RESUMES FOR SALES. Anne McKinney, Editor

☐ $16.95—REAL ESSAYS FOR COLLEGE AND GRAD SCHOOL. Anne McKinney, Editor

☐ $25.00—RESUMES AND COVER LETTERS THAT HAVE WORKED. McKinney, Editor

☐ $25.00—RESUMES AND COVER LETTERS THAT HAVE WORKED FOR MILITARY PROFESSIONALS. McKinney, Ed.

☐ $25.00—RESUMES AND COVER LETTERS FOR MANAGERS. McKinney, Editor

☐ $25.00—GOVERNMENT JOB APPLICATIONS AND FEDERAL RESUMES: Federal Resumes, KSAs, Forms 171 and 612, and Postal Applications. McKinney, Editor

☐ $25.00—COVER LETTERS THAT BLOW DOORS OPEN. McKinney, Editor

☐ $25.00—LETTERS FOR SPECIAL SITUATIONS. McKinney, Editor

☐ $16.95—REAL-RESUMES FOR NURSING JOBS. McKinney, Editor

☐ $16.95—REAL-RESUMES FOR AUTO INDUSTRY JOBS. McKinney, Editor.

☐ $24.95—REAL KSAS--KNOWLEDGE, SKILLS & ABILITIES--FOR GOVERNMENT JOBS. McKinney, Editor

☐ $24.95—REAL RESUMIX AND OTHER RESUMES FOR FEDERAL GOVERNMENT JOBS. McKinney, Editor

☐ $24.95—REAL BUSINESS PLANS AND MARKETING TOOLS ... Samples to use in your business. McKinney, Ed.

☐ $16.95—REAL-RESUMES FOR ADMINISTRATIVE SUPPORT, OFFICE & SECRETARIAL JOBS. Anne McKinney, Editor

☐ $16.95—REAL-RESUMES FOR FIREFIGHTING JOBS. Anne McKinney, Editor

☐ $16.95—REAL-RESUMES FOR JOBS IN NONPROFIT ORGANIZATIONS. Anne McKinney, Editor

☐ $16.95—REAL-RESUMES FOR SPORTS INDUSTRY JOBS. Anne McKinney, Editor

☐ $16.95—REAL-RESUMES FOR LEGAL & PARALEGAL JOBS. Anne McKinney, Editor

_____ **TOTAL ORDERED**

_____ **(add $4.00 for shipping and handling)**

_____ **TOTAL INCLUDING SHIPPING** *PREP* offers volume discounts on large orders. Call us at (910) 483-6611 for more information.

Would you like to explore the possibility of having PREP's writing
team create a resume for you similar to the ones in this book?

For a brief free consultation, call 910-483-6611
or send $4.00 to receive our Job Change Packet to
PREP, 1110 1/2 Hay Street, Fayetteville, NC 28305. Visit our
website to find valuable career resources: www.prep-pub.com!

QUESTIONS OR COMMENTS? E-MAIL US AT PREPPUB@AOL.COM